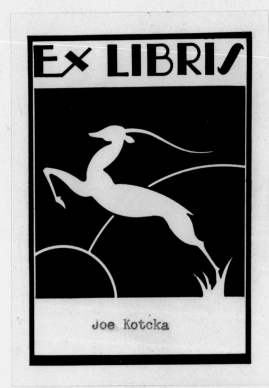

EX LIBRIS

Joe Kotcka

THOMAS EDWARD SHIELDS

BOOKS BY JUSTINE WARD

William Pardow of the Company of Jesus

MUSIC

Teachers' Manuals, 3 Volumes

Children's Song Manuals, 5 Volumes

Gregorian Chant

The Sunday Mass

Hymnal

Officium Pastorum, A Nativity Play of the
Thirteenth Century

Accompaniments, 3 Volumes

Thomas Edward
SHIELDS

BIOLOGIST, PSYCHOLOGIST,
EDUCATOR

By

JUSTINE WARD

Introduction by
Monsignor PATRICK J. McCORMICK

1947
CHARLES SCRIBNER'S SONS
New York

NIHIL OBSTAT
John M. A. Fearns, S.T.D.
Censor Librorum
IMPRIMATUR
✠ Francis Cardinal Spellman
Archbishop of New York

PREFACE

THIS is the story of a man who started out as a child incapable of learning. A victim of misunderstanding, of unsound psychology and prehistoric teaching methods, he was relegated to manual work on a farm. There, he rescued himself by the force of his innate genius, won for himself a tardy education, became a priest, a scientist and an educator. His ideas were so vast and, at the time, so new that they raised a storm of protest among his contemporaries. What he sought was a profound psychological renovation, ancient in its philosophy, modern in its method. He died with his task incomplete. Yet, "he planted a seed which is steadily developing into a great tree," wrote a successor in the Catholic University. "His point of view, which when first enunciated may have seemed bizarre and impracticable, pervades the whole of educational thought today. Any future historian of Catholic education in the United States must view his career and his labors as the turning point in the progress of our schools." [1]

Many great men who leave their mark permanently on the arts and sciences pass through a period of eclipse. This is but natural. A genius must create his own public capable of understanding his message, and it takes time for this public to reach maturity. Meanwhile, lesser voices prevail. Thus it was with the great Bach whose relatively flimsy sons basked in the limelight while the old man sank into oblivion. Time reversed the values, but it took a hundred years and

[1] Rt. Rev. Msgr. George Johnson, *The Sisters College Messenger,* Jan. 1929.

the zeal of a Schumann, a Mendelssohn and a Franz to unearth the giant and restore his music to the world.

Thomas Edward Shields has been silent for a quarter of a century. The strife that was raised around the living voice has died down. His name is seldom pronounced though lesser voices murmur snatches of his mighty themes without the master's genius. Is the seed still living? Is the leaven at work? Time alone will give the answer. Meanwhile, the silence can be broken, and educators can be given an account of a giant in their field. This book is a first step in that direction.

It is a pleasure to express my gratitude to the members of Doctor Shields' family for their kindness in providing much of the documentation necessary for the writing of this book; also to the authorities of the Catholic University of America and of the Sisters College for like cooperation, as also to the Catholic Education Press for permission to use copyrighted material. In particular I want to express my profound gratitude to the Reverend James M. Hayes, who urged me to write this book and who gave me constant encouragement and help during its composition, and finally my warmest thanks to the Right Reverend Monsignor Patrick J. McCormick, Rector of the Catholic University, for his kindness in reading the manuscript and for his invaluable criticism and suggestions.

JUSTINE WARD

TABLE OF CONTENTS

PART FOUR. CHRISTIAN EDUCATION

INTRODUCTION

T HE work and influence of the Reverend Doctor Thomas E. Shields may best be appreciated when the character and circumstances of the period in which he lived are known and understood. His great life work was accomplished within the brief space of two decades, between 1902 when he came to the Catholic University of America and his death in 1921; yet in that comparatively short time he profoundly affected Catholic education in the United States.

At the beginning of the twentieth century, Catholic education in our country was undergoing serious changes as it entered upon a period of rapid growth and development. The elementary or parish schools were increasing in number at an unprecedented rate, and the high-school movement was getting under way. Diocesan school systems hitherto governed by school boards were becoming better organized, and superintendents of schools were being appointed in important dioceses.

The religious communities of women were endeavoring to meet the needs of the schools for teachers, but the demand was greater than they could supply. In many places lay teachers had to be called upon to assist in staffing the elementary and high schools. The dearth of teachers was not, however, so great a problem as that of securing or providing for their proper and adequate training. The novitiate normals, which were intended to provide the spiritual and pedagogical preparation of novices, were harassed by the demand for teachers and themselves handicapped by insufficient teaching personnel. Many teachers had to be sent into the schools inadequately trained for their important office. Consequently, just as in many public-school systems of the time, there was a demand for instruction and help for those actually in service as teachers. This was one of the first needs of our Catholic teachers that Doctor Shields set about to meet in his correspondence courses and which enabled him to prepare the ground for his plans for teacher training, destined to be of such significance for Catholic education.

With this situation in mind one can understand how eagerly Doctor Shields entered into the planning and organization of the first summer session for teachers inaugurated by the Catholic University in 1911. He had come to know the needs of the teaching sisterhoods for pedagogical training and for the academic qualifications then required of them, and he planned accordingly. The Sisters found what they needed, and the first summer session was an undoubted success. The Sisters enthusiastically welcomed this opportunity, the first granted to them to pursue their studies under Catholic auspices, and through this initial enterprise the whole summer session movement was set in motion in Catholic universities and colleges, a movement which has continued ever since and has proved an immense aid in the solution of the teacher-training problem. Today, summer sessions for teachers are a regular feature of the work of the majority of Catholic universities and colleges in the United States.

The Sisters College, however, represented Doctor Shields' great achievement in the field of teacher training. Although he had long entertained the idea and discussed it frequently, although he knew that with the sisterhoods he was sure of support, Doctor Shields never anticipated the circumstances following the first summer session which made the foundation a sudden reality. He never had thought that the urgency of the demand would be shown by the Sisters themselves. Once encouraged by their appeals, Doctor Shields could not and would not regard any difficulties or obstacles as unsurmountable and with his tremendous energy pushed the project through. None can read of the beginnings of the College, as told in this biography, without marvelling at his courage and confidence that everything which would be needed, from ecclesiastical approval down to financial resources, would ultimately be forthcoming.

If the opening of the summer session for Sisters at the University were an innovation which did not escape some unfavorable criticism, partly because it was an innovation, and partly because it upset some traditions which prevented Sisters from associating with those of other communities, the opening of Sisters College was more emphatically hailed as such, and even viewed by some as a dangerous innovation. It had opened, however, with the full approbation of the Trustees of the University; Bishops had welcomed it and the Superiors of Communities expressed their gratitude for it. Furthermore, the Holy Father, Pope Pius X, had given the project his blessing and approval. The innovation proved eminently successful; the training of the Sisters was now associated with the work of the University and the latter's connection with the Catholic schools of the country definitely established. Viewed now in retrospect, the establishment of the College may be properly regarded as one of the best responses ever made by the University to a vital need of the Catholic school system.

It was through the correspondence courses which he conducted for Sisters, and especially the course in the Teaching of Religion, that Doctor Shields became convinced of the urgent necessity of better textbooks for the Catholic elementary schools, and with characteristic energy he set out to prepare them. The story of their making, from the early days of planning when he had the collaboration of Doctor Pace, through the period of their production, when he lectured on their methods at Teachers' Conferences and Institutes, down through the controversies which raged about them and about himself, forms the material for some of the most interesting reading in this biography.

The textbooks were the embodiment and the vehicle of the "Shields Method" at which violent shafts of criticism were hurled, as their popularity increased and the fine results of their use were recognized and publicized. Venturing into this field Doctor Shields was again the innovator and pioneer, blazing a trail which many others were afterwards to follow and profit by, but not with the same success, and chiefly because their aims and objectives were not the same. Doctor Shields had ever before him the purpose of making religion the central and foremost subject in the curriculum and a means of correlation with all other branches of knowledge. None of those who came after him has aimed as high or built his method on as firm a scientific or psychological foundation; none has so successfully drawn upon the teaching of the Divine Master for material as well as method of teaching nor sought to adopt the principles discernible in the organic teaching of the Church. Now, when other methods have been tried in the crucible of practice and found wanting, it is not rash to predict that there will be a revival of interest in these textbooks and methods which will give them again their rightful place in the classrooms of our Catholic schools.

This biography will undoubtedly awaken a new interest in Doctor Shields and his many enterprises. Appearing twenty-five years after his death, when the last vestiges of controversy about him have disappeared, and with that objectivity in presentation which the lapse of time and a better perspective permit, it will serve to place Doctor Shields in the position which he merited in the educational world of his time.

The author had the advantage of close association with Doctor Shields and collaborated with him in the development of his methods. She has produced a biography which graphically describes the early years and the heroic struggle of a dullard out from the darkness of illiteracy and misunderstanding into the light of learning and educational conquests. She has faithfully portrayed the development of a character which for tenacity of purpose, strength of determination and unselfishness, must be an inspiration for all who come to know of it. Depicting him in the various phases of his astounding career as the University teacher, lecturer, and college dean; as the prolific writer—propounding the philosophy of Catholic education to meet the fallacies and errors of his day, issuing manuals for the direction of teachers, and editing the *Catholic Educational Review;* as the scientist—bringing to bear upon the development of methods the most advanced biological and psychological data; as the innovator and pioneer inaugurating and organizing movements of national importance for Catholic schools; his biographer succeeds in showing that Doctor Shields should enjoy in the annals of the history of education for the first quarter of the twentieth century the distinction of being the outstanding Catholic educational leader of his time.

PATRICK J. McCORMICK
Rector of the Catholic University
of America

"He left us here that we may be as luminaries,
that we may be appointed teachers of
others, that we may be as leaven,
that we may be as seed, and
may bring forth
much fruit."

Saint John Chrysostom

PART ONE

SHIELDS' OMADHAUN

A faithful transcript of the record that was burned
into the heart and brain of the omadhaun and
read by himself after he had fought his way back
to the company of normal and intellectual men.
—*T. E. Shields*

CHAPTER ONE

CHILDHOOD

"IT'S a shame you don't try to do something for poor Tom!"

The Shields family had risen from the midday meal, but Bridget Shields lingered in the cool dining room exchanging impressions with her brother, who had come from Montreal to visit the farm for the first time. This land, so recently redeemed from the wilderness, was new to him. New, also, and fascinating was the bevy of thriving youngsters, his nephews and nieces. But why, he asked, was one boy among them treated so differently from the others? Why was this big, husky fellow, hardy and industrious, given no education, no schooling? Why was he treated as a mere farm hand among the hired men? His eyes flashed with indignation as he gazed down upon his sister. She defended herself sadly:

"We have done everything we could think of, but it seems hopeless. The teachers sent him home from school when he was nine years old. They said he could learn nothing and they feared he might pick up vicious habits from the bad boys who attended school."

John and Bridget Shields were Irish Catholics, like many of the early settlers in the Northwest who contributed so great a share to the development of the land which they adopted as their own. They arrived in America in 1850 and rapidly became Americans at heart in their love for our institutions, in their appreciation of this nation which gave them religious and civil liberty, which offered them boundless opportunity such as they could not find in the land of their birth. It is the spirit of America which creates Americans, and the immigrant pioneers of those days were often possessed of that spirit to an extent which might put to shame the descendants of the proud families that came to our shores on the *Mayflower*.

The new Territory of Minnesota drew them toward the great adventure. The land was little more than a wilderness. There were no railroads. The Minnesota River had only recently been opened to navigation by steamboats. The Shields traveled by boat and by "prairie schooner" with their two small boys, Michael Bernard, three years old, and John Joseph, a babe in arms. The life they were facing was neither easy nor safe. The Indians were far from friendly. A treaty, indeed, had been concluded with them "beneath an oak bower" on Pilot Knob in 1851, by which the Indians, after pressure, persuasion and threats, had ceded their land along the left bank of the river, but they had done so reluctantly, and now they watched with angry hearts as these newcomers cleared and cultivated the land which had been their tribal hunting ground. Incidents occurred and were spoken of with bated breath. A citizen of St. Paul was pierced with arrows, his scalp wrenched from his head. Indians broke into a farm house and murdered a little girl. Farmers returned from the fields to find their log houses burned to ashes and their wives and children assassinated after inhuman torture.

The two principal settlements faced one another on two heights: St. Peter and St. Paul, named in honor of the founders of the Church of Christ in Rome. St. Paul still retains its saintly name, but St. Peter had been replaced by

Mendota even before the arrival of the Shields. It was the most important town of the territory and could boast of one hundred and twenty inhabitants, a hotel and, above all, the central office and warehouse of the great fur company, a trust financed by John Jacob Astor of New York, whose agent, Henry H. Sibley, dealt with the Indians and was the big man of the region. He became the first Delegate to represent in Congress that "distant and wild territory," and was received in Washington with some curiosity as typical of the "rude and semi-civilized people who had sent him to the Capital." [1]

St. Paul was barely emerging from a haphazard con-glomeration of whiskey shops and birch-roofed cabins housing half-breeds and adventurers, but it had been selected as the Capital of the Territory to the amazement of the settlers since the real center of activities—business, social and religious—was the town of Mendota, six miles away, "the Meeting of the Waters." It was to this town that the Shields had come in 1854. The site was beautiful and dramatic, standing at the junction of the Mississippi and Minnesota rivers on the very spot which, according to Indian lore, was immediately over the center of the earth and below the center of the heavens.

The Shields did not stay long in town. They looked about for a farm, and showed their prudence by avoiding the more fertile lands along the banks of the river with their exposure to Indian attack, choosing a relatively safe position on the estate of H. H. Sibley within sight of Fort Snelling, the U. S. military post on Pilot Knob where they could take refuge in case of danger. Here, in this wild land, Bridget Shields took up her new life as a farmer's wife,

---

[1] Communication to Minnesota Historical Society by H. H. Sibley, as quoted in the *History of Dakotah County*, p. 116.

bearing and bringing up a generous brood of boys and girls, facing fatigues and dangers with courage and faith. And, thank God, the land was fertile, she explained to her brother, the climate healthful, the scenery of supreme beauty— he could see that for himself: that world of lakes, of forest, of high rolling table land. The little ones were grand children and helped their parents in the duties around the home and farm outside of school hours. All this she told her brother. Yes, indeed her life was full of responsibilities, of anxieties too, but also full of joys. As for Tom . . .

Thomas Edward was the sixth of her eight children. He came into the world on the 9th of May, 1862, during the course of the Civil War. In August of that same year there began the fearful uprising of the Indians, determined, at last, to exterminate the whites. The young men had left the region to fight in the Union army. The Indians seized their opportunity. The "week of blood" with which the Sioux opened their campaign was one whose horrors were burned deep into the memory of every settler. Up and down the river, the Indians spread in bands of eight or ten, carrying torture and death to the homes of all the settlers within reach. The latter were isolated and unarmed. They had no means of calling for help nor of warning one another of the impending danger: no telephone, telegraph, rare postal service, so that the Indians had things pretty much their own way with the unfortunate pioneers. The troops at Fort Snelling, in the outskirts of Mendota, were outnumbered and their early attempts at rescue turned into retreat. The years that followed were terrible ones for the farmers of what had by now become the State of Minnesota. Thousands of settlers fell victim to the Indians, most of them being foreign immigrants, peaceful, hard-working farmers engaged in turning a wilderness into a garden.

During the worst part of the massacres, many farmers sought refuge within the enclosure of Fort Snelling and it is highly probable that the Shields family were among the number. Thus the first few years of little Tom's life were perilous ones. The Indians continued their massacres until the young men returned from the war, and Bridget Shields had learned to face danger, daily and nightly, with courage and faith in God's providence.

Though he made his first appearance in this world at a time of danger and stress, little Tom was bright as a lark, quick-tempered and wilful, but soon learned to fit himself into a highly organized life. Each child must make himself useful: the boys in harvesting the crops, in chopping wood and in other small jobs fitted to their strength; the girls in aiding their mother in cooking, sewing and other details of household management, unending as they are in the routine of a large family. Each child had his or her allotted task and was responsible for its accomplishment. All arose early. Meals were served promptly: breakfast at six, dinner at noon, supper at six in the evening. Morning and night prayers were said in common before a little altar set up in a quiet spot. Sunday Mass was never omitted though the church—which still bore the name of St. Peter—was fully three miles away over rough roads, and the weather in winter could be rigorous. A child of the family remembers arriving for Mass with his ears solidly frozen, and the priest rubbing them mercilessly with snow before permitting him to enter the Church.

There was nothing soft in the training of the children, but, if discipline was strict, there was a touch of gaiety, too. Winter evenings were enlivened with games, and there was an occasional party for the neighboring families as the children began to grow up. Such was the life of this Irish-

American family of pioneering farmers; industrious, frugal, methodical, wholesome, with a profound piety bred in the bone.

How did it happen in such surroundings, with so sane a life, that their sixth child, this little Tom, should be at first so quick and active, so ready to learn, and then, by a strange turn of fate, become so dull, so incredibly dull as to become a byword among their friends and neighbors? The boy was known by a nickname that clung: "Shields' Omadhaun," [2] which reached the ears of the puzzled parents to add to their heartache and humiliation.

His mother sighed deeply as she continued:

"If we could only teach him reading, writing and arithmetic, just enough so that he might get along on the farm, we should be satisfied." And she added: "We sent him back to school last year—he was thirteen then—and the teacher did everything in her power to help him, but after three months she gave it up as useless."

The voices of the speakers carried through the open windows, from the cool dining room to the bench outside where an overgrown lad of fourteen was resting after his lunch before returning to his manual labor on the farm. Not a syllable was lost. Each tragic word struck him in the heart like an electric shock. "Poor Tom"—that was he! "Hopeless!" "Useless!"

[2] *Omadhaun* is one of the few Gaelic words that have been incorporated into our language. The word has long been in use as a term of contempt in Ireland and in the Gaelic-speaking parts of Scotland. If we accept the dictionary definition of an *omadhaun*, namely, "a fool, a simpleton, a madman," there was certainly no time in the childhood or early youth of Tom Shields when this name could be given him justly. When writing of those dark days of his life, Doctor Shields referred to himself as a *dullard*—a more exact word. Yet even this milder term is resented by many of those who knew him and considered the boy rather the victim of mistaken educational methods than a case of inherent stupidity or dullness. That he could have been known for years as an omadhaun can only be attributed to his unprepossessing appearance, his shyness and his halting, stammering speech.—*Author's Note.*

"It was the first intimation I had," as he wrote many years later, "of the reason which led my parents to keep me home from school. Although I knew in a general way that I had no talents such as other boys possessed, nevertheless my mother's words came to me like a sentence of condemnation and they crushed me utterly. I slunk away from the bench like a wounded animal and hid in the corn field."

The words he had overheard had not been intended for his ears. He realized this in the midst of his pain. Yet they set up a barrier between him and all the world of normal human beings. He retired into a solitude that was to be unbroken for many years. Any question that arose in his mind thenceforward could only be solved experimentally. There was no one to whom he could go and explain a difficulty without fear of ridicule. Highly sensitive, and not by any means the fool he was considered, the boy felt keenly every contemptuous look or careless word that underlined his supposed inferiority. There was no softness, no self-pity in the pain, but a deep humiliation that grew with the days, and a hopeless discouragement. His inner life, thrown back upon himself as he was, developed secretly and silently. Sometimes his brothers would find him hiding behind a hedge to pray or to say his rosary. His faith was simple and strong. His heart, imprisoned and solitary, found relief in appealing to a higher tribunal, full of earnest confidence. It was undoubtedly this strong faith which kept him from succumbing to the temptation of bitterness during the painful years which followed. No one around him suspected that the dullard was suffering keenly, and he never thought of expressing his loneliness and heartache. He built a wall to protect his inner life against ridicule. At the age of fourteen, he had become a hermit, living in a family but apart from it. He was alone.

When there was a litter of pups on the farm and the men

wished to determine which pup of the litter to raise, they used to catch each one by the scruff of the neck and hold it out at arm's length. The pups that squealed were drowned; those with grit enough to keep their mouths shut were raised.

Did the lesson remain fixed in Tom's mind? Certainly he was not the kind of boy to squeal. The few incidents that remained in his memory from the days of his early childhood, those days when he was considered a clever child, advanced for his age, would seem to show a grit and tenacity that were anything but soft. The emotion connected with the incidents caused them to remain engraved on his mind some fifty years later. He writes:

"When I was three years and ten months old, our family moved three or four miles to a neighboring farm. I can see the kitchen of the old house . . . the empty wood box behind the stove. Outside the door was a broad step at one end of which was an inverted, broken shovel that had served for many years in scraping the mud from the family shoes. There was a light snow on the ground and in the front yard, a mule team hitched to a wagon was piled high with furniture and boxes; behind this there was an ox team hitched to an empty bobsled. My parents intended that I should ride in the bobsled with my mother and younger members of the family, but I resisted with so much anger reinforced with kicks, tears and sobs that I finally obtained my own way and was allowed to take my place beside the driver on the high seat behind the mule team."

Once upon this dizzy height, his nerve was put to the test. Had he been put there without having struggled for the privilege, the child might have cried out in terror as the wagon got under way, begging to be taken down as the wheel struck the first stone and the icy ridges. But, having committed himself, his pride was aroused and all his strength of will was summoned to control his fear during the perilous journey. The emotional tension was so high that a permanent record was made on his memory: each trivial incident that occurred, the crossing of the railway track newly laid at the time, with its two bright bands of steel seeming to touch one another in the distance, his feelings of terror as he clung to the back of the seat while the wagon jolted over the frozen ground, his relief when Jake lifted him down from the high seat, his little limbs numb from the long, cold ride—each was recorded on his mind with the accuracy which emotion only can provide.

The Shields family had tried farming in another locality for a few years and were returning to the Sibley farm when the perilous ride took place.

Another incident stood out in his memory which took place some eighteen months later:

"At that time I was the proud possessor of two pair of homemade rusty breeches. . . . It was an autumn day and I was keeping guard over the pair of breeches that had just left the wash tub and was drying on the clothes-horse behind the kitchen stove. I had determined that my wardrobe should not be depleted even to rescue my little brother from the ignominy of petticoats. But alas, courage was never yet a match for women's wiles. One of my sisters promised to mount guard for me while the other induced me to accompany her to the corn crib where I stood fascinated by the golden ears as they came in showers and rolled down the pile of corn. On my return to the house I found I had been basely betrayed; my little brother was strutting around in my newly ironed trousers and my anger rose to the breaking point."

If these two incidents are hardly of a nature to advance

a cause for canonization, they are characteristic of a nature that could stick to a point doggedly in spite of personal danger, a trait which was highly characteristic of the man, who, furthermore, resented deeply anything like deceit or encroachment upon what he considered a personal right. The child in this was father to the man.

How shall we bridge the gap between this child, high-strung, quick-tempered, perhaps a bit spoiled, and the boy hiding in the cornfield like a wounded animal? How could a few years have brought about so great a change?

Dullness among children is usually attributed to certain definite causes such as heredity, poor physical environment, undernourishment, child illnesses, imperfect senses or some moral shock such as fear. In the case of Tom Shields none of these causes can account for his condition. Heredity was entirely in his favor. He came of a long-lived, fecund race. His grandparents lived beyond the allotted four score years; his father lived to the age of eighty-four and his mother to the age of ninety-eight! There was no sign of hereditary disease in any branch of the family, his ancestors having been well-to-do farmers as far back as the family can be traced. The physical environment of his childhood and youth were all that could be desired. Born and raised on a large farm, with plenty of outdoor life, air fresh and invigorating, soil wonderfully fertile, scenery beautiful, each changing season bringing its variety of occupations, the boy kept close to nature and generated a hearty appetite which was appeased five times a day by an abundance of wholesome food.

There were poultry and fresh eggs all the year round with homemade preserves; fresh fruits and vegetables in season from the garden; beef and mutton of their own raising and home-cured ham and bacon. Tom's mother was an excellent cook, moreover; never did he taste in after years bread and butter to compare with those she used to make. But things often look better from a distance! Things were daintily if simply served, with immaculate table linen. Three times a day the children sat down to table; in addition a bulging lunch basket was sent out to them in the fields at ten and again at four. Fresh milk was Tom's usual beverage and from the time he was eight years old until he was sixteen, he would finish his share of the milking each day by draining a brimming quart of warm milk, which habit linked with his lanky appearance, gained for him the nickname of "overgrown calf."

His health was excellent. Except for the usual childish siege of measles and whooping-cough he never had a day's illness during the first twenty years of his life. His senses were normal, indeed above normal. He was not a timid child by nature, nor could he remember ever having been frightened nor having suffered any accident that could account for his period of dullness. Finally, no one could ever accuse him of being lazy. Thus, by process of elimination, the case of Tom Shields narrows down to a single cause: *the dullness which arises from alternate phases of physical and mental development;* that, and mistaken methods in its treatment.

At the time of his childhood, this problem was almost unknown to educators as were most of the phenomena involving the physiology of the nervous system. If they are better known today, it is due in large measure to this particular victim of mistaken educational methods, who, looking backward over the experiences of his childhood and youth, read the record " that was burned into the heart and brain of the omadhaun" and based upon it many of the discoveries which have helped to make school life less odious to the child, less crushing, in particular, to the retarded child.

Stripped of technicalities, the important facts in such a case are these: all vital functions are controlled by nerve currents. Both bodily and mental development rests upon high tension in these currents. A child who grows very rapidly will make such demands upon this nerve energy for his physical organism that the cortical tension is lowered and there is not enough nerve energy to carry on the work of rapid mental growth. A conflict takes place between mental and physical development. Seldom is a perfect balance preserved between the growth of the body and that of the mental processes. One or the other is sacrificed, unless great skill is shown in dealing with such cases.

Thus if the children in a third- or fourth-grade room be ranged according to size, it will be found as a general rule that the brightest children mentally will be the smallest, and the largest, the dullest. The eagerness and ambition of these smaller pupils coupled with their quickness of movement indicate high cortical tension. Now if these children be constantly overstimulated, their physical development may be retarded for many years; and if the precocious little ones escape disease and death, they will finally reach a time in which the balance swings in the opposite direction. Physical development, so long retarded, sets in with great rapidity. The ensuing phase is characterized by lack of energy which to the uninstructed *appears to be dullness* or even laziness. Pupils who are intrusted at such a time to incompetent teachers are likely to be driven into discouragement so great as to degenerate into permanent dullness from which these unfortunate children make no further effort to escape.

This was precisely the state into which mistaken methods

drove Tom Shields. Looking back in later life over those distressing years of his childhood and youth, he took to heart his own tragic experience and made up his mind that all his life was none too great a gift to devote to saving other children from a like fate. All his studies were aimed at equipping himself for this task. All his later life was spent in imparting to teachers the principles of education based on the results of proved scientific data on the psychology of the nervous system in so far as it applies to education. He was not evolving theories in a vacuum. He could touch the living flesh—his own—on which had been carved by pain and humiliation the lesson which he must pass on to others.

CHAPTER TWO

SCHOOL AND FARM

TOM SHIELDS was sent to school for the first time at the age of six. The educational facilities were rudimentary in the new State, the children of the settlers were gathered together in groups of disparate character. Tom found himself in a little schoolhouse at Mendota which consisted of a single room containing sixty to seventy pupils of all ages and one teacher to attend to them all.

The boy had learned to read at home. For his misfortune, he was the only child in what, by courtesy, we might call the First Grade. There was but one child in the Second Grade. For the sake of convenience, the teacher promoted Tom—then a bright child—into the Second Grade Reader in company with his older fellow student. Then, for further convenience, the teacher promoted the two little fellows into a higher class, thus eliminating the elementary reading classes. From the pupils' standpoint, it was a fatal mistake. It represented precisely the kind of overstimulation which a competent teacher would have avoided. The new book was made up of selections from the English classics and was entirely too difficult for a child of six. Tom had no comprehension of the subject matter, and the words themselves were too difficult for him to pronounce. He found himself pitted against children much older than himself. His hesitations, his stumbling over words, developed rapidly into a defect which his teacher and his parents referred to as a "stoppage in his speech." The daily humiliation of defeat began to settle into a violent and permanent distaste for reading.

In other branches he fared better, his work in spelling and arithmetic was considered good. He had finished long division, was working on fractions before his ninth year, and was considered a child of normal intelligence. The only subject in which he had a sense of complete failure was reading, due to the overstimulation, but this failure caused him a deep sense of shame and discouragement. His dullness came on gradually, and it was not until the closing months of his ninth year that he noticed that the other boys kept teasing him, playing tricks upon him and provoking him into frequent fights. He was growing very rapidly during that period, and this, as well as the discouragement, must have accounted for the fact that he ceased to progress in any of the school subjects.

On the completion of his ninth year he was taken out of school and put to work on the farm. "I was not sorry for this change," he writes; "I had grown to dread the school and hate it. I was given a team to drive and, dressed in an overall suit, I felt myself quite a man. I used to climb up into the manger to put the bridles on the horses and had some difficulty in harnessing them."

He worked on the farm for four years, which, as we shall see, was time well spent as regards his mental development. He fell and broke his arm when he was thirteen, and his parents decided that during the time of enforced inaction, he might be sent to school once more, as they wished him to be prepared for Confirmation. They still nursed a lingering hope that he might be taught the elements of the "three R's." Evidently, they were convinced that

Tom's dullness was a permanent infirmity to which they must resign themselves with Christian fortitude. They never suspected that his mental condition was due to a temporary phase of abnormally rapid physical development combined with mistaken methods at school. This physical state had come to an end at the period when he was sent to school for the second time. Had he been handled intelligently, his mental life would have awakened. Unfortunately his second experience at school was all too similar to the first. Whether it was the same teacher or another of equal pedagogical genius who received the thirteen-year-old boy has not been recorded, but this time the drama was of a more tragic nature.

He was three or four years older and much larger than any of the other pupils in the reading class, and was undoubtedly the poorest reader of them all. To make matters worse, during his four years' absence from school, he had had no contact with other children. His intercourse with them was shy and awkward. Under these conditions, a new and favorable beginning in the difficult art of reading could hardly be expected. As a matter of fact, the experiment proved to be one long-drawn-out humiliation. Each day recorded a fresh failure. While the pupils did not laugh at Tom openly, as he towered above them in size, their pity was more galling to the embarrassed boy than would have been their laughter.

Worse was to follow. During class one day, the unfortunate boy committed some slight offense against good manners which he regretted instantly. He hoped that the teacher had noticed nothing, but the next day she called him sharply to account and reasoned with him insistently. Sincerely penitent but inexpressive, Tom hung his head in shame and let the torrent of words roll over his silent regret. Speech was not easy to the *omadhaun*. The teacher continued her lecture and finally made the unpardonable blunder of drawing a comparison between his clever brother and himself. At this, all his contrition turned to defiance. The teacher saw the change in his attitude without understanding its cause and concluded, as she said, that since scolding was ineffective, she would see what a whipping would do. We have Shields' own account of what followed:

"She was a muscular woman and enjoyed a well-deserved reputation for her ability to wield a black walnut ruler two feet long, an inch and a half wide and a quarter of an inch thick. She ordered me to hold out my hand and, rising on her tiptoes, she came down with all her might. No boy in school was ever known to wait for a second application of that ruler. But I sullenly held my hand in the same position and looked the defiance that I felt. I believe that I would have stood there until she had exhausted her strength, but she ordered me to leave the room. The blood was just trickling through the skin and my hand was swollen for some days afterward."

This was the teacher who, according to Bridget Shields, had done everything in her power to help Tom. Perhaps, according to her lights, she had done so, but the results were not commensurate with the effort. After that occurrence, the boy ceased to make any effort. He was in a state of sullen defiance and his old hatred of the school revived with increased violence. Once more, he felt pleased when his parents took him out of school a few weeks later and put him back to work in the fields. No doubt his broken arm had had time to heal.

Yet his old light-hearted joy in the work was overshadowed by a growing realization that he was different from other boys, different even from his own brothers and sisters. He could plow and mow, sow and reap as well as any of the grown men on the place, but there were things which were hidden from him. He could not imagine what the world was like to those around him who were clever, who could read the papers and keep track of events in the outer world.

It was at this precise moment that the blow fell, more crushing than that of the teacher's ruler, his mother's words overheard at the noon hour. At last he understood. Too well. The gloom and despondency which settled upon him during the years that followed were deep indeed. He used to look at the workmen on the place with a feeling of reverent wonder as at beings of another sphere. They had brains and were like other people, whereas he, Tom, was Shields' *omadhaun*, a monster. From that time on he made no attempt to read, he forgot the multiplication table and he could not have written so much as his own name when sixteen years old. He shrank from all contact with strangers and became silent and sullen. Yet in spite of his sullenness, he was a pious boy and remained so during the dark years that followed. No matter how tired he might have been after his hard day's work, he never went to bed without saying his night prayers and his rosary. "God and the Blessed Virgin, my Guardian Angel and the Saints were as real to me as the people who surrounded me," he records. "Whenever I particularly wanted anything, I dropped on my knees behind the plow or in the wagon box and asked for it with far more confidence of being heard and answered than I would have had in making any request of my earthly parents."

"Sometimes," he continues, "I used to dream of my future. A religious vocation occasionally teased my imagination. Of course I did not dream of being a priest, for I knew that a priest had to have brains . . . I had heard people talk about lay brothers whose duty was to work in the fields and to take care of the cattle, and I imagined that I might become a lay brother. Sometimes I used to wonder whether I would be a farmer, but I found it impossible to complete the picture for I could not imagine a farmer without a farmer's wife, and I never dared to hope that any girl would look with favor upon *Shields' omadhaun*."

Tom's mental life had sunk to its lowest ebb a short while before his mother's words reached his ears. The boy had acquired his adult weight and height when only fourteen years old. In the years when he had been growing so rapidly his condition had caused him little worry because his intelligence was not sufficiently active to realize his condition. The pain began with his awakening intelligence at the beginning of his fifteenth year, but many long years dragged by with leaden feet before he understood that pain was the harbinger of salvation. Those around him had as little knowledge of his awakening mental life as they had of the humiliation from which he was suffering. Crushed by the memory of his repeated failures at school, mortified by the contemptuous attitude of those around him, Tom reached the conviction not only that he knew nothing, but that he was incapable of ever knowing anything as long as he lived. The struggle that began at this time between that abiding conviction and his growing mental life, of which he was totally unconscious, continued to his twenty-first year.

It is all too easy to imagine the state of mind of Tom's family, though, from a distance, it seems singularly unenlightened. They had witnessed a first inexplicable transformation, that of a clever child turned into a dullard. That a second change could take place, that the dullard might one day become a normal member of society, simply did not cross their minds. We can hardly blame them if we consider the wall of silence which enclosed the adolescent lad as in a cell. The "stoppage in his speech" was a slight barrier compared to the greater obstacle to all intercourse built up out of discouragement and fear of ridicule. A boy with a less solid foundation of faith might well have despaired and have been drawn into the ranks of young criminals of whom we see so many. That he did not do so must be attributed in part to the healthful outdoor life which he led, the poetry of the natural beauties which surrounded him and to which he responded in his silent way, but principally to his deep piety and sincere attachment to those invisible friends who had his confidence and to whom he could carry his distress and sorrow. Thus his days were spent, painfully enough, surrounded by a group of gay, clever brothers and sisters who may have pitied him but never for one moment understood the boy who was struggling up out of the darkness.

Meanwhile a strange transformation was taking place. The first ray of self-confidence reached Tom through his muscles, which had hardened into strength by the time he reached the age of fourteen. It was no little thing for him, who felt himself so inferior in every other respect to the immigrant laborers on his father's farm, to pass from the lighter occupations assigned to the boy to the harder work of the man. To compete successfully in strength and endurance with men who had passed the golden line of twenty-one, while he was still a boy of fourteen, was to gain a measure of self-respect and to lay the foundation of self-reliance. Yes, he could chop as much wood in a day, hoe as many rows of corn, shock as many acres of grain as the best man on the farm! He did not connect these activities with education, fortunately perhaps, but they gave him a sense of satisfaction that more than compensated for the fatigue entailed. Thus, while the state of profound discouragement and the condemnation of his mother's words barred every other gateway to the exercise of his mental powers, Tom's budding conscious life found here an avenue of growth.

From these rude employments he gradually progressed to others which demanded more skill, such as plowing a straight furrow, making a load of hay or pitching bundles of grain to the top of a high stack. Other occupations developed rapidity of movement, such as husking corn, or binding on a harvester. He delighted in feats of horsemanship in which he acquired no mean skill. He learned the use of the simpler carpenter tools and his eye was trained to accuracy of measurement. Indeed, no other years of his life brought him treasures comparable in value to those gathered so casually during those years on the farm, when he believed himself cut off forever from the things of the mind, from books and from human companionship. Those years left him with a sensory-motor training of a high order, with a robust constitution, an enduring love of work, and they built up in him self-reliance and a determined will. No small treasures indeed.

The constant variety of scene and of occupation that came with the changing seasons provided the best possible motor training for the boy, and became the basis of all his subsequent mental development. The value of such things to mental life was hidden from him and from his parents, yet such was their power that, without them, he would probably never have come up out of the darkness. It was later in life that he realized they had been his salvation.

All these things were real work, not play. But the circumstances surrounding that work happened to be of the most favorable kind for a boy in his condition. Fortunately the work was not mere drudgery, as would have been the case in a factory. The deadening effect of monotony was totally absent. Tom was kept out of doors and in close contact with nature. All his senses were appealed to in turn. He writes:

"The smell of the upturned soil, the perfume of the wild rose and the odor of the new-mown hay are still with me; the call of the catbird, the whistle of the bobolink, the humming of the bees and the familiar spectacle of the prairie chicken inviting death by shamming a broken wing in order to divert attention and avert danger from her young. . . . With these sights and sounds of nature are inseparably entwined in the tangled skein of memory, the outward signs of human activity that blended with nature's processes. I can still feel on my feet the soft, wet moss, hear the swish of the scythes through the soft grass and the music of the whetstones on the steel blades.

"Another great advantage attaches itself to the sort of training that we received on the farm; the work is not done for the sake of the training; there is no make-believe about it. It was animated by an earnest purpose; something real was being done at every hour. The absence of this motive is one of the chief drawbacks of all artificial systems of training. There is nothing that develops character and self-reliance in youth so surely as real occupations and real responsibilities."

CHAPTER THREE

MIND AND MUSCLES

FROM the age of nine to sixteen, the farm became the only school of Tom Shields. If we are to understand the drama of his development, we must examine briefly the experiences which contributed to his formation. No schedule of studies was announced on a bulletin board, no teacher stood over the boy to encourage his efforts. Yet the cure for his peculiar condition could hardly have been better planned by an educational expert. The number concept, special relationships, truths which grew vivid through close contact with nature, all these things contributed to the development of his mind and led him by slow degrees to a grasp of the germinal truths of mechanics through which he reached his ultimate mental salvation.

When he was first taken out of school, his duties on the farm were not confined to the jolly task of driving a team. Tom's father used to raise several thousand bushels of grain for the market. As a boy of nine or ten it was Tom's task to "hold the sacks," that is to say, Tom held the bag at arm's length while his father emptied into it three half bushels of grain. Each time the measure was emptied, the boy lifted the bag so as to pack down the grain. In this way he learned through the sense of sight and through the muscle sense the size and weight of a half bushel, a bushel and a bushel and a half of grain.

It was also his task to count the sacks as they were lined up against each other, and he learned to recognize accurately the twenty sacks that made a load. A correlation between sight and muscle sense was being built up in this way and others too numerous to mention.

At the age of fourteen when he was taken out of school for the second time, hemmed in by discouragement and thrown completely on his own interior resources, the farm was still his best friend and educator, standing by as though in sympathy and offering its aid. At fifteen he was one of the strongest men on the place and was assigned the task of hauling in the grain. He used to lift the bags containing a bushel and a half each into the wagon box, and arriving at the granary, raised them to his shoulder and, running up a ladder some ten or twelve feet high, emptied them into the bin. In the winter season when the grain was marketed, it was Tom's task to tie the sacks and pile ten of them on the scale. He knew the weights and could call out the total for the ten sacks. His brother John entered these weights in the books while Tom regarded him with reverence for his ability to discover from these weights the number of bushels and of pounds in each "batch." He longed for the ability to work out this problem himself, but as he had forgotten the multiplication table and the system for doing a problem in long division, it baffled him for a long time.

It must be remembered that the stage had long passed in which Tom's physical development was such as to handicap him mentally. His mind was keen and eager for information, curious and persistent in his search for truth. But mental tools were totally lacking. Not to be defeated in his research, he formed the habit of counting on his fingers, calculating the weight of bags in "batches" with that same inner necessity of arriving at a fundamental truth which characterized him later as a man. Each bushel that he added in imagination was a *real* bushel known to him through thousands of individual muscular efforts. For all that, the result of his calculations was a failure; it differed from the total at which John had arrived.

Should he ask John for an explanation? The idea did not even occur to him. Since his second failure at school he spoke very seldom, and on the rare occasions when he attempted to speak, even the members of his own family found it hard to understand him. Could he ask one of the boys of the neighborhood? They all mocked and made fun of him, so much so that he grew ashamed of the sound of his own voice. He did not even dare to hum a tune or to whistle. He had no playmates, and when the boys gathered on Sunday afternoons to play ball in the Shields' pastures, Tom was forbidden to join in the game. He was never allowed to visit nor to leave home. To whom, then, could he put the question that was teasing his mind? Would any workman on the place have risked ridicule by explaining a problem in arithmetic to the dullard? For more than a year the problem baffled him, yet his curiosity and sense of logic gave him no rest. At last one day chance came to his rescue. He overheard John calculating out loud. He listened and found the key to the riddle; John had subtracted ten pounds for the weight of the sacks! It was Tom's first discovery in pure science, the first in an intellectual development that was to lift him one day into the companionship of the learned.

From that moment of discovery he tied and weighed many thousands of bushels of wheat, but never once without calculating mentally the bushels and pounds. He soon learned to dispense with his fingers in counting and dealt wholly with sense images; but they were images of real bushels of wheat and not artificial symbols such as those on which children's minds are often fed.

It was chiefly the muscle sense that formed the basis of *number* in his mind. The sense of touch and that of sight each contributed to the formation of the mental images, indeed, but their chief content resulted from the constant repetition of muscular exertions.

Nor were these the only lessons supplied by the farm to contribute to the growth and development of his mind. During the summer months, between his tenth and fourteenth years, Tom helped to build several miles of board fence around the farm. He learned to use the square and the hand saw. His eye was gradually trained to judge with considerable accuracy small variations in the length of boards without needing to measure them. He frequently helped the carpenters with the rougher work of building barns and outhouses, an occupation that taught him the use of carpentry tools and familiarized him with various dimensions.

He advanced in knowledge unaware of his own progress. Everything had to be discovered for himself by experiment. He performed fantastic feats of interior visualization based on cubic feet: scantlings split or laid side by side became his tools. Sometimes he cut off (in imagination of course) a two-inch strip from a two-by-eight and added it to a two-by-four, thus converting the two pieces into a pair of two-by-sixes. Sometimes he converted three two-by-eights into four two-by-sixes. In this interior world of his, Tom was creating his own set of mental tools, and one can but wonder how many men on the farm or which one of his clever brothers and sisters could have carried through successfully such complicated feats of concentration and visualization! Yet all his progress was secret, hidden, as though in shame, from any indiscreet glance.

John Shields was growing old and had turned over the active management of the farm to his second son, John Joseph, who was ten years older than Tom. Michael Bernard, the elder son, who was twelve years Tom's senior, was married and engaged in setting up an establishment of his own with his young wife on a neighboring farm. These two brothers, each in his own way, performed for Tom, quite without intending it, some of the functions of a teacher. Of his two brothers, Shields writes as follows:

"It would be difficult to find two men who, in their mental life, offered a more complete contrast to each other. John was a calm, decisive, imperturbable man; he was an omnivorous reader; he was boss on the farm at the time of which I speak, and his orders were final, his decisions irrevocable. John dealt only in conclusions; his processes of reasoning and his data were all reserved for his own exclusive use. Michael, on the contrary, was a mechanical genius and while he had a fair education and was fond of reading, his mental life was built up largely of his own experiences. He was never content with assertions; he had to see things. If you differed from him, he proceeded at once to find out the reason for the difference. With him there were twenty correct ways of doing everything instead of one, and it was only a question of choosing which of the twenty was best."

The play of these two influences in the education of Tom Shields can be gauged by the following incident which we give in his own words:

"When I was about fifteen years old we hauled two or three carloads of lumber from a siding a few miles from the farm, to build a barn. I drove one of the teams and helped to load and unload the lumber. One day we loaded some green sills onto my wagon. Before the load had attained its usual size, my brother John remarked that I had eight

hundred feet on, which, owing to the bad condition of the
roads, was quite enough for my team. I knew that the
load was heavy enough for my team but his remark that
there were *eight hundred feet* of lumber on my wagon
puzzled me sadly.

"At that time I could measure off a foot with my eye with
great accuracy, and I had just as accurate an idea of what
constituted a square foot, but in my mind, neither of these
things had anything to do with solids. I was familiar with
the cube in putting up ice and in measuring cord wood. I
had hauled many a cord of wood and I knew its dimensions;
eight feet long, four feet wide and four feet high; and I
had frequently counted up the one hundred and twenty-
eight feet which it contained. But this load of lumber which,
to my eye, did not seem much more than half as large as a
cord of wood, contained, according to my brother's statement, *eight hundred feet*."

John, of course, would vouchsafe no explanation, only
repeating drily that the load contained eight hundred and
sixty-four feet. It was a clear case of conflict between
evidence and authority and, as usual, authority had the best
of it. But the problem stuck in Tom's mind. He could not
get rid of it. That evening at supper he mentioned the
matter again, telling his brother that he had measured that
load of lumber and it contained only seventy-two feet.
John smiled his usual pitying smile that Tom remembered
so well, doubtless considering the remark as another proof
of Tom's hopeless idiocy.

For a whole year this problem tantalized the boy. Every
time he handled lumber, he counted the feet, and when he
could get someone to measure it, he was always faced with
the same baffling contradiction. The result confirmed John's
statement and contradicted the tangible evidence of his

senses. It never occurred to him to question the accuracy of his own idea as to what constituted a foot of lumber, and those around him failed to understand the nature of his difficulty, or simply brushed it aside as one more of the *omadhaun's* vagaries which it would have been worse than folly to seek to understand.

Characteristically, he refused to let go of the problem, and finally it was his brother Michael who gave him the key. Tom was helping Michael put a roof on a barn. They ran short of lumber and as John was leaving for town, Michael called to him to bring home two hundred feet. Tom had noticed the shortage and had counted the amount of lumber that would be needed. He protested that seventeen feet, not two hundred, was all that would be required.

"How do you make that out?" asked Michael.

The unfinished strip of roof was seventeen feet long and twelve feet wide, so the probem was easy. Tom called Michael's attention to the fact that seventeen boards one foot wide and twelve feet long, each of which contained, according to his calculation, but one foot of lumber, would just finish the roof.

"What do you mean by saying that there is only one foot of lumber in each of the boards?" asked Michael. When Tom explained the matter, Michael told him that he must be thinking of a cubic foot, whereas a foot of lumber was only one inch deep. At last Tom had the solution of his problem.

A word of explanation! It is the first that is recorded in the history of Tom's childhood and youth. A little light coming to him from the outside. The thing was simple enough in itself and Michael, no doubt, gave the matter no further thought. Not so with Tom. This incident became a landmark in his education. His mind was hungry and his intellectual curiosity was out of all proportion to the available data upon which to work and from which to draw conclusions. Thus, each new fact that he acquired was put to immediate use. No talents were hidden in a napkin. From that day forward he made the foot-wide board his standard of measurement. His feats of interior visualization took on an ever-increasing complexity. His mind was active while his muscles worked in the fields. Where another boy of his age might have been absorbed in sports, dreaming of romance or of adventure, he was busying himself with a concentrated effort to calculate the amount of lumber contained in every fence on the farm; the amount of lumber used for the barn —and this last was a baffling problem because of those two-by-four studdings and rafters, those two-by-eight joists, those eight-by-eight sills. For several months these dimensions defeated him, but, with bull-dog tenacity, he finally triumphed by the process of splitting and putting together —mentally, of course—until all the various values were converted, strip by strip, into one-foot boards. With the accomplishment of these supreme mental gymnastics all difficulties disappeared in calculating quantities of lumber.

He did not know the meaning of the words *angle* or *triangle*. He had never heard of geometry, yet he was solving many practical problems in geometry nevertheless. Moreover, the fever of investigation had taken a deep hold upon his mind. The areas of irregular corners presented themselves; how could he reduce them to some shape that he could deal with? The sheeting of the gable ends of buildings compelled him to deal with triangles, and he noticed, in so doing, that when he fitted a piece of board into an angle of the gable there were two triangular pieces cut off which, if put together on their square edges, would just cover the same space. He discovered that by calculating every board on one gable as having the same length as the longest board, there would be enough lumber to cover two gables. It was many years before he learned that the scientific way of stating that simple truth is: *The area of a triangle is equal to one-half of the base times the altitude.* How fortunate it was for the "dullard" that no one attempted to instruct him by rote!

Again, he used to nail the jack rafters to the middle of the rafters and they were always level. Of course he learned much later that the right way to state this truth is: *A line dividing two sides of a triangle proportionally is parallel to the base.*

Thus the number concept was built up and the boy advanced in knowledge without the stultifying effect of memorized formulae. Tom's growing thirst for knowledge, his ardent experimental passion, which could rest only when the truth had been attained, were hidden from those who surrounded the boy called *omadhaun.* He himself had no thought of education. All those mathematical visions were, to his mind, a sort of daydream. His mental powers, having been thoroughly discouraged in every other direction, fastened themselves upon these problems of space and proportion and grew along those lines without suspecting that there was growth but rejoicing in activity.

Today many teachers use, in a methodical manner, some of the devices for building up the number sense with which Tom Shields educated himself in so haphazard a manner. Yet there is a difference. The school work, being systematic, may give a child more useful information in a month than Tom acquired in many years, but, as he points out himself, "Every little bit of truth that the growing mind discovers for itself has more real value than many times that quantity if fed to it. There is a development of self-reliance and originality in discovery that is seldom attained in systematic instruction."

It was precisely this originality and self-reliance, the fruit of the lonely years, which became a vital characteristic of the man who was destined to lead future educators along new paths.

CHAPTER FOUR

MECHANICS IN GERMINAL FORM

IT IS so easy for most of us to acquire information that we are apt to confuse the shadow of knowledge with the substance, mere intellectual tools with intellectual power, memorized formulae with the living growth of the mind. Yet is there any man so trite, so uninteresting as the one who knows everything, is looked upon by his contemporaries as a walking encyclopedia, and gets all his knowledge out of books? If Schiller is right in his theory that "the mind possesses only what it does," then Tom Shields was becoming very rapidly an educated man. This tall, raw-boned, lanky fellow with the frame and muscles of a man was still a child as regards information. He could neither read nor write. He could dig no facts out of books. He had no friends with whom to exchange ideas. Those who surrounded him seemed denizens of a higher order who had brains and the advantages of an education; he did not expect them to engage in any futile attempt to lift a brainless boy to the mental plane on which they lived. He was only conscious of their pitying contempt in his regard. Yet in spite of all this, his mind was active and constantly struggling, his energy was limitless. Fortunately, no drab memory loads clogged the development of his mental faculties. At least he was saved from that one handicap by his absence from school. Each discovery of truth was an original discovery and brought with it the joy of undiluted light. Yet, during those years between fourteen and sixteen, the contrast with this vital mental activity and the deep-seated conviction of his own hopeless inferiority was a constant torture.

"It is difficult," says Joubert, "to live despised and virtuous. We need support." We might add to this thought the observation of Madame de Sévigné: "Strength often requires more support than weakness. Feathers, unsupported, will sustain themselves for a long time in the air." Tom Shields was a strong boy; strong in body, strong in will. We look in vain for any human support during those years of his childhood and youth. God was his strength, his support was in the everlasting Arms as he recited his rosary behind a haystack or knelt in prayer before the Tabernacle of the village Church. And thus, with no external support, he lived despised yet virtuous, the mere fact of his strength hidden from all who surrounded him, a closely guarded secret between himself and God.

He lived, also, in a world of beauty. God's creatures, animate and inanimate, spoke to his imagination and delighted his senses. He writes with poetic insight of the teeming life that surrounded him, where nature's processes became familiar to him, and where he entered into nature's moods. There, on the banks of the Mississippi, stood armies of fine old lindens and stately elms, clusters of cottonwood and willow. There the wild grape grew in profusion, reaching high in festoons upon the lofty arches of linden and elm. There were wild plum, sumac and hazel bushes in tangled masses. But his chief delight was a shallow lake half choked by water lilies, bulrushes and wild rice. Marshes edged the lake covered with moss and luxuriant grasses. He sought out the springs of clear, cold water that bubbled up through the peat, wandering at leisure toward the open lake in little streams that gurgled and murmured between overhanging mossy banks, or lingered in the open sunshine, to be filled with watercress, or again, tumbled over some slight obstruction in mimic waterfalls. These beauties of sight and sound were stored in his imagination to reappear many years later in his beautiful story for children, *Silver Brook*. He delighted in the color of the tiger lily, the iris and the wild morning-glory. He followed the antics of the fish, watched for the coming of the birds, listened for the familiar whistle of the meadow lark and the red-winged blackbird, knew the habits of the snipe, the crane, the wild duck and the loon. The spreading meadows, that paradise for snails and frogs, had no secrets for Tom, and he watched the humblebees laying their store of honey in each high tuft of moss safe from the ravages of the field mouse. Nature herself was his teacher, explaining to him the many-sided struggle for existence going on about him. Thus the germ of many a natural truth took refuge in his mind which grew and bore fruit in after years.

Doctor Shields' own record of his boyhood states plainly that his education on the farm was his salvation. "Experience of twenty years with dullards," he wrote, "has convinced me that we are here in the presence of a natural law. The dullard's one hope of salvation is bound up with the phase of his mental development that is directly related to concrete reality. The sensory-motor reaction lies at the basis of mental life and until this is developed and made the standard of interpretation, the knowledge contained in books and language remains sealed. But once we have secured a vigorous development along these lines, it will be found comparatively easy to divert the flow of mental

energy into other channels. . . . There is no surer way to
defeat all purposes of education than to cram book learning
into a boy's mind before he has any desire or capacity for
such knowledge and while all his being is crying out for
the elementary things involved in sensory-motor experience." And he adds: "It is not improbable that the world is
indebted for the genius of Shakespeare to the fact that he
escaped too much formal drill in school and to the further
fact that many of the happiest hours of the boy's life were
spent in the woods listening to the song of birds and to the
murmur of breezes in the treetops, with his senses bathed in
the perfume of wild flowers, while he chased the squirrel to
its nest or watched the wounded fowl creep in among the
sedges. Had he been forced to spend those hours . . .
seated on a hard bench, his feet dangling, trying to engrave
on the tablets of his memory the a, b, c's while his soul was
in angry revolt—his heart never could have been the source
of the sweet songs that charmed the world."

Have we here an analogy, a glimpse of the happier and
richer moments of Tom's own childhood during which no
sense of inferiority haunted his heart? Those moments
which made the rest of the day alive with joy amid humiliation?

Meanwhile no boy at school ever took such pains to
attain knowledge as did the discouraged dullard in his solitude. He grappled with each problem that presented itself
with a dogged perseverance that would not let go until it
was mastered. We find this quality as clearly defined in the
upward surge of the outcast boy as, later, in the man of
science.

His education was one of muscles, touch, sight and hearing. Upon this foundation was based the awakening of his
mental faculties, which developed rapidly with the experi-

ences in simple mechanics which he acquired while working on the farm.

Farm machinery had been a necessity in Minnesota even in territorial days, due to the large tracts of wheat under cultivation. During the Civil War, machines became even more important because of the shortage of labor and the increased demand for wheat. Finally, with the building of the railroads, the farmers increased the acreage under cultivation since they could ship their crops to the markets of the whole continent. Thus machines took on an ever-growing importance. Even as a small child, Tom had watched the indispensable monsters with the respect which was their due. His young hands were taught to manipulate many a screw and nut before delving into the highly complex virtues of the machines which later fascinated him. But long before any of this, the observant child may have had as teachers the see-saw, the pump with its pulley and lever and other simple objects from which to absorb solid if germinal verities. Many a child astride a see-saw can grasp the principle of the lever with arms of equal or unequal length; can realize by experience that downward pressure on one arm of the lever is changed into an upward pressure on the other arm; can notice that when one child sits on the far end of the see-saw he will balance two or more children seated near the fulcrum of the other arm, and though the child's mind would be incapable of grappling with abstract definitions or mathematical formulae, he can realize that the longer the arm, the larger will be the movement.

"When we begin to teach mechanics with deductions from abstract principles we are simply reversing the natural order of the mind's growth," wrote Doctor Shields, the teacher. "Modern science and modern inventions have all grown out of actual contact with nature and not out of the speculations of philosophers. To obtain satisfactory results in the teaching of any subject we should begin with *germinal truths* which contain the body of knowledge in somewhat the same manner as seeds contain fully developed plants." A germinal idea, an expression borrowed from biology, is the first form of a living structure out of which the organism grows, which is capable of development from the very start, and whose development comes from inner, not external forces.

Had a machine been defined to Tom Shields, the child, as a transformer of energy, the definition would have conveyed little of what he learned by observing the see-saw. He grasped, in this simple game, a germinal truth, rudimentary as it was, which became the initial stage of a long series of mental processes; by observation of this and other sights around him he laid a foundation for the future study of mechanics. The story comes to mind of a young man who went to Darwin for the explanation of a difficult problem. "I shall think of what you have said," the young man remarked as the interview came to a close. The great scientist replied: "For Heaven's sake, do not think, *observe*."

There was an old-fashioned well near the farm house which whispered into the ear of little Tom a germinal truth. Ninety feet of rope passed over the pulley which was suspended from the roof that covered the well. To each end of the rope was fastened by a bit of chain an "old oaken iron-bound, moss-covered bucket." Tom remembers pulling the wet rope when he was scarcely tall enough to reach it, remembers, too, his fatigue before the seemingly endless rope finally brought the bucket into view. He had a clear realization of the fact that the bucket was heaviest at the bottom of the well, but he attributed this to the great depth of the well itself without suspecting that the ninety feet of wet rope added its weight to that of the bucket of water at the beginning of its upward journey and that this same rope acted as a counterpoise as the bucket neared the surface. The lesson, vague as it was in outline, was conveyed through the muscles and other senses. Tom was perceiving, as so many little children do, certain truths of a fundamental nature in their concrete setting without troubling to analyze their hidden causes.

As the boy grew older, the germinal idea of the lever developed by use of the hay-pole and the pitchfork. Out of the marshy fields, too soft for other means of transportation, Tom and another man would lift and carry the hay on two poles. Here the horizontal position was maintained, whereas with the pitchfork the lever rotates through a half-circle. In the hay-pole the weight is in the center of the lever, whereas with the pitchfork it is at one end, the power and fulcrum being in the hands of the haymaker. Thus, with the relative position of his hands constantly shifting on the handle, Tom learned through his muscle sense the meaning of the relative positions of the lever as it moved around the axis of rotation. One more germinal truth acquired by observation and experience.

The next transition in Tom's education was from the pitchfork and the pulley to the wheel and axle. He began to sense dimly that the lever affects energy in any one of four ways. It can shift the point of application, reverse the direction, increase the intensity acting through a diminished distance or diminish the intensity acting through an increased distance. He was dealing, now, with machines which embodied the use of the lever in these different ways. From familiarity and close observation, from admiration, too, he passed to meditation on the possibility of modifying some of the forces with which he was dealing. From germinal truths acquired by the handling of simple levers, he began to delve into mechanical first principles. This was the crucial moment when the walls of the cocoon began to split.

To use Doctor Shields' own words in looking back over the past: "As long as we use a machine in the form in which it is given to us and for the attainment of those ends which were contemplated by the builder, the machine remains our master. Our mastery over the machine dates from the moment in which we learn to modify it and adapt it to our purposes. My attempts to modify a few of the simpler farm machines produced in me the first discernible germ of self-reliance, the dawn of faith in my own mental powers."

It seems such a sudden leap from the dullard to the inventor, from the illiterate and lonely boy to the young enthusiast meditating upon the modification of machines, that we are inclined to wonder whether we should not, ourselves, modify our own ideas about what constitutes a dullard. Tom's first experiment took place in his thirteenth year, one year before his second school experience. This was the boy whose intelligence was judged so mediocre by his teacher. It had been his task to turn the grindstone on which the mowers sharpened their scythes. Now, a new grindstone is large in diameter; a low speed of the turning crank suffices to keep it in motion but as the stone wears down to a small core, a progressive increase in speed is required for the attainment of satisfactory results. This increased speed adds considerably to the fatigue of the arm that turns the crank. The arm was that of Tom Shields.

One morning toward the end of the haying season when the stone was worn down to a small core and the mowers were in a hurry, his patience reached its limit. The urgent haste and his tired muscles both cried out for a remedy, the first suggestion for which came to him from previous muscular exertions which, throughout all human progress, have been the prolific source of inventions. He knew what was needed—it came to him in a flash: a device that would cause the grindstone to revolve faster than the crank! Why had no one thought of that before? He remembered that such an end actually was obtained in a fanning mill that he had spent many a long day in turning. His powers of visualization showed him the handle of the mill attached to a large cogwheel each revolution of which caused a small pinion attached to the shaft of the fan to revolve several times. Why should he not transfer that wheel and pinion from the discarded fanning mill to the grindstone? What a saving of time and of muscular fatigue!

Full of enthusiasm, he attempted to carry out his idea. He failed and the failure brought down upon his head the ridicule which greeted any attempt by the *omadhaun* to depart from the trodden paths. He quailed under the ridicule but was not crushed. He was convinced that the failure was due to his lack of mechanical skill. As a matter of fact the bearings on which the grindstone turned were of such a nature that they could not hold the shaft in position in the new arrangement. As Tom attempted to turn the grindstone, the pinion slipped away from the larger wheel. There were other causes of the failure, but in the course of the experiment, Tom had obtained a clear view of a mechanical truth that neither failure nor gibes could obscure. There was a change in his mental attitude. Far from abandoning his idea, he busied himself eagerly with seeking out a remedy for the cause of the failure. He remembered that there was another grindstone on the farm, an heirloom of territorial days. It weighed several hundred pounds, the shaft was made in a forge and it turned in metal boxes. Perhaps this would serve? Tom made haste to transfer the wheel and pinion to this grindstone and, by strenuous efforts, he succeeded in making the grindstone revolve at a very high rate of speed. His triumph, however, was of short duration, for this rapid rotation soon shook the old frame to pieces.

It was another failure, yet this time the failure was not complete. He had accomplished his purpose; he had actually made the grindstone turn more rapidly than the crank, and, in the experiment, he had come upon two new bits of knowledge, the play of inertia and the function of a balance wheel in mechanics. His mind was enriched even though he could make no immediate application of these new conceptions.

Yet this new failure—for so it seemed to him—with the ridicule that followed it, made him pause in his experiments. His second school failure filled part of the interval, and two years passed before his next attempt to become an inventor.

These first crude experiments, far from appearing to his relatives as signs of an awakening mind, merely reinforced their settled conviction concerning the limitations of Tom's intelligence. The boy had shaken to pieces the frame of an old grindstone without obtaining any practical results. What else could one expect? They turned with a shrug to more serious preoccupations which were worrying the farmers of the region. A plague of locusts had descended upon the fertile lands of Minnesota, devouring the crops, ruining the owners. "They came," reports an eye-witness, "like an immense snowstorm, a vast cloud of animated specks glittering against the sun," or like a "dust tornado." When feeding, they made a noise like the roar of a prairie fire. When they had finished feeding, the wheat fields looked as though they had been burned, even the roots eaten. Not a leaf on the trees. For five years the pests had triumphed over the farmers and their combined efforts. It was precisely in this year, 1877, that the Governor of the State bethought him of appointing a day of public prayer throughout the State. The day was faithfully observed and, almost at once, the locusts disappeared as mysteriously as they had come. The farmers drew a sigh of relief. To the Shields family, what could be the significance of the frame of an old grindstone in this time of providential deliverance? They dismissed the incident from their minds.

CHAPTER FIVE

A DAYDREAM

THE year 1878 was a memorable one in the life of Tom Shields. It was during that year that the first ray of hope penetrated the gloom of discouragement in which he lived. As we have seen, his mind had been growing steadily during the preceding years but in a manner to escape recognition by those around him. He himself, at that time, had a more poignant conviction of his mental incapacity than at any other period during the last seven years. Hemmed in by the narrow horizon of one debarred from letters, his mind busied itself with combining and recombining memory pictures derived from muscle experiences and the sense of touch and sight. He would have been astonished indeed had he been told that his mind was awakening and giving promise of a development that would make him, one day, the equal of the farm lads in the neighborhood.

He had just completed his sixteenth year, but his size— five feet ten inches—made him look much older. His one hundred and sixty-five pounds were well disposed with no superfluous flesh in a strongly built frame. His dreamy brown eyes were overshadowed by luxuriant auburn brows. The forehead was broad, the nose large and strong, but the lower part of the face gave an impression of weakness, due, not to the chin itself, which was well developed, but to the lack of muscle tension, which caused the mouth to hang open habitually and the lower lip to protrude.

"In the summer of 1878," he writes, "I had a daydream that issued almost immediately in practical results of the greatest importance to me. It was early June. My brother and I were hauling timothy hay to market. For eight miles our road wound along the margin of the high bluff on the right bank of the Mississippi. My team—Jenny, a large dun-colored mule that had been dismissed by the government ten years previously on account of old age and rheumatic joints, and Lame Jack, a big bay draft horse that had acquired a stiff leg and a swollen knee during one of his many winter campaigns in the northern pineries—followed slowly along behind my brother's load from which they munched contentedly."

Wearing loose, well-worn brown jeans and a battered straw hat, Tom sat relaxed, tailor fashion, on the load of hay, his head sunk between his shoulders. As the team reached the top of Pilot Knob, an elevation of some five hundred feet above the river, the view which greeted the eye was one of surpassing beauty. On every side were well-tilled fields big with the promise of the coming harvest. Beneath, on the opposite bank of the river, lay St. Paul spread out over a group of low hills, while to the north-west, the spires and chimneys of Minneapolis stood up against the blue of the summer sky. To the left he could look down into the broad expanse of the Minnesota valley, where for thirty miles the eye could follow the river as it meandered between its wooded banks. In the foreground, Fort Snelling crowned the high promontory, marking the spot from which, in ages past, the Mississippi leapt over the precipice into the bed of the Minnesota three hundred feet below.

Tom Shields was not unresponsive to such beauty, but today the magnificent lines of the landscape and the delicate tints of the wild rose by the wayside were equally lost on the boy who sat dreaming on the top of the load of timothy hay in the June sunshine. He was absorbed in building a mental world of his own, crude and undeveloped but filled with the vigor of unmolested natural growth. His daydream made him impervious to the joyous song of the bobolink in the hedges of hazel and briar that edged the road, and to the lazy drone of the bee returning to his hive laden with the spoils of the clover field. What was the subject that so absorbed his mind and his senses? Was he dreaming, perhaps, of a religious vocation, of a future life as a farmer, or of a future farmer's wife? No, none of these things mastered his mind. The mental picture which shut out the natural beauties spread so alluringly before him was more prosaic. He was absorbed in contemplation, obsessed by the vision of a machine. A chain-rake reaper had so mastered every faculty of this youth of sixteen that, as the teams reached the top of Pilot Knob, his imagination was occupied in visualizing and following the motion of the drive wheel through the train of wheels and spur gearing to the sprocket wheel that drove the rake.

In those days, each farmer swore by his own reaper and discussed its points of superiority at the crossroads, in the market place or around the church doors on a Sunday morning. Tom's brothers were loyal to Wood's Chain-Rake-Reaper. No other machine, they claimed, was so light in running, no other dropped so neat a bundle. Other agents discovered that it was useless to propose their wares at the Shields farm. In the eyes of Tom Shields this reaper was the very embodiment of mechanical perfection. "It had not occurred to me that by taking thought, I might add one cubit to its stature . . . an attempt on my part to improve this paragon of perfection would have seemed to me a presumption so colossal as to render me a fit subject for the insane asylum. And yet, on that morning, my mind was possessed by Wood's Chain-Rake-Reaper.

"From the time I was a child of seven until my weight became too great to be added to the horse's load, it was my task, during each harvest, to drive the pair of leaders on my brother's reaper. I rode bareback on the nigh horse, and every time the reaper broke down (and it broke down pretty often in those days) I jumped from the horse's back and helped Michael to make repairs. Sometimes I held the sickle-bar while he riveted on a new section, or again I helped him to replace a broken link in the rake-chain; at times it was even necessary for me to crawl under the machine and lie on my back on the ground so as to hold a bolt firmly with a big monkey wrench while he unscrewed its stubborn nut.

"My ear soon came to recognize unerringly the sound of a loose nut or a broken sickle section. Every wheel and journal, every bolt and screw of the machine reached my consciousness through eye and ear, through muscle and sense of touch. In fact, during my childhood, Wood's Chain-Rake-Reaper laid hold of my senses and filled my imagination. To me it was the symbol of harvest. It was the heart of those bustling, anxious days on which the fruitage of the whole year's toil depended, and it naturally became the center of my conscious life during the silent years that followed.

"On the morning of which I speak, I had practically nothing to do during the two hours occupied by our trip to town. I simply sat idle in the sunshine on the top of my load of timothy and let my horses follow my brother's load.

I did not need to touch a line until we reached the crowded city streets. The discouragement resulting from my failure to improve upon the grindstone had prevented me from seeking to embody in concrete form the mental life that, from day to day, was growing in vigor and that finally held my imagination captive in the day dream. Whenever present circumstances ceased to hold my attention, I simply could not keep my imagination from playing with the various parts of the machines with which I had grown familiar."

Why it should have been the reaper that dominated his imagination on that particular morning, it would be hard to say. It was early summer and the reapers had not been touched since having been dismantled after the preceding harvest. Yet he watched that reaper with concentrated attention, his inner eye saw each wheel revolving in its place, traced each reversal of motion in the gearing until his imagination rested satisfied in a picture of the rake traveling around the platform. How like it was to the interior concentration of a musician silently following with his inner ear the complex movements of a fugue. For Tom Shields, it was a fugue for the inner eye.

"Having exhausted this material," he continues, "my imagination busied itself for a time in picturing the relative velocities of the several rotating wheels. . . . The sizes of the wheels were such as to involve fractions, so, after a short time, I turned my attention to another part of the machine in an attempt to picture the number of times the sickle turned to and fro to each revolution of the drive wheel." Baffled, however, by his inability to multiply and divide, he began at the other end of the problem. He pictured each revolution of the crank shaft, counting them, until they resulted in one complete revolution of the bevel gear. He continued this process, as he tells us, while "with the other eye" he watched the small gear creep slowly around the circumference of the drive wheel. Still counting carefully he finally triumphed. He had pictured and counted in imagination the one hundred and forty-four strokes of the sickle that corresponded to a single revolution of the drive wheel!

The glow of satisfaction caused by this success lifted his mind, for one brief moment, to a higher plane. What artist has not known these sudden golden showers of insight? From this new height Tom found a further problem before him based upon the memory of an incident which had taken place during the previous harvest. The scene was etched on his memory. He had been binding and had stepped aside to let the reaper pass. The grade was steep, the horses were drawing the reaper down the hill at full speed when, suddenly, a little twig caught in the sickle and locked the whole machine. The drive wheel dug into the soft earth and the heavy pole team broke their doubletree. In some way the picture of the one hundred and forty-four strokes of the sickle to each revolution of the drive wheel had brought this incident vividly to his mind, and as he visualized the scene, he felt, dimly, that, in some way, velocity and power were connected. Of course he did not know the meaning of those words, but only wondered whether or not it might be true that because one round of the drive wheel produced one hundred and forty-four strokes of the sickle, one pound of resistance in the sickle would hold out against one hundred and forty-four pounds of power in the drive wheel.

He was unable to reach a conclusion as to whether or not this were so, but he decided to put the matter to the test. If what he imagined turned out to be true, by taking hold of the wrist of the crank shaft, he should be able to turn it with ease while it caused the machine to move forward or backward. Satisfied that this would be a crucial test, he resolved to try the experiment on his return home.

That same evening he went to the machine shed and found, to his delight, that by turning the crank shaft, he could easily move the reaper forward or backward on the shed floor.

The psychological effect of this success was out of all proportion to its practical importance. Tom's supreme need was faith in his own mental power. He had lived too long under the shadow of early failures and rejections. "Hopeless, useless," rang in his ears like a refrain. He was convinced that he had no brains, that he would never be like other people, would remain an outcast all his life. And now, suddenly . . . as the reaper moved over the shed floor in response to the touch of his hand on the crank shaft, thus confirming the vision of his daydream, he slaked his thirst for the first time at the fountain of purest joy set up by the Creator for the refreshment of those who seek the truth and find it.

He had made no contribution to physical science. The truth involved was considered elementary ages before he was born. But, as far as Tom was concerned, he had made an original discovery. He had thought out for himself the relation of power to weight in a simple gearing and had verified his conclusions by actual experiment. The result yielded him all the joy of an original discovery and something more besides. For perhaps no discoverer had ever hungered and thirsted more ardently for some assurance that his mental processes were sound. The daydream had carried him upward into a new realm. Strong with this new sense of power, he took his first steps out of the darkness.

The daydream played an overwhelming part in rescuing Tom Shields from his condition of inferiority, but his daydreaming was not an effortless floating on the tide of sensation and memory. It was active, concentrated; a condition of the mind characteristic of the frontiers of thought in which the attention is wholly absorbed by the play of eager elements of growth, in which the phenomena of sense are transfigured by the light of truth. Every artist, every musician knows this type of daydream. To use the words of Doctor Shields himself: "The play of fecund memory pictures, born of the embrace of mind and matter, has ever been man's inspiration in the conquest of truth. In this apparently aimless play . . . the mind catches glimpses of beauty and hints of unrevealed truths that rouse the whole man to that eager and persistent effort in pursuit that has ever marked both the artist and the discoverer in the realm of pure science. Yet the day dream is seldom articulate enough to issue in language. It is thought in embryo and it should see the light of day in action before being clothed in words. Its soft outlines rapidly fade from the memory unless they become sharply defined in some concrete embodiment."

CHAPTER SIX

THE INVENTOR

DAYDREAMS such as that of the reaper followed by experimental verification were only a prelude, though a necessary one to give confidence to the lonely boy. During the summer that followed that daydream, Tom Shields became the inventor of a grubbing machine that worked.

His parents had bought a farm on the shores of a small lake close to the property of their eldest son Michael. They were building a new home and clearing the land meanwhile. The story of the invention must be given in the words of the inventor:

"On the bank of a beautiful little inland lake that skirted the southern extremity of my father's farm, there once stood a majestic grove of black oaks that, for more than a century, had sheltered the wigwams of the Sioux. In the early fifties the finest of these trees fell before the axe of the pioneer, who converted their straight trunks into logs with which to build his hut, or split them into rails with which to enclose the first few acres he had hewn from the primeval forest. But the life of these trees was beyond the reach of his axe in their wide spreading roots, where it lay safely hidden from the frosts of winter. At the first call of spring the sap rose to the surface, and not finding its accustomed channels, built for itself around each stump a clump of suckers. . . . At the time of which I speak, a quarter of a century had transformed these suckers into clusters of vigorous young oaks whose trunks had grown together at the base and whose roots were intertwined in an inextricable mass.

"Under a scorching July sun, with scarcely a breath of air stirring and with a crew of half a dozen workmen to help me, I was engaged in clearing this field for the plow. The roots of the dense underbrush of hazel and sumac that had been cut during the previous winter formed a close feltwork in the loose soil that prevented the use of the spade and made difficult the work of laying bare the roots of the trees for the axe. . . . On a former occasion I had seen Michael make use of a team of horses and a block and tackle to bend the clusters to one side and thus facilitate the cutting of the few central roots. I was tempted to resort to this expedient, whereupon I remembered my daydream about the relation of power to motion, and my experiment with the reaper. This led me to the conclusion that a combination of the pulley and the wheel and axle would yield better results. The more I thought over the matter, and the more exasperated I became at the slowness of our progress the more firmly did this idea take possession of me. . . . I went to the shed and began to dig out discarded farm machinery in search of wheels and shafts which I needed for the construction of the machine that I had planned while on the grubbing field. . . . I worked feverishly all day during the course of which I was questioned more than once by the workmen and by members of the family as to what I was doing. . . .

" 'Nothing, just fooling!'

"My previous failure had taught me prudence. Realizing the possibility of another failure and shrinking from the ridicule which it would be sure to bring upon me, I resolved to satisfy myself that the machine would be a success before telling anyone of my plans and hopes.

"Among the old machinery was the body of a mowing machine that had been built in Baltimore in 1859 and shipped to Mendota by way of the Chesapeake and Ohio Canal and the Ohio and Mississippi Rivers. The sickle bar had been lost in transit . . . consequently the machine had never seen active service. One of the first of its kind, it was heavy and clumsy in construction; its shafts and wheels had many times the strength needed for mowing, but they just suited my purpose. . . . Before I went to bed that night I had my grubbing machine well under way and by working after supper into the late hours of the night, I had it ready for trial inside of a week; but the test could not be made while others, who would discover the purpose of the machine and be witnesses to a possible failure, stood around.

"The following Sunday morning I remained at home to 'mind the house' while the rest of the family went to early Mass.

"The machine was mounted on two wheels and, as soon as I was left alone, I ran it out of its place in the shed and anchored it to one of the trees in the yard. With a piece of new half-inch rope I connected the drum with a neighboring tree and began turning the crank. The rope gradually tightened and almost before I felt the pressure on the handle, it snapped!

"A tide of joy surged over me such as only those who have lived through long years of discouragement will ever understand. I had brains! I was an inventor! The desire for concealment was now changed into a feverish impatience to exhibit the machine to the family. The time until they returned from church seemed interminable.

"My imagination was on fire with the wonderful things

that the grubbing machine would surely accomplish. I thought of the forests that were still to be grubbed and feared that they were not extensive enough; and of the patents that were to be taken out, and of the money that was to be made, and I am afraid that before the hour had drawn to a close I was a millionaire in imagination." Then the dark, humiliating years rose up, as in a nightmare, before him: the failures at school, the condemnation of his teachers, the blow with the ruler, his mother's words that had seared his soul as with a red hot iron; all this was past history now. They would see that he was not wholly useless nor hopeless. He was an inventor! And in the midst of this immense surge of feeling, "the thought came continually obtruding itself that, whatever might be my shortcomings in other respects, there was at least one thing for which I had brains! A glorious career as a machinist and an inventor seemed to stretch out before me." Even his terrible brother John, once convinced of the machine's value, would permit him to get the improvements he needed. Yes, surely, even John!

A rumble of wheels, and Tom leapt to his post. The great moment of his life had come.

"At last the family arrived. The carriage stopped just in front of my machine. I was standing with my hand on the crank, with my heart ready to burst with joy, not to mention the condition of my head; but to my surprise and disappointment, not one member of the family would bestow even a single glance on me or my machine. As John threw the lines over the dashboard and stepped from the carriage, I tried to tell him about my wonderful invention. But I was chilled by the reception which the others had given me, and the unsympathetic look on John's face caused the words to stick in my throat. He turned towards the house with the peremptory order: 'Tom, put up the team right away.' "

Was he to be thrown back into the darkness? No, those days were gone for good. It was a bitter disappointment that not one of his family would consider, even to the extent of a casual glance, that which he had evolved for the general good of them all, but this could not crush him. His great invention was a reality which filled his heart and brain to overflowing. His joy and triumph were no longer dependent upon outside approval. He would not give up.

"The next morning I hitched the grubbing machine behind the wagon intending to take it with me to the grubbing field but John appeared on the scene and forbade the procedure. I remember his words still; they hurt and angered me more than anything he had ever said to me:

" 'Unhitch that thing and leave it here, and quit wasting the men's time with your fool machines.'

"In my experience, no one had ever questioned John's authority; his word was law on the farm. So, with a heavy heart and a rebellious will, I unhitched my grubbing machine and went back to dig out the clusters of young oaks without its aid."

He had not accepted defeat, but bided his time.

"At noon I found that John had gone to town so I again hitched the machine behind the wagon. Whatever the consequences might be, I was determined to see the thing through and to give my machine a fair trial. My father was going to Michael's house and he rode with me as far as the grubbing field. He scolded me all the way for my disobedience to John, but he did not himself forbid me to take the machine to the field. When we reached the grove, I wanted him to wait to see the machine work, but this he positively refused to do."

The fact that his father did not formally forbid the experiment was enough for Tom. He proceeded at once to anchor his grubbing machine to a stump and to attach the pulley to a cluster of oaks. It was the great moment. What would happen? He turned the crank and to his great joy, the oaks came out without any difficulty. All his dreams came rushing back: the triumph was complete! He was an inventor! So powerful was his machine, indeed, that the available ropes and chains were too weak to withstand the tremendous strain put upon them. Half a dozen times they broke. The difficulty would be to find anything strong enough to hold. . . .

"About four o'clock in the afternoon, my brother's hired boy happened along, apparently by chance, but he told me *sub rosa* that my father had sent him down to see whether the machine was working, and had cautioned him not to tell me that he was sent. We had results to show him which made his eyes bulge. . . . He told me there was a coil of new rope in Michael's barn and volunteered to bring it to me. Half an hour later he returned with the rope and with him was my father who watched the operation of the grubbing machine with unfeigned delight.

"When we reached home that evening, John was eating his dinner. He had just learned of my disobedience and for the first time in my memory, he seemed genuinely angry. Notwithstanding the fact that there were strangers in the dining room when I entered, he turned sharply and reprimanded me for disobeying orders. But my father stopped him, saying:

" 'Never mind, John; Tom did more work this afternoon with his grubbing machine than the crew could do in a week without it. You had better hitch up in the morning and go to town and get him everything he wants for it.' "

A word of praise! How long the boy had thirsted for such a word. His heart must have leaped with joy, hope and gratitude. In his own story of the cloudy, dark days of his boyhood, these are the only recorded words of encouragement that we read. Had they been left unsaid, we may well wonder whether Tom Shields would ever have reached his high calling as a teacher of youth and a savior of souls. "Strength needs support more than weakness." With the grace of a gentle word, a little sympathy, "the mute inglorious Milton" that the poet buries in his country churchyard might have taken his place in English literature among the most glorious of the sons of light.

CHAPTER SEVEN

OUT OF THE
DARKNESS

THE invention of the grubbing machine was the turning point in the life of Thomas Edward Shields. An insignificant thing in itself, it was decisive in its psychological effect. Triumph had replaced failure, self-reliance and a consciousness of mental power had driven out the vacillating uncertainty caused by the conviction of his own stupidity. But this was not all.

The child naturally obeys the individual. He begins to be a man in that hour wherein he learns to transfer his allegiance from individuals to principles. There comes a moment in the life of each boy when he faces the parting of the ways which lead to freedom or to slavery. The incident of the grubbing machine had brought Tom Shields to such a moment. He did not realize, on that critical day, that when he defied the unjust decision of his brother, he had taken one of the most important steps in his life and one which involved far-reaching consequences to his character. The defiance, on his part, had been instinctive. It was his job—not John's—to do the grubbing. In his brother's prohibition, Tom saw nothing but prejudice and injustice since he had condemned the machine without taking the trouble to look into its merits. John's action was that of a tyrant, and it stung the younger boy into his first act of open rebellion against tyranny.

Often it is success that measures the distance between treason and patriotism. Had the soldiers of George III triumphed in our war of revolution, the body of George Washington might have dangled from the gallows tree like that of Robert Emmet, who failed in his struggle for the freedom of Ireland. Tom Shields, in his act of rebellion, had succeeded. Had it been otherwise, had the grubbing machine failed him, the very glow of emotion which accompanied his act of defiance would have burned defeat deep into his soul. It would have determined the course of subsequent events as definitely as his success determined them in a contrary direction. For the worst effect of failure is not its immediate sting, but the permanent memory of failure which blocks the way toward future success. Had Tom failed, his brother's rebuke would have crushed him utterly. Never again, perhaps, would he have followed his convictions when they led him beyond the boundaries traced by the narrow letter of the law. Now, however, that he had succeeded, he knew that he was right. From that day he was sure of himself. Never in the presence of duty or in the face of opposition would he falter. This was the secret of the success that crowned his life. He never faltered, he never retreated, once he was sure of being right. Retreat is difficult and dangerous at best; in most cases it is fatal. These were truths which were asserting themselves in the mind of Tom Shields on that day of defiance and of triumph.

Suddenly the grubbing machine appeared to its inventor to fill the whole heavens. He was tempted to strut. "At sixteen years old," he remarks, "all the pent-up struts which my childhood should have known, suddenly rose up within me and, in their frantic efforts to exhibit themselves simultaneously, left me paralyzed and devoid of speech." His family had gathered around him, pleased and astonished at the unexpected originality and initiative of the *omadhaun*. They questioned him about the workings of his machine, asked him to state what further improvements were needed. He stood before them speechless. He had grown morbidly self-conscious during the years of discouragement and now, in the moment of exaltation and of excitement, the little power of expression which he possessed deserted him. He could not put his thoughts into words. Perhaps it was fortunate that he could not pour out the ambitions which were boiling within; dreams of the patent office, fears that someone else, seeing the working of his machine, might anticipate him there and rob him of the fruits of his great discovery which was to make the family fortune and his own fame.

The incident, strangely enough, did little to change the estimate his parents had formed of Tom's mind. It failed to awaken in their breasts the long-buried hope of teaching him the elements of the famous three R's. "This state of affairs must not be thought strange," as he himself remarks in retrospect. "The invention, objectively considered, was trivial to a degree and it could hardly be expected that any of those around me would understand its subjective value. After all, are not the subjective values the real values? It would be hard to overestimate the value of this poor grubbing machine to my mental life, and it is just as well to remember that this value was due almost wholly to the fictitious importance which I attached to it. I can never be sufficiently grateful to Providence that there were none of those well-meaning fools at hand to enlighten me concerning the real value of my invention. Had I been able to see the naked truth, it would have shattered my bubble of conceit and left me in the slough of despond.

"Mud pies, houses of cards, doll houses, popguns and kites are, to us grownups, trivial matters; but they are often filled with tragic importance to the child. Perhaps some day when we view all things in the unchanging light of eternity, our adult hopes and large ambitions, our latest discoveries, our railroads, canals and games of empire will seem as trivial in their objective importance as do these games of childhood, and we shall come to understand that the only real importance of achievement is the subjective importance."

We are reminded of the widow's paltry coin that, falling into the treasury box at the temple door, made a noise that still sounds to the music of the Savior's benediction. The widow's mite had little objective value. Its subjective value was sufficient to purchase the Kingdom of Heaven.

At least the Shields family had the good sense not to disillusion the boy. They had a word of praise for the machine whenever it was mentioned, but exercised a firm restraint when he talked of taking out a patent. If Tom had had the money, he would have applied for a patent, but John held the purse strings. Thus his illusion was allowed to run its course. As he wrote himself in after years:

"It has seemed to me many times that illusions are our salvation. I feel sure that it was so in my case at least. The truth would have left me paralyzed to the end of my days. It was the bright, flashing illusion, a mere rainbow of ambition, that led me up out of the valley of darkness and discouragement. . . . By the time that I had grown out of my illusion concerning the importance of the grubbing machine, I had learned to form a juster estimate of my own powers, and the germ of hope had begun to set its roots deep in my nature. Error and illusion, after all, are but the natural limitations of the mind's growth; they drop away as naturally and as inevitably before the light of growing truth as do shadows before the rising sun. You cannot build with naked truth; the mind cannot look upon it and live.

"If on the evening of my first success with the grubbing machine, someone had made me realize its paltriness, and had shown me what little significance it had for the world at large, I would have been crushed and have had nothing to fall back upon. But as it happened, I was allowed to dream dreams that night of my wonderful achievement."

The next day John took him to town to purchase the needed improvements, having found it impossible to obtain from Tom an accurate description of what he needed, tongue-tied and timid as he was before that dreaded brother whom he had defied only yesterday! They visited the largest foundry and machine shop in the city, and there, with wonder and delight, Tom contemplated, for the first time, lathes and drills, planing machines operating with quiet, irresistible strength, moving with what seemed like almost human intelligence. When he returned to the farm, his grubbing machine had begun to shrink. Still it remained unique: "There were no grubbing machines in the shops and I, Shields' *omadhaun*, was the inventer of one!"

He conceived a burning desire to become a machinist. Could he but learn his trade, what great things he could accomplish! He appealed to his father, again and again, to obtain for him a place where he could serve his apprentice-ship, but in vain. His father would not consider the matter seriously, so the boy determined to run away from home and learn the trade on his own account. He actually visited every shop in the Twin Cities, offering his services free to the foreman if he would only take him and let him learn the trade. He met with discouraging rebuffs, and was rejected at each shop. What was the reason? His rough appearance? His difficult speech? Or was his father consulted behind the scenes? At all events, Tom's self-confidence was strong enough to carry him over this trial without discouragement. He knew that the grubbing machine had been a success. During the summer months it had enabled him to pull out hundreds of trees by the roots with a slight motion of his hands. Again and again he had snapped a two-inch cable with the multiplied power of his own muscles. Each time that a great oak bent over under the strain, each time that root after root snapped a hundred feet from where he stood and shook the earth beneath his feet, he felt himself to be the source of a mighty power. The energy that went out from his arm over the cable and chain returned in a tide of strength to his will, building there the foundations of self-reliance. And so, when the foremen refused his application for a job, he attributed their refusal to his uncouth exterior and comforted himself with the thought that there was something in him much better than anything that had hitherto appeared on the surface.

Had he been accepted, he would have become a mechanic, a good one perhaps, if this term can be applied to an illiterate man, but he would never have gone back to school. Back to school? He, the hater of books, he, the inventor of grubbing machines? Yes, at the age of seventeen, he was to return to school. Meanwhile, with his deep religious faith in God and his reliance on Divine Province, he must have prayed fervently for a place in a mechanic's shop. God answered his prayer by refusing his request. In Eternity, how many of us will thank God for our unanswered prayer? we shall see, then, in the Divine refusal the Divine wisdom and love.

During this time, Tom taught himself to read. Obviously,

there was nothing in the library of the Shields family to tempt the curiosity of the average boy, to say nothing of one in the condition of young Tom. On the shelves of the bookcase were to be found such ponderous and solemn works as Lippincott's *Gazetteer*, the Bible, Milner's *End of Controversy*, Nathan's *Church History*, Spalding's *History of the Reformation*, Rodriguez's *Christian Perfection* and a few others of the same weight. It is true that these volumes did not furnish the customary reading matter for the members of the family. Lighter literature was purchased or borrowed but these volumes never found their way to the library shelves. They were passed to neighbors from whom other stories were borrowed in return. Bridget Shields was a stern censor of any stories that might leak in through the pages of weeklies. Whenever they fell into her hands she confiscated the papers and burned them but not until she had read the stories to be sure that her condemnation was entirely justified. As a rule, each one read to himself, in the Shields family; an occasional news item was all that was ever read aloud. Had it been the habit of the family to read aloud it is possible that Tom's interest might have been awakened and that he might have understood that reading was something more than a disagreeable drill in which the clever might show up to advantage.

During Tom's sixteenth year, this situation was changed. John had joined a circulating library and as he could keep the books for a week only it was decided that all the family should profit by them. John read them aloud during the long winter evenings. At first Tom took no interest, but, little by little, an episode would catch his attention, something containing action and excitement. Affairs reached a climax on Ash Wednesday night. John stopped reading as the clock struck: night prayers were still to be said. Lent was a time of early-to-bed and early-to-rise for the Shields family, so John determined to finish the story for himself alone. But the robbers had been left in a cave in the midst of a highly exciting situation. Tom's imagination had been fired by the story so he begged John to finish it for him. John paid no attention. The next day Tom found his mother at leisure and begged her to read him the end of the story, but she replied: "What interest can it have for you?" He tried his sister next, but she was afraid of being caught reading aloud to the *omadhaun*. Tom took the book to the barn. Fortunately the story was nearly finished, the print was large, and Tom began to spell the words out for himself, studying each letter in turn and pronouncing each syllable. His progress was slow but he managed to finish the story.

As a matter of fact he was not learning to read. He could have read much better eight years previously and, as he plodded his way through the closing chapters of the novel, he was aided by no sense of triumph, but was conscious only of having lost the little ability he had once possessed in this line. Nevertheless, the spelling out of those words was a turning point in his life, the full significance of which he did not understand until he took up the study of pedagogy many years afterwards.

Perhaps the most significant element in the experience was the *motive* that prompted this attempt to read. In school, the form had been all that mattered in reading: correct pronunciation, pauses, emphasis, inflections; it was a purely gymnastic drill and the meaning was neglected. What should have been the means was made the end. The lessons were along false lines, offering shadows for substance. There was no soul, no life; it was another instance of the fact that "the letter killeth; it is the spirit which giveth life." Now there was life indeed: Tom was reading for content alone and his interest in the thought pressed him on to make the effort of technique required. In this respect, his bungling attempts to read without the aid of a teacher at the age of sixteen, pondering each syllable in turn as he lay upon the hay mow, had in it something infinitely better than could have been produced by the best achievements along the old lines where form replaced substance in the focus of attention. His reading was wretchedly poor yet it represented a germ of mental life that was destined to have a vigorous growth. It opened the door to new worlds that contained the accumulated treasures of the ages.

Soon he began to crave from books the companionship and the excitement which were denied him in real life. He discovered that they could supply his need and turned to them in his loneliness.

Obviously, it was not on his parents' bookshelves that he could look for stories of romance and adventure. He discovered another source of supply out of reach of his mother's censorship. Many of the workmen on the farm came from the pineries of the north or from the mining camps of the west. They were rough in manner and speech. As they sat smoking during the lunch hour, they told many a story of drunken brawls in the wild life of the frontier. Tom listened to these stories. He knew those men and liked them; he had heard them joke and seen them fight. Rough as they were, they were Tom's friends. He found that they had an abundant supply of wild west literature which they were ready to lend him and to which he turned when the blue devils laid hold of him. The stories were short; the print was large; the paper was poor; the language was ungrammatical and vulgar; the moral tone was low. Indeed they were cheap in every sense of the word, but the stories were all action. There was not a dull line for Tom, nor a passage beyond his comprehension. This state of affairs continued for a year or more. Naturally, had his parents known of it, they would have forbidden such reading matter but they were lulled into a sense of false security against danger from books in Tom's regard due to his presumed inability to read.

However, in the fall of 1878, all those workmen, Tom's friends, were discharged. The Shields were moving into their home on the lake side and the new farm was smaller than the old, requiring no outside help. This land had been the scene of the grubbing and of Tom's triumph. With the disappearance of the workmen, Tom's supply of wild west stories was cut off, but it had fulfilled its mission. It had built up in the boy a habit of reading that had become a passion. "Something to read" became a necessity, especially in moments of dark depression which were not infrequent. Lacking the literature that he would have preferred, he was forced to seek other sources. In the spring of 1879, two books fell into his hands which marked a new stage in his development.

Many a life has been changed by a book before Tom's day. Augustine opened the Scriptures and became a Christian; Ignatius, the wounded soldier of Pampeluna, read the lives of the saints and became a soldier of Christ, father of a vast multitude fighting in the army of God. The reading of *John Inglesant* influenced Robert Hugh Benson, the son of the Anglican Archbishop of Canterbury, and led him to the Catholic Church. Shelley's poems, strangely enough, gave Alice Meynell her first impulse toward Catholicism. The novels of Walter Scott with all their inaccuracies in the portrayal of Catholic life, yet, by investing the Ages of Faith with a glow of romance and splendor, prepared the

English people for the revival of interest in Catholicism. The novels of Dickens, Hood's "Song of the Shirt," Elizabeth Browning's "Cry of the Children"—all these gripped the hearts of the English people and gave the impetus to a movement for the alleviation of England's submerged masses.

Ishmael or In the Depths by Mrs. Southworth and its sequel, *Self-Raised or From the Depths* were the two books which fell into the hands of Tom Shields and left a profound mark upon his character. He saw himself reflected in Ishmael; Ishmael was a companion in misery! Hand in hand with him, Tom climbed out of the gloom into the sunshine of hope. It was possible, then, to come out of the depths! This was a matter of supreme importance to Tom Shields. As he closed the book he resolved with all the concentrated energies of his whole being, that he would rise from the condition of inferiority in which he had lived so long; that he would conquer his fierce temper, his surly resentment and that he would acquire what knowledge he could. The ascent from the depths would be slow and difficult, he had no illusion on that score, but no difficulty could have daunted him in that moment of exaltation.

And thus it was the reading of a book which determined Tom Shields to go back to school.

PART TWO

VOCATION

Who will be to thee a lamp between the truth
and the understanding?—*Dante*

There is a center in us all
Where truth abides in fullness; and to *know*
Rather consists in opening out a way
Whence the imprisoned splendor may escape
Than in effecting entrance for a light
Supposed to be without.
　　　　　　　　　—*Browning*

CHAPTER EIGHT

TENACITY

I N his autobiography, *The Making and Unmaking of a Dullard*, Doctor Shields has emphasized those phases of his life which are directly of interest to educators. Little is recorded of the more secret and subtle side of the boy's life, his simple piety, his religious faith. Yet it was precisely those things which saved him from bitterness, revolt and despair during the dark years of solitude and humiliation. The intense inner life of this outcast boy was known to one man only, his confessor and spiritual guide. It was to him that Tom Shields revealed the tortures of humiliation, the sting of daily and hourly contempt and his own angry reactions, his surliness, his stubbornness which he was striving to conquer. Thanks to the fatherly guidance of this priest, Tom's spirit, unlike his mind, was nourished. Enlightened by wise counsel, Tom's faith stood between him and total disaster in childhood and during the trying years that followed. He learned to use the daily miseries as spiritual exercises. Even in his childhood, he had experienced the consolation and the power of prayer as he knelt in the field to appeal to a higher Tribunal. Now, as an adolescent, the generosity of his nature, his warmth of heart began to crystallize in a desire for self-sacrifice, for devotion to a great cause, and these aspirations were encouraged by his spiritual father who discerned in this ardent nature the seeds of greatness.

No great action takes place without a strong emotion as its motive power. Whether that emotion is harnessed and transformed into a permanent force depends upon the will. Tom Shields was now seventeen years old. Under the force of a deep emotion he had determined to come up out of the depths. Already he could count to his credit the success of his grubbing machine with that of several other small devices of his invention which had followed. These had provided a ray of hope, a sense of power. Yet, apart from their effect upon his own spirit, he found no reflection of their success in the attitude of those around him. To his own people he was still the pitiful dullard, he was still Shields' *omadhaun*. A struggle was ahead which would put to the test every ounce of his will power.

Tom's ambition to become a machinist's apprentice had been a passing fancy based, to some extent, on his passionate longing for independence, for an escape out of that atmosphere of pitying scorn that had become intolerable. As the fumes of excitement blew away, he looked upon another destiny. Already as a child, he had played in imagination with the picture of a lay brother. The vision had not faded but was transforming itself into a dream of a higher vocation. He wanted to be a priest and, in this desire, his confessor encouraged him. The dream of the child was now the fixed determination of the young man.

He knew that there would be difficulties in his path. Every vocation encounters difficulties; they are the test of its validity. But Tom's difficulties would be different from those of the ordinary boy. He would have to face and overcome the contemptuous unbelief of his parents and their friends. He shrank from the ordeal but braced himself to meet it. Then again, education of some sort would be required, though just what this would mean was not clear to his mind. It would certainly cost money, and his brother John was the custodian of the family exchequer. If John had refused to invest a small sum on a patent for the grubbing machine, what would induce him to risk a greater sum in educating an *omadhaun* for the priesthood? The apparent hopelessness of the struggle would have appalled a less generous heart, a less stubborn will.

A new parish priest succeeded Tom's earlier confessor at Mendota. Father Eagan was a Dominican, a man of superior education and culture, with long experience to enlighten him on the type of souls that came under his influence. To him, Tom was no enigma. He believed in this boy. He was certain of Tom's vocation and urged him to study for the priesthood, offering to help him to obtain the consent of his parents. There would be no difficulty: these people were good, pious Catholics, he argued, who would not grudge the gift of one of their children to the service of God. True, Tom felt, but that was not the point. He knew that his parents had been pinning their hopes of a vocation to the priesthood on his younger brother who seemed to possess all the aptitudes required. How could they be brought to accept the *omadhaun* as a substitute? Father Eagan consoled him: parents, he said, rarely pick the winner in this type of race; God mocks the judgment of men—even that of women—choosing the weak things to confound the strong. The classic arguments were excellent, but Tom knew all too well that his parents would refuse to accept him as the privileged child of the family, chosen by God for His service. It was too much to expect. He knew that he must face a long, hard struggle requiring patience and grit. He was determined to win, so he braced his will to meet the struggle.

As it turned out, Father Eagan's intervention changed

nothing in the preconceptions of the Shields family. They admitted that Tom was developing more than they had ever dared to hope, but to dream of so high an ambition as the priesthood with its duties and responsibilities was pure absurdity. Father Eagan, they thought, must be a bit odd himself to encourage the poor boy. Prejudices are tough masters and the situation remained unchanged. But Tom was prepared for all objections. If his parents could see in his project nothing but failure for him and humiliation for themselves, Tom opposed a will of iron. His very silence was a force. Finally, before the boy's tenacity and the insistence of the priest, Tom's parents agreed to give him a few acres of land to cultivate for his own profit. The money he made would be set aside for his education.

It was perhaps a mere device for gaining time during which the fancy might pass. The fancy did not pass. No change of heart took place in Tom, nor change of mind in Father Eagan. The latter insisted:

"You will not only become a priest but you will be one of the Church's great teachers because of your thirst for fundamental truth!"

These prophetic words did not hasten matters. One day, with the thought of taking matters out of the realm of theory, Tom went to call upon the Bishop, offering himself as a candidate for the priesthood. The Bishop received the country lad with kindness and questioned him as to where he had made his classical studies. Evidently Tom looked older than his years. Here was a difficulty that Tom had not foreseen.

"Classical studies?" he faltered. "What are they?"

The Bishop hastily closed the interview and showed the young man to the door.

What were these classical studies Tom wondered. Father

Eagan must know. He discovered the bitter truth: he would need three or four years of classical studies before he could even apply for entrance into an ecclesiastical seminary. A college course! He looked at his potato patch ruefully. It would be a long time before the crop would cover that college course. But the course he must have. So, to the potato patch, was added a "sugar field" as recorded in the Day Book under the date of August 2, 1882. He was not yet twenty years old. He wrote in a childish hand:

> T. E. Shields invests in cane business this day with the following resources and liabilities:
> Resources: Real estate, 4 acres, presented by
>   by J. Shields Jr. valued at $400.00
>   M. B. Shields owes us on a/c
>   Goods on hand, valued at............... 50.00
> Liabilities: Balance due to St. Paul Book and
>   Stationery Company 12.50
>   Balance due to M. G. Haggerty for tuition 5.00
> T. E. Shields, net capital ....

The entries were not such as to offer any immediate hope of paying for his studies, but the figures are not the most important feature of this brief record in the Day Book. We come in contact for the first time with a name that was to mean much in the preparation of Tom Shields for the life that lay before him. The name was that of Michael Gamble Haggerty, a man who, like Father Eagan, believed in this boy from the start and saw, under his crude exterior and lack of educational advantages, the sign of hidden genius.

Haggerty's influence, in this stage of Tom's life, was of primary importance in bringing the boy up out of the darkness. Was there ever, indeed, any real darkness in the mind of Tom Shields? There was certainly no mental deficiency. One questions whether those who surrounded this boy were not suffering from a greater darkness than his, the fog of prejudice. Certainly the testimony of these two men, the only men of superior culture to that of the pioneer farmers of the neighborhood, with whom Tom came in contact at the time, would seem to disprove the possibility of mental inferiority. They alone knew the boy from the inside. To them, he was not afraid to reveal his thoughts. They were not afraid of the ridicule which held others away from the *omadhaun*. They bored through the crust of prejudice that surrounded and hemmed him in.

"He was a brilliant student *from the start*," said Haggerty in later years, having heard with amazement that Doctor Shields had written of himself as a dullard; "It is *impossible* that he could have been a dullard at any time." But then Haggerty was a bit different himself from the village people of Mendota, from the simple farmers and pioneering families of the region. He taught, indeed, in the village school because he loved to teach, but he was *different*. He was a stranger, had not been brought up in the State, but came from afar and was looked upon with curiosity not unmixed with criticism. Yes, he was different and would have queer notions, naturally.

Michael Gamble Haggerty was born in Ireland. When he was a boy there were few educational advantages to be found in Ireland for a Catholic. To keep the people in ignorance was the policy of the English government at the time in its campaign to crush the Irish national spirit. Many of the families who could afford it sent their children to France to obtain the education denied them at home. France welcomed these exiles seeking knowledge. She had not forgotten the days of old when Ireland was the University of Europe, when her learned men were the first school masters to bring the rich store of their learning to the youth of France. Far back in the days of Charlemagne, Irish scholars came to France and became the leaders in every intellectual activity throughout the Empire. Indeed, when Charlemagne founded schools, it was to Ireland he looked for masters to impart the new learning, and in the beginning of the Carolingian renaissance, the Parisians looked with awe and wonder at the Irish monks who walked through the streets of the city crying out: "Knowledge to sell!" In his History of Philosophy, Doctor William Turner relates that these Irish masters were found, at the time, in every cathedral and monastery of the Empire as well as in the court of the Frankish kings and were so identified with the new intellectual movement that the teaching in the newly founded schools was characterized as *Irish learning*.

Michael Gamble Haggerty was sent by his parents to France at the age of twelve years, turning his back upon his native land, that he might obtain a higher education while retaining his faith. He followed the courses in the French secondary schools and through college, finally graduating from the University of Paris. He spoke French like a Frenchman, had absorbed the French ideas of civilization and culture and, after graduation, he had spent several years in teaching languages in the French governmental "lycées" before emigrating to America in 1870. Once there, he studied law in Iowa, passed the bar and might have practised law save for his profound love of the teacher's art which brought him to Mendota as School Principal at the precise moment when Tom Shields took up his interrupted studies.

Mr. Haggerty taught Tom in school during the day and gave him private lessons in the evenings. Latin and Greek were the subject matters to be mastered but it is easy to imagine that Tom Shields mastered many things that were not on the schedule from contact with this man of experience, of general culture, who seems to have been a master in the art of correlation.

Haggerty loved books, good books and even fine bindings when he could afford the luxury. His library was stocked with works on travel, history, philosophy, poetry. He could quote his favorite authors by the page—from Dante to Dickens. He had traveled extensively, far more, at least, than anyone else in the neighborhood, and could talk entertainingly about what he had seen and heard in foreign lands. All this was queer enough, but there were worse things: Mr. Haggerty was a man who loved the arts with a discriminating if catholic taste. He was the possessor of a clear tenor voice and liked to sing or whistle the tunes of the latest operas that were popular in Paris; melodies from Trovatore and Rigoletto could be heard rising from the hills of Mendota—Verdi being then at the height of his popularity. The voice of this strange teacher would give out—and this may have been more to the taste of the farmers—the strains of many an Irish folk song: *The Exile from Erin, The Valley Lay Smiling Before Me,* or *The Wren, the King of All Birds,* for the owner of the sweet tenor voice was an ardent Irish patriot. Every now and then, he would return to his native land as visiting correspondent for the *St. Paul Globe.* He could be fierce in his Irish sympathies and gloriously wrathful over what seemed to him to be matters of principle. It is quite easy to see that Mr. Haggerty must have created something of a stir in the village of Mendota.

This was the man who was to open out the world of knowledge to young Tom Shields; a professor who loved to teach with a student who was starving for knowledge.

The combination could hardly fail, for the contact of mind with mind is more important than what is taught. How much more than dry texts must have illumined the mind and heart of Tom during those years. Perhaps he may have accompanied his teacher on his long walks, climbing hill-tops for distant views, for Haggerty delighted in the beauties of nature; knew the names of flowers and trees, and delved into the varied riches which that beautiful country-side had to offer.

For two years and a half Tom studied with Mr. Haggerty and if the latter had "knowledge to sell" it is evident that he sold it at a price commensurate with what the young pupil could pay with the slim profits of the potato patch and sugar field. We can well believe that the master threw his library open to his pupil and that Tom's taste was formed on different models from those of the early wild west tales. Was Tom encouraged to travel after the fashion described in Bayard Taylor's *Views Afoot*, the book which was a favorite with his master? Was he permitted to browse along that long shelf devoted to Hume, one of Haggerty's favorite authors, or dip into Locke's *On Human Understanding*, borrow volumes from the shelf devoted to Whittier or from the works of Washington Irving, pore over the poems of Tom Moore, or turn the pages of Dante's *Inferno* with the fearful fascination of Gustave Doré's illustrations? A teacher such as Haggerty would undoubtedly throw the riches of his library open to a student such as Tom Shields.

When at last in the spring of 1882, Tom graduated from the village school in the presence of his parents, brothers, sisters and friends, he was a very different Tom Shields from the *omadhaun*. Much credit is certainly due to his teacher, yet his own explanation of the change from his former condition is this: "I simply grew out of it."

Already in the spring of 1880, after his first six months of study with Haggerty, his parents had been present at his commencement exercises and had been enthusiastic over his progress. That evening he wrote on a slate and slipped the message to his youngest sister: "I wish to be a priest. Pray that I may succeed." Now, on this day of his graduation, his mind was occupied, not so much with a momentary triumph, as with the fact that now he could begin his college work, could prepare himself to enter the Seminary.

As a matter of fact, Tom's studies had given him but little difficulty. He had been building better than he knew during those long years on the farm. "The sensory motor reaction is the first element to be developed in the child's conscious life and its importance throughout the entire developmental process can scarcely be over-estimated," as Doctor Shields wrote later in his *Philosophy of Education*. "It lies at the base of all other modes of expression and even cognition itself does not proceed far in advance of it. The constant relation between impression and expression, between cognition and action has been stressed in all the leading works of modern psychology. . . . Before loading the child's memory with truths to be assimilated, it is highly important that he be given freedom in his movements and accuracy in their coordination. It is also well that he be given some measure of skill in handling instruments and in dealing with materials." All this Tom Shields had been given in abundance. He found, when he began to study, that mathematics came to him easily. The problems of geometry stood out from the printed page like transparencies. He could never see wherein lay the difficulty, due to his habit of dealing with actual objects instead of artificial symbols.

On the other hand, he retained for the duration of his life, certain handicaps from his early experiences. Writing had been too long delayed and remained difficult; spelling, even more so. He wrote the words as they sounded to his ear and it is amusing to look over his college notes and contrast the maturity of the thought with the childish writing and spelling. This he conquered, of course, in later years, but it remained an obstacle requiring concentrated effort. A still greater inconvenience grew out of his experiences in teaching himself to read. The fact that he had to stop, spell out the words and pronounce each syllable aloud as his eye rested upon it, created a habit which gradually hardened into a locked synergy (an inseparable joint action) between the movements of the eye and those of the vocal organs. It was many years before he discovered the evil consequences of this habit and then it was too late to remedy it. Throughout his life, if his eye wandered to the last syllable of a word while he tried to pronounce the first, he would stumble hopelessly. In music, he could not look ahead, as is so necessary in phrasing, for the moment his eye passed from the actual note he was singing, his vocal organs refused to hold the pitch. These were some of the handicaps which he carried through life as a result of his solitary struggles as a boy.

The following autumn, Tom Shields entered the College of St. Francis at Milwaukee as a sophomore. This college served as a minor or preparatory seminary and he remained there for three years, throwing himself into his studies with every ounce of energy and will power which he possessed. He made a number of close friends among the students, with many of whom he corresponded affectionately during vacations. Others, those who lived far from their homes, he invited out to the farm where the young fellows spent long days exploring the beauties of the Minnesota hills. During those three years, the change from the outdoor life of a farmer to the sedentary life of a student had an unfortunate effect on his constitution from which his health never entirely recovered.

We find among his notes at College an elaborate Compendium of Universal History, a series of charts arranged by dates and nations which enabled the eye to pick out at a glance the chief events all over the world in their mutual relation. His desire for correlation was finding expression at this early date: indeed the Compendium was an invention which filled a place in his studies not unlike that of the grubbing machine in his farming. He graduated with highest honors.

In contrast to his success in his studies, the ghosts of past years would rise up at times to torment him. On one occasion it became his turn to read aloud to the other students in the refectory. He opened the book and began to stumble through the words, syllable by syllable, while burning with shame. The old "stoppage in his speech," the wretched locked synergy between the eye and the vocal cords, were rising up and asserting themselves from out of the past. He realized that it was a pitiful effort, that the results were lamentable, but he only knew how very bad it was when the professor snatched the book out of his hand, remarking in a loud voice: "Mr. Shields, this is the very worst reading I have ever heard. You will please never read again in this room."

Tom graduated from St. Francis College in Milwaukee in the spring of 1885. He was now ready to enter the ecclesiastical seminary. It would appear that, by this time, Tom's parents had accepted the idea of his vocation for the priesthood and they helped him financially, putting aside a certain part of the income from the farm to meet the expense of his education.

CHAPTER NINE

SEMINARY DAYS

NOW, for the second time, Thomas Edward Shields presented himself before the Bishop of the Diocese requesting admission to the Seminary as a student for the priesthood. Who would have recognized in this thoughtful student the crude country lad who had applied for the honor some years earlier, ignorant of the classics, unaware of their very existence? This time he came armed with letters of commendation from the Director of the College at Milwaukee where he had completed brilliantly those preliminary studies which included the famous classics. He received a warm welcome from the successor of that prelate who had dismissed the young man so unceremoniously. It was the first time that Tom Shields came into contact with one of the great figures in the Church, one who was to have a decisive influence on his career—Bishop Ireland—later Archbishop of St. Paul.

John Ireland was a native of County Kilkenny, Ireland. Like so many of his compatriots, he was forced to seek his education in France. In 1849, he came to America and gave his complete devotion to his adopted country. A chaplain in the Union army during the Civil War, Rector of the St. Paul Cathedral, Bishop, then Archbishop, he threw his full energies—which were great—into the interests of Church and State, becoming a national and even an international figure. Education received his immediate attention and one of his dearest projects was the opening of a theological seminary to train the priests of his diocese. This project was about to be realized when young Shields presented himself. Tom, himself, had cherished the hope that he might be sent to Belgium to study at the Seminary of Louvain, but the Bishop decided otherwise. He was to be enrolled among the first students of the new seminary. Little did the Bishop realize that, after half a century, this simple country boy would be looked upon as its most illustrious graduate.

The Seminary of St. Thomas Aquinas, opened in the autumn of 1885, no longer exists. It gave way to its successor, the Seminary of St. Paul, a few years after the ordination of Father Shields. Strangely enough, the funds to build and endow it were given by James J. Hill, the empire builder of the Northwest, and the relations between these two pioneers in contrasting fields—Archbishop Ireland and James J. Hill—throw an interesting sidelight on the history of the Church in America. Here was a man ready to donate a vast sum to build and endow an institution to educate priests for a Church of which he was not a member and by so doing to become a silent partner with Archbishop Ireland in providing young apostles to make the spiritual conquest of that vast empire which his genius had drawn out of the boundless prairies and forests of the Northwest. It was the character of the Archbishop, his intellectual and moral greatness, which drew this extraordinary response from the heart of the man of business.

On the day when Thomas Edward Shields was enrolled as a student for the priesthood, his heart was overflowing with enthusiasm. It was a dream at last realized, for which he had labored so long and overcome so many difficulties. At last he had obtained what he sought—a right to devote his whole mind and soul to an ideal of greatness. He was turning his back definitely on any selfish interest that might have beguiled him; on family life, home ties, personal ambition, his chance to make a name for himself as an inventor; in a word, the things that he felt to be transitory in order to devote himself to the interests of God. For this he was to discipline his soul, fortify his will, store his mind with knowledge—he was not a man to do things by halves.

Under date of September 2, 1885, Tom Shields wrote to a Swedish friend, probably one of the ex-workmen on his father's farm, whom he addresses as "My dear Friend John" and reminds him that "five years have glided by since together we picked our way over the hills of Mendota," as follows:

> I had looked forward to the day when I could stand on Swedish soil and clasp the hand of my dear friend. But men before me have laid plans, built gigantic castles in the air which the rude hand of time shattered to their base. I suppose then, I cannot grumble if my plans meet a like fate. I was calculating to go to Louvain toward the beginning of last month, when things suddenly took a complete change. Just the other side of Fort Snelling, there opened up a Seminary that has every indication of being one of the best on our continent. The many peculiar advantages it offered joined to the earnest wishes of all my friends, determined me to renounce for the present at least, my intention of visiting Europe. My course in this new Seminary will occupy six years; two in the study of philosophy and four in that of theology. Together with those, we of course take up other collateral branches such as courses of elocution, business, law, etc. . . .

The hours are long in the Seminary. The day begins at five in the morning and closes at nine in the evening. Four hours are devoted to spiritual exercises in common and three to classes. The subjects taught are philosophy, the history of philosophy, science, dogmatic and moral theology, Church history, the holy Scriptures, Canon law, Liturgy, Gregorian chant, ascetical theology and, finally (during the two years which precede Ordination), a thorough course is given in pastoral theology in which practical application is made of all that has been studied heretofore in the light of its relation to the management of a parish both from the spiritual and temporal standpoint. This, roughly, was the canvas on which Tom Shields was to work for the next six years.

In opening this Seminary, the mind of the Archbishop was dominated chiefly by one idea. He wanted learning to be fostered, but above all he wanted this institute to be a hotbed of holiness. The Archbishop met the students frequently and informally and always reminded them that they were to become "other Christs." Their first duty was to form their lives according to the Divine Model. No sanctity was too high for those who were to exercise in the ministry that tremendous power over the real and mystical Body of Christ, as "dispensors of the mysteries of God." Six long years of study, of meditation, of prayer, should enable each student to say with St. Paul, "I live—now not I —but Christ Jesus liveth in me." One student at least listened and the lessons were assimilated. Doctor Shields held a nation-wide reputation as a learned priest, but to those who knew him well, he was above all a holy priest, living his everyday life according to the high ideal of sanctity which had been his goal as a seminarian. His was a deep and lasting assimilation of the riches acquired during those six years of intense activity, mental and moral.

Fellow students remember Tom Shields as intelligent

and studious, spending his leisure time in the library or in the laboratory making experiments. Some of them dubbed him a bookworm, he who had so hated books as a boy. Yet he made a number of warm friends among the students as his correspondence shows and he kept in touch with the young men who had studied with him at St. Francis College and were preparing elsewhere for the priesthood. Nor did he forget the friends of earlier days. To his Swedish friend "John" he writes an account of his life at the Seminary:

> They feed us better here than at most colleges, in fact it is such board as would be obtained in a two-dollar-a-day hotel. My chief attention this year is directed to mental philosophy, although we devote four hours a week to 'Die Deutsche Sprache' and a few hours to other lighter branches. The same faculties of my mind that produced the grubbing machine are now exercising themselves in the highest planes of human thought, ramping the universe, traversing space, prying into the operations of the multifarious natural forces, following out the triple principle of life, ascending from created things to the contemplation of the Great First Cause. You see I have plenty of room to expand and grow and there is no fear that I will be reduced to the extremity of Alexander who sighed for more worlds to conquer. My conquests are conquests of the mind, and there is an infinite field at our disposal to explore. The further we advance in our conquests of truth, the fairer, the more enchanting become the fields spread out before us and behind, to the right and to the left, constraining us to cry out, "It is good for us to be here."

He did not always write in so ecstatic a vein. His vocation demanded stern renunciation. After the summer vacation, in September 1886, as the moment approached to leave his home, he writes to a cousin:

> I am about to begin my second year's philosophy and will likely have five more years to study before you can call me "Father Tom.". . . I start for the Seminary to-morrow to spend another four months without seeing home: I have the blues thinking of it.

And later, that same year:

> This is the hardest year's studying I have ever done since I have been going to college, and though I still enjoy good health, I have never needed rest more than at present.

At the Seminary, he came to be regarded both by members of the faculty and by his fellow students as remarkably talented and even brilliant. The students would often quote the opinions of Shields as though he had been one of the professors. Father Eagan and Michael Haggerty had not been bad prophets. Since young Shields had thrown off his sense of inferiority, he had become a natural leader of men over whom he exercised a totally unconscious attraction. He may have been conscious of a danger from the many voices raised in flattering appreciation as the pendulum swung to the opposite extreme from the crushing discouragements of his childhood, for he writes to his "Cousin Emma" in 1888:

> He who praises your virtue is your greatest enemy . . . I am very careful about bestowing my praise when speaking to my friends. If they were always as careful of their praise when speaking to me, they would not be opening the gates of hell so wide to receive me. Do you not know it was by the sin of pride the Angels fell?

Why, then, should you suppose us poor mortals to be
proof against it? Our friends, in all things else, are often
our greatest enemies in this, with their flattering tongues.

During the years that Tom Shields had spent at St. Francis College, he had been thrown with teachers and students
who were foreigners and whose English was far from idio-
matic. This same condition prevailed, to some extent, at
the Seminary. A fellow student recalls that on Bishop
Ireland's return from Europe in May 1887, the students
greeted him by an impromptu reception. "Addresses were
delivered in English, French, German, Latin, Polish and
Slavic," he notes, but does not record in how many languages the Bishop "thanked the boys for their good will in
his regard." Whatever may have been the advantages of
this melting-pot and its varied contacts, it was not creative
of a pure English style. Shields determined to help himself, resolving to improve his style and his means of expression by composing each day at least one phrase that would
express a thought clearly in the fewest possible words. He
would use this exercise for a further purpose, namely, to
set down his own ideals and purposes in life. He began to
keep a book of *Daily Thoughts* on January 8th, 1887, and
continued to write in it during the remaining years of his
Seminary life. These thoughts remain of peculiar interest
in a biographical sense because during the winter of
1921–22, a few weeks before his death, Doctor Shields happened to come across the faded pages of the old copy book
and, glancing through it, was amazed to find there many
ideas, which he had imagined to be the experience of later
life, had sprung from the heart of the *omadhaun* as he was
just coming up out of the darkness. These were his own
words and, those who are interested in this curious phase
of the Shields process of development, will find a number

of these thoughts reproduced in the Appendix.[1] They give an indication of the trend of his mind at the beginning and end of his career.

Under the date of February 7th, we find copied among the *Daily Thoughts,* this passage by Abraham Lincoln which Doctor Shields was fond of quoting in later years:

> No man resolved to make the most of himself can spare time for personal contention. Still less can he afford to take all the consequences, including the vitiating of his temper and loss of self-control. Yield larger things to which you can show no more than equal right, and yield lesser ones though clearly your own. Better give your path to a dog than be bitten by him in contesting the right. Even killing the dog would not cure the bite.

The young man who wrote the *Daily Thoughts* had cast off whatever might have remained of his early inhibitions. We see already a man of mature mentality and sound judgment.

While still a seminarian, in the year 1888, Thomas Shields published his first book. It was an encyclopedic index or filing system in book form for ideas and facts. Like his earlier inventions, it grew out of his own immediate needs. Its cumbersome title was INDEX OMNIUM, *being a reference book designed for the use of students and professional men on a plan intended to save time and facilitate access to knowledge acquired by reading and study.* The work was divided into two parts: the first was an Index; the second, a catalogue. A system of letters and numbers enabled the user to find at once the subject, book and page; each being arranged under as many headings as there were subjects dealt with.

The *Index Omnium* served its chief purpose in its effect

[1] Appendix I, p. 287.

upon his own mind as he composed it; for he found that when he had entered a thought under all the possible headings under which it might be of use, he had already developed a habit of thinking of each subject in a rich and fecund way and of correlating it with everything else that he knew. To the composition of the *Index Omnium* he attributed many of the habits of mind which were characteristic of his later work and showed forth so brilliantly in his lectures. Indeed the *Index* was a milestone comparable in importance to the grubbing machine. The Superior, Father O'Gorman, gave him a written approval:

> Having examined *Index Omnium*, a reference book designed for the use of students and professional men by T. E. Shields, a student of this Seminary, I recommend it as new in its line and most useful for whom it is intended.

The President of the University of Minnesota declared in writing that he considered the book "very useful and helpful to all who wish to reap the fruits of their reading by keeping a record of the places where the most important subjects are treated" and two other members of the faculty commented on the originality of the book. Professor Mac-Lean wrote:

> Mr. Shields' ingenuity has invented a plan for the most compact and convenient Reader's Reference Book of which I know. Every student appreciates the need for such a book and will be glad to avail himself of it.

and the Professor of History, H. F. Judson, commented:

> It is a very ingenious arrangement and one that students, I am sure, will find very valuable in their work. I have seen nothing like it.

Armed with these reinforcements and with the approval of his Superior, Shields took a trip to the East during his summer vacation in search of a publisher, but was obliged to return to St. Paul without a definite assurance that his masterpiece would be brought out. In the following April, however, he wrote to his cousin:

> Nims and Knight of Troy, N. Y., have it in hand. Their offer is pretty fair and I have concluded to accept it. . . . Perhaps the next time I write I will be able to tell you about what date the work will appear on the market.

When the little book appeared, it was bought up rapidly by the students. Indeed its sale continued for some time; letters reached the author from Rome as late as 1897 asking for copies. But the edition was exhausted within the first year of publication. Strangely enough, in view of its popularity, the book that was destined to be the salvation of busy men of affairs and of students, never went into a second edition. The *Index Omnium* faded from sight. Yet the psychological effect on its author remained.

"There is no development without labor and no discipline without pain," we find in the *Daily Thoughts*. About a year before his ordination, Thomas Shields went through a crisis. A strange illusion took possession of his mind. He could no longer question the fact that he had brains, for the evidence was cumulative. What tortured him now was an idea—a veritable *idée fixe*—that he was devoid of all imagination, feeling and human sympathy. Sympathy was necessary in the confessional: how could he hope to help souls with so fatal a defect? Should he continue his studies? It was the first and only time that his resolution faltered. He consulted his Superior, opening his heart freely and frankly.

The latter advised him to continue his studies on the ground that he, Shields, was obviously cut out to be a teacher and would, in all likelihood, have little active parochial work to do. The argument was tranquillizing, perhaps, to the student, though it seems as strange, in retrospect, as the illusion itself. It was not until after Father Shields' Ordination that this disturbing illusion was dispelled and that he discovered by experience in the confessional that he was able to help his penitents chiefly through his power of vivid imagination and warm sympathy. Difficult cases of conscience were very apt to be brought to Father Tom because of his excellent judgment as well. At the time of which we speak, he decided to continue his studies on the advice of his Superior.

"Peace of soul," he wrote in the *Daily Thoughts*, "is essential to all really spiritual or intellectual progress. Peace is the kingdom of God, disquietude, a living hell. The union of our will with God's builds around us an impregnable castle of peace. When God's will is the sole motive of our actions, we are never disquieted over the result."

During the winter of 1890, Tom Shields had a serious breakdown, whether caused by overwork or anxiety over his vocation is unknown. For some time his life was despaired of, but a summer vacation passed among his beloved hills and plains of Mendota restored his health to the point that he was able to return to the Seminary for the final months of work preceding Ordination. Archbishop Ireland had watched the progress of this particular student with immense interest. He recognized, even in seminary days, that here was a young man of promise. He accepted him for Ordination, and in the month of February, 1891, Tom Shields writes to his old friend and beloved teacher, Michael Gamble Haggerty as follows:

Seminary of St. Thomas Aquinas
Merriam Park
St. Paul, Minn.

Feb. 28, 1891

Mr. M. Haggerty
My dear Friend:

The work of preparation for the Priesthood which you began in me ten years ago has about drawn to a close. I will receive Holy Priesthood on Saturday, March 14th, at 8 A.M. I would feel honored by your presence should you care to witness the ceremony. I will celebrate my first Mass in Mendota next day at 10:30. I will be at home at Father's in the afternoon.

Your sincere friend,
T. E. Shields

CHAPTER TEN

THE PRIEST

THE large stone church overlooking the town of Mendota opened wide its doors on that bright spring morning, March 15, 1891. Every seat was already filled, and still the crowds kept surging up the hill from far and near toward the Church. Was it piety, friendship or mere curiosity that drew them? A young priest was to celebrate his first Mass, a young man whom they had all known as a boy, that strange boy, whom they had called Shields' *omadhaun*, now, as all men knew, one of the brilliant students of the Seminary whose special talents had been recognized by the Archbishop himself, and whose proud parents were even now sitting, like venerable patriarchs, in the front pew, surrounded by their sons, Michael, John and Henry, each with his wife and children clustered about them, not far away. There, too, could be seen the youngest daughter in the habit of a Sister of St. Joseph, for the Shields had found that sacrifices do not come singly, and they had cheerfully given another child to the service of God.

The great bells of St. Peter's began to call the stragglers. Long years before that time, Saint Peter had been robbed of his river which was re-named the Minnesota; he had been defrauded of his town which was re-named Mendota; but his church remained loyal and proudly bore his name So much had happened in the span of a single life time.

Among these worshippers, there might still be found some old-timers who could remember the day when Bishop Loras of Dubuque had arrived in a canoe (his diocese including all that wild northwestern country) and had administered baptism, confirmation, holy Communion and the nuptial benediction to many of those one hundred and eighty-five Catholics who had never before seen a priest in those remote regions. They could remember his stay in their town of St. Peter on that first trip in 1839. They liked to recall that the Bishop had not forgotten the spiritual needs of those same Catholic pioneers, for one day—so the story ran—the whistle of an up-bound steamer stopping at Dubuque, brought vividly to the Bishop's mind the needs of the Catholics in those wild regions whither the steamer was bound. He had lost no time. Within an hour he had consulted Father Lucien Galtier, newly arrived from France, had appointed this devoted pastor as missionary priest to that faraway field; the latter had accepted the charge, had completed his preparations and had embarked on the very steamer whose whistle had jogged the Bishop's memory.

Many could still remember that, hardly a year later, on November 1, 1840, Father Galtier had completed the log chapel of St. Paul which gave its name to the capital of Minnesota. They could recall how, two years later, he had erected the first building in Dakotah County destined exclusively for religious purposes. It was another log chapel, and this one he named the Church of St. Peter. It was situated at the base of the hill which is now crowned by the new stone church. The modest little chapel had been forced to make way for the St. Paul and Sioux City railway and had been relegated, after its removal, to serve as a school house while the permanent St. Peter's was situated on a high bluff, built of stone, founded on a rock as was but fitting.

Until the early years of the 1870 decade, the Catholic Church of Minnesota had received much financial support from the missionary organizations of Europe, in particular from France and Austria. Gradually, however, the Church grew strong both in numbers and in leadership, and could support itself. One of these leaders who stood above the others was the great Archbishop John Ireland, who had just ordained Father Tom. Indeed, as the old-timers looked around them, there were changes great enough to make them rub their eyes. But these changes had come to stay. Had not the War Department put aside twenty acres of land for the Catholic Church and Cemetery of Mendota in the year 1870, when settling the boundaries of the Fort Snelling Reservation, giving the Catholic Church the land actually occupied by St. Peter's Church and burial ground? Never again would the Church have to cede its place to a railway nor to any other material force. Upon its rock it stood firm.

As they crowded closer, many of the younger parishioners thought of the days when they had sat on school benches beside the hesitating, floundering dullard. Others recalled that they had worked side by side with the young farmer through long summer seasons. He was not proud, in those days, that son of the boss; what would he be like today?

In the medley of old friends and acquaintances, one familiar face was lacking, one that was peculiarly dear to the newly ordained Priest, that of his dear friend and advisor, Father Eagan, who had retired from the active ministry because of advanced years and ill health. But Tom's teacher, Michael Haggerty, was there with his young wife and little daughter.

Now every eye was fixed on the door of the Sacristy. First came the Sub-Deacon, the Deacon, the Assistant

Priest and finally, Father Tom himself, the Celebrant, vested in a golden chasuble, erect, calm, totally absorbed and seemingly unconscious of the stir his presence created. How natural he looked, the same Tom Shields they knew so well, without a trace of affectation or pious mannerism, yet subtly different, in a way hard to analyse. There was a new dignity of bearing stamped upon him by years of meditation, prayer and study. . . . Here was the eternal Sacrifice offered by a new apostle, one of Mendota's own boys, now fully dedicated to the life of self-sacrifice which he had chosen and for which he had struggled so hard. When his aged parents received the Body of their Lord from the hand of their son, all shades of past doubts must have passed from their minds forever.

After the Mass, the family and friends approached the altar rail to receive the benediction of the young Priest, and that afternoon, the house of John Shields was crowded with neighbors who rushed out to the farm to congratulate Father Tom and his parents. "I can remember nothing of that day," wrote the youngest daughter, many years later, "save the smile on my father's face." To have become the center of attraction in his home was a new experience.

Father Tom, unaccustomed to such a crowd which filled every corner of the farm house, had difficulty in finding a quiet spot in which to read his Office. He needed quiet, too, for the preparation of the sermon he was to preach at Mendota, his first. How should he face all those familiar friends and neighbors without letting the shades of the past rise up between himself and those to whom he must now speak in the name of Jesus Christ? He would try to forget, to ignore the past, would speak to them like a newcomer. But no, that was impossible, it would be insincere, artificial. He must meet the difficulty frankly. He drew a

little notebook [1] from his pocket and jotted down the ideas
as they occurred to him. He would greet these people as
old friends, tell them of his joy to have returned among
them, beg them to bury all memories of the faults and shortcomings of the life he had led among them beneath their
love for Him in whose Name, he—Tom Shields—was coming to them today. Yes, that would be his opening phrase.
Then he would plunge into the subject of his sermon,
Charity, as described by Jesus Christ Himself in St. Matthew
xxv: the kingdom prepared for those who have exercised
true charity in almsdeeds, the condemnation of those who
have failed to do so. He would show them the life of
practical, enlightened charity of the Catholic priesthood
and religious orders, "the great arteries of the Church of
Christ, carrying the life blood of alms to all its members, to
the foundling and the orphan, to the aged and decrepit,
bringing forgiveness and the glad tidings of the Gospel to
the sin-laden and oppressed; instructing the ignorant, ministering to the sick and dying, bringing consolation to the
prison cell, rescuing the waif. No danger, no difficulty re-
tards them; they reach out and alleviate human misery
wherever it exists. There is no human want too insignificant for their care, no disease too loathsome for their tender
ministrations. They are lines of light and love illuminating
and warming the Church of Christ with the quick pulses
of her Founder's charity." He would describe this life of
unselfish devotion whose ideals were now his own, but he
must also make a direct application of these truths to the
lives of those who would be before him, who were neither
priests nor religious. They might say: "I have no opportunity of giving alms, no beggars come to my doors in this

[1] This notebook was found among Doctor Shields' papers after his
death.

land of plenty where nature bestows abundantly on all who wish to take. There can be no obligation for me to give alms." "And yet, without alms, it is useless for us to call ourselves followers of Jesus Christ. He declares to us that we shall have no part in His glory." Therefore this group of successful, self-satisfied persons must be told that "alms-deeds consist not alone in money bestowed on beggars, but in ministering to every need of our neighbor. There are none so rich in gifts of God that they are not poor in something, nor are there any so poor that they may not give abundantly of the treasures which God has bestowed upon them. Christ intended that His followers should be a brotherhood, not of equality nor of likeness, but of giving and receiving: souls that are unlike, natures that are unlike, each receiving from the other's gifts." He would try to make them understand the greater excellence of conferring benefits than of receiving them, it being the very nature of perfection to communicate itself. He would explain that, "It was the transcendent beauty of communicating good to others that moved God to create the world. The very purpose and essence of the Blessed Trinity is the infinite inter-communication of good." Would that be too profound a subject to touch upon? Could he explain to this congregation that "God has made us a mixture of perfection and imperfection; that it is our imperfection and dependence that renders it possible for us to receive, and our perfection that gives us a share in the special glory of the creative act by allowing us to communicate good to our fellow creatures?" He filled the little notebook with material for a dozen sermons on charity, but he did not intend to read from his notes. He would say what he could, what he felt would be understood, when he faced his hearers.

Whether it was this first sermon or a later one that was heard by a child of Michael Haggerty while still rather young, we do not know. She noted, with a childish wonder, that Father Tom's brothers went to confession to him before the Mass, and made the reflection that she would not care to go to confession to one of her own brothers. As for the sermon, she found it difficult to understand. "Father Shields spoke very rapidly and there seemed to be some impediment in his speech. But it may be that the sermon was over my head."

During the short interlude of home life after his Ordination, Father Tom had time to wonder what would be his first assignment in the Diocese. It was not long in coming. In June, he was named Curate at the St. Paul Cathedral. There, two remarkable gifts became apparent: the first, his extraordinary intuition as a confessor. His confessional was framed by long lines of waiting penitents, some of them coming from long distances. He himself knew that he could see straight into the hearts of his penitents and that, after the first few words, he seemed to know more about their lives and characters, than they knew themselves. The second gift was for preaching, and despite the fault noticed by the child, he was in great demand, which is unusual for so young a priest. One of his sermons, delivered at Easter, 1891, is printed in the Appendix.[2] It is the only one we know which he wrote out from the beginning to end. In later life he never wrote his sermons or lectures. He did not even make written notes, feeling that all such things raised barriers between the speaker and his audience. The time that others gave to written preparation, he gave to quiet meditation on his subject, so that he might speak only after he had so absorbed the thoughts that his discourse would

[2] Appendix II, p. 289.

be like an inevitable overflow. This one written sermon, however, remains to demonstrate that, had Doctor Shields been willing to devote himself to activities other than those of education, he might well have obtained renown as a preacher.

Some of his friends may have been astonished to find him scheduled for parochial work instead of the work of a teacher, for we find a letter from him to one of these friends under date of September 17, 1891, which is characteristic:

> I thought you knew me well enough to know that I am never pained at disappointments which happen to myself. . . . But are *you* pained and disappointed at the turn affairs have taken? If so, it is surely but the thoughtlessness of a moment on your part. You must bear with me—I am in a moralizing mood this morning . . . and I have determined to let it have full swing even if I am compelled to make a general confession on paper.
>
> I think I have often told you that the world of spiritual grace and the over-ruling Providence of God were to me far more intensely real than the world of ever-shifting material phenomena that surround the organs of the body. There is one desire in my life, the purest of all others (did I detect within my soul one desire not its legitimate offspring, I would tear it out, did it take with it half my heart)—the desire to do what God wants of me.
>
> Now this is all very fine in theory, but I do not expect you to believe that I carry it out to the letter, God help us! It is rarely that we can actualize our ideals; and when, in practice, I fall short of it, I trust to the clemency of a loving Master who knows the weakness of our nature. No achievement, no matter how splendid it might appear, would have aught of value for me did I not

believe it was what my Master wanted of me. I refuse to recognize any other standard of excellence in our lives and works but the degree in which they embrace the Divine will in our regard. When the finger of God points the way, should we not, with a heart overflowing with joy, cry out from the bottom of our souls: "Lead kindly light, lead Thou me on." What though it be "through encircling gloom?". . . Our Father knows best what is for His glory . . . and what more can we desire? The words of St. Paul are ever ringing in my ears and making sweet melody in my heart: "Of myself I can do nothing, but I can do all things in Him that strengthens me." Does anyone imagine that this resignation to divine dispositions may un-nerve resolution and rob the soul of courage? Let him find his answer in the life of this same Apostle, the epitome of indomitable courage and unconquerable resolution.

CHAPTER ELEVEN

THE MAN OF SCIENCE

FATHER TOM was not destined to remain long in parochial work. If Archbishop Ireland had assigned the young priest for fourteen months to a relatively humble task, he had not forgotten the man whose qualities had interested him from the first. He had important plans in mind for Father Shields, having selected him to teach the natural sciences in the new Seminary then under construction. For this task, Shields must be given the best preparation that this country could provide. It was unusual, in those days, to send a young priest, so newly ordained, to study outside his own diocese and in a secular university. That the Archbishop decided to do so is at once proof of his own broad spirit, his determination to make his Seminary a center of solid culture and, incidentally, a demonstration of his confidence in Father Shields.

Shields went directly to Baltimore, stopping at St. Mary's Seminary, which had the distinction of being the first Pontifical University in the United States. There he obtained a degree of Master of Arts after which, in October, 1892, he entered the University of Johns Hopkins to undertake graduate study in biology and the physiology of the nervous system. While he continued to reside at St. Mary's Seminary, he carried on his studies in the Biological De-

partment of Johns Hopkins where he remained until
1895.

This University ranked, at that time, among the highest
in the United States for its academic standards and the
distinction of its faculty. It was devoted exclusively to
post-graduate work. Within its walls the German science
of experimental physiological psychology was first introduced to America by G. Stanley Hall, a student of Dr.
Wundt of Leipzig, who opened the first psychological
laboratory in this country and who gathered around him
a group of distinguished students such as James McK.
Cattell and John Dewey. The graduates and their students
spread the science far and wide and, by 1894, no less than
twenty-seven institutes of higher learning were engaged in
research work in experimental psychology.

The results were valuable in the field of science but open
to question when some of these graduates undertook to
popularize their conclusions and to apply them to elementary education. It was in this latter field that Doctor Shields
was to meet them in later years, recognizing the importance
of the principles at stake but disagreeing with their applications and with their materialistic philosophy. He openly
condemned many aspects of their psychology. In his judgment, the very importance of these men's work in the
realm of science increased the danger that lurked in their
materialistic application of this science to the realm of education. He was destined to become a champion in this field
who could hold his own with the best of these modern
scientists while demonstrating that sound laws of the mind
could be combined with a sound philosophy.

Meanwhile the young priest carried on his work in the
physiological laboratory. His research in biology and physiology centered on the study of a problem which had been

the subject of earlier experiments by Mosso and Lehmann. According to their theory, pleasant sensations were accompanied by a diminution of the blood supply to the brain and unpleasant ones, by the reverse effect. Shields made his own experiments, invented and constructed his own instruments, and came to different conclusions. He worked assiduously for nearly three years on this subject and on the effect of mental and emotional stimulation on the blood flow.

A fellow student remembers him at this time as "an awkward, somewhat gaunt, wiry body, farm-trained to bear strain and steady effort; an intellect (strangely co-cooned for a period of boyhood) realizing and developing by leaps and bounds immense abilities and capacities; fearless as the pioneer stock from which he sprang, yet balanced by the caution which pioneer labors and dangers are wont to effect; eagle-eyed and sure in reaching facts and stripping them of fallacies, with a logical instinct for their correlation and analogy that bordered on positive intuition. I do not believe he ever learned a definition by heart; by reasoning or experiment, he worked the thing out and then told you what it was. The evidence of extraordinary faculties was this, that no matter how original his methods, his results would be correct. In mental and physical action he was quick as a flash—to a fault it would seem to those for whom completeness or reverence should curb speed. A heart as capacious of companionships as his intellect of ideas, Celtic in its warmth of feeling and power of sympathy, bridled and curbed and held to the path of the Commandments by a will through which functioned the supernatural life of his soul. Ingenuous and simple as a child, he knew not pride. Incomplete, and in the rough, this is a glimpse of Thomas Edward Shields as I knew him during his course at the Johns Hopkins University in the early and middle nineties." [1]

The Catholic University of America at Washington was not far from the scene of Father Shields' activities. Archbishop Ireland had been a strong supporter of this University from its foundation in 1889. It may well have been part of the Archbishop's plan in sending Shields to Baltimore that he should establish contact with some of the more prominent professors of the Catholic University. This is precisely what happened. While Father Shields was carrying out his own experiments at Johns Hopkins, Professor Edward A. Pace, of the Catholic University, was working on somewhat similar lines in experimental psychology. Pace was one of the first Americans to repair to the famous psychological laboratory of Wilhelm Wundt at Leipzig. There, in 1891, he obtained his doctorate in philosophy. Special courses in biology at Louvain and in psychology at Paris were also included in preparation for his teaching career at the Catholic University. One of the greatest Thomistic philosophers of his day, Doctor Pace was, at the same time, a modern psychologist and an upholder of the new experimental school.

Temperamentally, the two men were at opposite poles. Pace, though intelligent and thorough, was slow, ingrowing, plodding, as diffident in action, as hesitant in decision as Shields was rapid. In spite of this, they respected one another and became friends and collaborators, each contributing to the experiments of the other. Father Shields made it a habit to spend his weekends in Washington, working with Doctor Pace in the house at Eckington which the latter occupied with Doctor Shahan, later Rector of the

[1] Rt. Rev. Mgr. Joseph V. Tracey of Boston, in *The Catholic Educational Review*, Apr. 1921.

University, and devoting his Sundays to aiding the parish priest at Hyattsville, a suburb of Washington, staying at the rectory with the pastor.

During the first six years of its existence (1889-1895) the Catholic University had functioned merely as a school of theology. In 1895, however, the year in which Shields was completing his studies at Johns Hopkins, the University entered upon a new phase by establishing Schools of Philosophy and Social Science. The appointment of professors was no easy task. For the departments of Biology and Psychology, few competent men were available. Among these, Shields headed the list. In view of his outstanding ability, his friends at Washington tried to draw him into their ranks. At the time, however, Shields felt himself under obligation to his diocese and could not consider any such proposition. He was concluding the work on his Dissertation for the Doctorate based on his three years of experiment in the Physiological Laboratory of Johns Hopkins University. In his thesis entitled *"The Effect of Odors, Irritant Vapours and Mental Work Upon the Blood Flow,"* Shields pointed out that the experiments of his predecessors had been made under unfavorable conditions and with inaccurate instruments. Through an ingenious modification of the plethysmograph, Shields obtained more exact results. The experiments and conclusions of Shields are still quoted with those of Binet as late as 1923 in the monumental *Traité de Psychologie* by George Dumas [2] as important contributions to science and as disproving the conclusions of Mosso and Lehmann.

In his summary, Doctor Shields states:

> The most important outcome of this investigation has been the completion of various improvements in the con-

[2] *Traité de Psychologie.* Librairie Felix Alcan, Paris 1923. Chapter "Les Etats Affectifs," p. 427.

struction and use of the Plethysmograph by which numerous errors attending the use of the instrument have been eliminated.

The new and successful apparatus was invented and constructed by Shields himself. His printed dissertation includes photographs and diagrams of the instrument. He describes the various experiments in detail, illustrates the results by elaborate graphs and concludes that odours have little or no effect on the blood flow in so far as the experiments testify, but that mental and emotional stimulation have a definite effect on the blood supply to the brain.

His dissertation was published and submitted in view of a Doctor's Degree in Philosophy majoring in biology. He received the degree in June, 1895.[3]

The work of Doctor Shields was greatly appreciated at the Johns Hopkins University. Although faculty and students were surprised, at first, to find a young Catholic priest working among them, devoting himself to the study of science, they soon learned to like and respect him. The feeling was reciprocated. On the other hand, Shields found himself in an atmosphere of preconceptions and false notions regarding his religion. An incident which occurred during his first year at the University throws light on his loyalty, his love of truth, his sincerity, and his frank but courteous manner of dealing with those who did not share his views.

In the course of a lecture some reference had been made to the Catholic Church as tyrannical in its treatment of certain men of science. The situation was embarrassing for the young priest; his own honor as well as that of the Church was under attack; he could not let such criticism pass

[3] At that time Johns Hopkins University gave a general Ph.D. in imitation of the German system. A man could work for this degree while majoring in any subject.

unanswered. The next day, Shields arose to continue his series of lectures on the nerve-jerk. He remarked:

> No one can be more keenly alive than I am to the fact that this time and place should be sacred to Biological Science. But circumstances compel me to request a few minutes of your attention to a subject whose connection with Biology I am unable to discern. Yet I have too much confidence in the integrity and fair-mindedness of my professors and fellow students of this institution to believe for a moment that they would willingly deal unjustly with any man.

In this disarming fashion he opened his argument. It was evidently unfair to condemn any man for inconsistency or any institution for tyranny without first investigating the matter or hearing them in their own defense. He continued:

> I believe that all fair-minded men who are not pessimists will readily agree that when any large body of intelligent men are represented as holding doctrines or following practices that are inconsistent, dishonest, absurd or tyrannical, it is our duty to suspect the representations as mistaken or false until we have thoroughly investigated the matter, just as any prudent scientist would suspect startling or improbable discoveries until they are verified. This is especially true when the representation comes from a hostile source or from certain newspaper reports which too often sacrifice truth to a craving for sensation.

He set forth vigorously the difference between the standards that should be applied to the study of science on the one hand, "where reason is the supreme arbiter" and the study of Revelation, on the other, "which, from the very nature of the case is purely a matter of authority."

Reason, he explained, could in its freest and fullest exercise, prove beyond the shadow of a doubt the existence of an Authority which guarantees us:

> that Christ was God, that he delivered to us a body of truth concerning our relations to himself and the conditions of life beyond the grave; that he fulfilled his promise of sending into the Church the Pentecostal Spirit of Truth to remain with her, calling to her mind whatsoever he had said and showing her the things that are to come.

This body of truth, he pointed out:

> lies beyond the possibility of investigation by the human intellect. The absolute infallibility of this authority in the premises having been made evident to the intellect, pitiless logic compels us to accept its statements. The article in question deals with a question of Authority and Authority only. If the author fails to represent the doctrines of the Church correctly, she certainly has the right to disavow his statements without thereby incurring the reproach of tyranny; and this independently of any question of infallible authority. Has not any man or institution the right to disavow a presentation of his or its tenets which is perceived to be untrue? To interfere with this right would certainly be tyranny.

He then concluded courteously:

> I would have much preferred not to feel obliged to speak of this matter here, especially as I am convinced that no offense or injustice was intended—however much was done. Yet my silence would have appeared to give tacit consent to what I know to be untrue. I thank you, Gentlemen, for your kind attention which I trust I will not again be compelled to infringe upon. We will now return to the nerve-jerk.

His fellow students seem to have respected Shields the more for his uncompromising stand regarding his own faith and his insistence on its being treated with justice. As for the University authorities, they went so far as to make serious efforts to keep this young priest permanently on the faculty. It was urged upon Doctor Shields that if he would devote his life to science, he could become one of the leading biologists of the age. But Shields had other ideas. So had the Archbishop. To Shields, himself, science was of value only in so far as it was a means of doing God's work more effectively. Laborious research was all very well, brilliant achievements might have their use, but were of little value in themselves, precious only if they provided a solid scientific basis for the theories of education which were taking shape in his mind and which, from a dim outline, were to become a clear vision of the principles which he found exemplified in the teaching methods of our Lord Himself. He declined all offers of change and returned to his diocese leaving behind him staunch friends both at Baltimore and Washington.

The new Seminary of St. Paul had been opened the previous year (1894). Its curriculum included, besides the usual courses in philosophy and theology, a serious study of the natural sciences. For this line of work, Doctor Shields, with his brilliant record at Baltimore, was well fitted. Indeed, the Archbishop had been counting on him for the organization of the Biological Department together with the equipment of its laboratory, a task which was entrusted to him immediately upon his return to St. Paul. Thus, for some years, his activities were directed in this definite channel. Doctor Shields threw himself into the work with passionate enthusiasm. His power as a teacher was quickly recognized by his students and fellow professors.

Their discussions of scientific and philosophical problems had a stimulating effect upon the entire faculty, and the new Seminary at once took high rank among American institutions for the training of the clergy. Doctor Shields was recognized as an authority in what, for the moment, had become his special field. He became prominent in Catholic circles and in the larger sphere of scientific activity. The Minnesota Academy of Medicine elected him to honorary membership and other associations, particularly those interested in education, welcomed him to their discussions. He was known as a man of wide knowledge, deep culture and as an independent thinker who saw in religion the safeguard of intellectual freedom.

The death of his father, John Shields, cast a shadow over the joy of the son's return from Baltimore. Besides being a personal sorrow to Father Tom, this death entailed many a family adjustment in order to plan for his mother that independence which her strong nature required. She must have her own part of the house divided off from the rest where she could lead her own life, do her own work, receive her son, Father Tom, and her personal friends. This was arranged and the great old lady continued to live alone, do her own cooking and housework until the advanced age of 98, when, after a three weeks' illness, in full consciousness, she died.

There were not only his mother's affairs to adjust. His brother, Michael Bernard, had organized on a large scale a business enterprise known in the whole region as the "Shields Sorghum Company." The farmers of the region had planted a considerable acreage of sugar cane and they brought their produce to be manufactured into syrup by the Shields Company at Mendota, "the purest syrup on the market." Shields Mendota Sorghum was known all over the state. The plant had a capacity of fifty thousand gallons. It had grown up from small beginnings at the time when Tom Shields had worked his "sugar field" to pay for his classical education. Father Tom still took a vivid interest in the whole proposition, feeling that a home industry of this nature would be of benefit to the farmers as well as to his brother. Some thought that the whole idea had been Father Tom's, but however this may have been, his interest was keen. The best holiday for him was to spend an afternoon on the farm. He bought a bicycle. By leaving the Seminary immediately after the midday meal, he could pedal those nine miles over crowded roads, out of the city, through the suburbs to Mendota, which was becoming almost a suburb itself of that great, spreading city of St. Paul. There his brother Michael and a bevy of young nephews and nieces greeted him with delight on his frequent visits to the factory. Father Tom did not come as an onlooker, for with sleeves rolled up, he helped his brother to handle the sugar cane and tinkered with the machines as of old. It was good to be using his muscles once more, good to be breathing the air of his native hill, good to find himself, for a few hours, in a home environment, he who had been compelled by his vocation to live in an institutional atmosphere for so many years. No man ever loved a home and fireside more than he, and in the years to come, we shall find him struggling to create around him a home atmosphere within the possibilities of his vocation. These very nephews and nieces who watched eagerly for his coming to Mendota were to be the nucleus of that home life of the future. He could not know this as he sat for a few moments to rest under the branches of a spreading oak, joking with the children and talking business with his brother until—with a wave of farewell—he mounted his bicycle to pedal back over those nine miles of road that led to the Seminary of St. Paul.

In addition to his work at the Seminary, Doctor Shields gave regular conferences to the Sisters at the College of St. Joseph, where the Archbishop's sister was Superior. He lectured on biology, psychology and education, lectures which many of the older Sisters still remember for the profound spirituality of the doctrine. Then, in 1898, another sphere of activity was opened to him when he was assigned to parochial duties at St. Joseph's Church in the city of St. Paul, an experience which brought him into closer practical contact than hitherto with people of all types, particularly the poor, giving him abundant opportunity to apply to concrete examples all knowledge of the human mind which he had gained through long years of study. Not of the human mind, only, but of the human heart through generous alms both spiritual and material. He won distinction as a preacher by the forcefulness of his exposition and the method of developing his subject by parable, arguing from the homely and the familiar to the supernatural, basing his method on that of Christ. As a spiritual director, once again, he was able to exert an immense influence for good by his almost uncanny insight into the human soul and his quick sympathy, which drew penitents from far and near, quite outside of the parish limits. It was a career, it would appear, of uninterrupted success. Yet in the heart of Doctor Shields there burned an unsatisfied longing; he knew that his real work had not yet begun.

Whether the incident of which Doctor Shields often spoke in later years, occurred at St. Joseph's Church or elsewhere we do not know. It must have been during that period that he invented a painless project for financing a parish, and, like the grubbing machine, it worked. At the time it was considered wholly original; since then, it has been tried elsewhere. Doctor Shields loathed the support of the parish expenses on what he called "the beggarly five-cent system"; it was beneath the dignity of the parishioner, still more of the priest, to meet the necessary expenses of the Church by constant appeals from the pulpit. He called the men of the parish together; showed them an outline of the budget; together they discussed it; decided then and there what each one could contribute, and the parish expenses were made to tally with the contributions. Doctor Shields agreed to send each one a monthly bill, just such a bill as they received from their butcher and baker. The plan worked like a charm. No mention of money was made from the pulpit; no collection was taken up. When the people went to Mass, they received doctrinal and spiritual teaching. The finances were otherwise disposed of. "They were not rich people," Doctor Shields would add, "mostly poor miners, workingmen who had no surplus over and above their daily earnings which were meager in those days. But they never missed paying their bills; they knew the expenses had been reduced to a minimum for they had taken part in making up the budget. They liked the system and did their part promptly. The House of God, for priest and people, was strictly a House of Prayer."

Meanwhile his friends at Washington had not forgotten him. He received frequent letters from Doctor Thomas O'Gorman (later Bishop of Sioux City) who had been his Superior in Seminary days and became Professor of Church History at the Catholic University. Now that the Biological Department at St. Paul's Seminary was well established, he argued, why could not Doctor Shields think of joining the University faculty where his ideas would reach a wider audience? He outlined ways and means for bringing this about. Doctor Pace, too, was working hard at the other end to bring about the appointment of Shields.

One fine day a telegram from him advised Doctor Shields to make an immediate formal application for the position of Instructor in Biology at the Catholic University of America. Due to a local complication, it was later decided that he should rather apply for the Chair of Physiology and obtain the necessary consent of his Archbishop to his transfer to Washington. Accordingly, in the spring of 1902, he wrote as follows:

> To the Right Reverend Thomas J. Conaty, D.D.
> The Catholic University
> Washington, D. C.
>
> Right Reverend Sir,
>   I beg leave hereby to put into your hands my application for the Chair of Physiology at the Catholic University of America. I inclose the letter of the Most Reverend John Ireland granting me permission to accept the professorship if the University should honor me with the appointment.
>
>   I am, Right Reverend Sir,
>   Yours very respectfully,
>   Thomas E. Shields, Ph.D.

It was in the autumn of 1902 that Thomas Edward Shields went to Washington to become Instructor in Physiological Psychology in the Department of Philosophy at the Catholic University of America. There he was to start a movement which was to revolutionize educational methods in the whole Catholic education system of America. There he was to struggle, to initiate, to gather round him a group of collaborators; to suffer opposition and misunderstanding, to expend the last ounce of his strength, and to die.

PART THREE

THE EDUCATOR

The great benefactors of the race have been the men who cause each generation to rediscover for itself the great fundamental truths that constitute the life-blood of every civilization.

—*T. E. Shields*

Blessed is he who has found his work; let him ask no other blessedness.—*Thomas Carlyle*

CHAPTER TWELVE

PREPARING THE SOIL

LESS than twenty years lay before him. He might have settled down to a comfortable academic routine, teaching and carrying on research work. But that was not his plan. He had an objective which grew more vast at each step forward. Interlocking activities multiplied with the years. Though he covered the ground with astounding rapidity, twenty years were too few for the work of this man whose destiny it was to revolutionize the standards of Catholic education, who saw the needs of his time with so broad a vision, with so warm a sympathy and to whom vision and action were one.

He belonged to the Faculty of Philosophy and gave courses in Biology and Physiological Psychology. Those were his official activities in the early days at the University. But, pioneer and promoter, he organized a Catholic Educational News Service, a Correspondence School for Catholic Teachers, lectured on educational topics from coast to coast, contributed articles to educational reviews and encyclopedias, headed the Department of Education at the University, founded and became Dean of a Catholic Teachers College, wrote books, founded and edited a Catholic Educational Review, founded and managed a publishing house, organized a system of affiliation of Catholic colleges and high-schools with the University, wrote a masterly series of textbooks for the primary schools, his boundless resources of hope and enthusiasm carrying over rough ways and plain.

He became something of a financial wizard, carrying his enterprises "on a shoe string" as more timid contemporaries complained, but never hesitating, trusting in Providence to supply what was essential to his purpose. Working like a dynamo, serene under attack, meeting opposition from the wise and prudent with a smile and a shrug, overcoming obstacles with tenacity and diplomacy, smarting under the delays of men with average intelligence but limited vision, he left behind him an indelible mark on the trend of Catholic education. Within the limits of a single volume, only a rapid impression, a bird's-eye view, can be given of what the ex-dullard accomplished for the Church and for the education of her children.

Already in his Seminary days, Shields had noted among his Daily Thoughts:

> A reconciliation between faith and science must be brought about, a reconciliation so valuable to the cause of truth, so conducive to real scientific progress. There is but one way to accomplish this. We must make ourselves masters of the science of our day, retain all the truth it possesses, disprove its errors on scientific grounds and supply what is wanting from Philosophy and Revelation. By this means only can we hope to enter into the thought of our age and influence it for good.

This had been his plan of action. The first part of the program was an accomplished fact. Doctor Shields had made himself a master of the science of his day. His teachers at Johns Hopkins had noticed Shields' tendency, even at that time, to correlate science and scholastic philosophy. Today the second part of the program must be carried out. His knowledge of biology and psychology was the opening wedge, useful indeed, but only as an introduction to his real work which was to cover a wider field.

For several years Doctor Shields lectured on biology and psychology. His predecessor in the Department had been a specialist in plant biology and had left, taking with him his whole botanical collection to another University. Shields had inaugurated courses in animal biology but without laboratory equipment. Consequently his work was limited to lectures. His students found him a magnetic if somewhat informal teacher judged by the standards of the day. "His was an intense nature. . . . For him there were no half-hearted interests; he could do nothing without being wholly absorbed in it," wrote one of his early students.[1] But did he want to be totally absorbed in biology? Other interests soon pressed upon him.

For several years Doctor Shields lived in the house of Doctor Monaghan in Brookland, a suburb of Washington in the northeasterly section. It was in the parlor of this little frame cottage that he gathered his students for the weekly seminars at which he presided. Between times, he lectured far and near, the prestige of his Hopkins doctorate casting a glow about his name, for, in those days, a degree from that University was held in high consideration. Shields did not disappoint his audiences; he interested them, excited them and opened out vistas in fields that were unfamiliar. But his own heart was elsewhere. His mind was turning more and more toward education as the great need of the day. The application of psychology to the art of teaching was still in a tentative stage. No one realized better than did Doctor Shields the benefits which education could derive from biological science and from modern psychology, but, on the other hand, no one saw more clearly than he did

[1] Rt. Rev. Mgr. Patrick J. McCormick in the *Catholic Educational Review*, Apr. 1921.

the dangers that were inherent in a false application of these very principles to the science of education. The transfer of thought and theory from biology to teaching should be undertaken only by men who were competent in both fields, otherwise the transfer would be fraught with grave dangers. It was all too rare, he felt, that workers in one field had a sufficient knowledge of the other to be able to verify the theory in its original field and also judge of its suitability in the related field. Doctor Shields became convinced that his own life work was to consist in this transfer of science to education. Other men could carry on the research work he had begun, others could teach biology. His contribution was to be in the field of education. He bided his time, however.

Meanwhile the field must be fertilized. Why should not the influence of a small group of forward-looking men at the University make itself felt beyond the limits of the campus? Why not meet the public with well-planned publicity of ideas? The educational field was sorely in need of fresh seed. The pioneer and promoter in Doctor Shields rose to the occasion. His friends agreed that the plan was sound and timely. They were ready to think it over. But with Shields, thought was equivalent to action. He believed that delay is fatal to those who are prepared—and he was prepared. His plan was ready. He organized *The Catholic Associated Press* which was formally incorporated in the District of Columbia with Doctor Monaghan as President and Doctor Shields as Secretary and Treasurer. Across the vast continent, all the more important organs of the Catholic Press began to sound a new note in Catholic thought.[2]

[2] Among the writers who contributed articles more or less regularly were Doctors Shahan, Pace, Kerby, Maguire, Monaghan and Shields—the latter contributing the lion's share. Among the periodicals that subscribed for these articles were *The Telegraph, Tidings, Union & Times, Standard & Times, Sentinel, Monitor* and others.

The work grew in volume and the new ideas attracted attention in educational circles. It was like the sounding of a pitch pipe to give the tonality before the singing starts.

Soon the little house of Doctor Monaghan became totally inadequate for lodging Doctor Shields and his works. A home had to be found for the Catholic Associated Press, the working material, the duplicators, the secretaries. On a wooded hilltop near the northeasterly boundary of the District, stood a shabby but spacious frame house bearing the dignified name of Dunbarton Hall. Doctor Shields rented it and moved his records and papers from Brookland to Pierce Mill Road. The shabby frame house became the home of the Press, of Doctor Shields, his collaborators and his friends, for he was not a man to keep a good thing to himself. The old house, while commonplace, must have seen better days for it was surrounded by noble trees and commanded a wide view of rolling hills and fertile valleys bringing to mind memories of his beloved Mendota.

Looking back over those early days Doctor Pace wrote of him: "We discern in his life the gradual unfolding of a plan which became more definite as time went on—more definite and more absorbing. It attained proportions which far exceeded its earliest conception. Even in his enthusiastic thinking, the full scope of what he intended was not at first visible. But with each step, it grew upon him. His horizon widened. New projects took shape in his mind. New problems arose and, with them, the thought that contained their solution. His career was a development, slow and painful at first, then rapid and vigorous, a living exemplification of the principles which he applied to educational theory and practice."

Thus already another and larger plan had engrafted itself upon the first. The new venture was a Correspondence School to be conducted by the University professors for the benefit of the teaching Sisterhoods. At that time no Catholic center of higher education had opened its doors to meet the needs of the Sisters for an adequate professional education. The need was recognized by all, but no action had been taken in the matter. Though the Correspondence School was far from being an ideal solution of the difficulty, the need itself was so urgent that Doctor Shields decided to grasp at the only solution within his reach. Moreover he viewed it as a mere stepping stone. With perfection still on the horizon, he worked eagerly at the best thing that could be done at the time. Courses were offered in Philosophy, Psychology, Logic, History of Education and the Teaching of Religion. This last, with Psychology, were his own courses. Religion must be made the center and heart of all education; a germinal truth to be planted in the heart of the child, the central thought around which all else must be correlated; the method, that of Our Lord Himself when on earth as Guide and Teacher—the parable. Things of nature must lay a foundation for the things of God as in the parables of Jesus Christ.

The work became overpowering. He needed help. An S.O.S. to Minnesota brought young hands and bright faces from the "Shields Sorghum" to the "Shields Education." Two of the children of his brother Michael, who had watched their uncle come and go on his "bike" between St. Paul and Mendota, were ready to lend him their enthusiastic support in his new venture. Thus, living at Dunbarton Hall were his niece, Rose Shields, who kept house for her uncle, Joseph Shields, who helped with the mimeographing, assembling and mailing, two secretaries and his intimate friend Doctor Turner.[3]

In addition to this work at Dunbarton Hall, Doctor

[3] Later Bishop of Buffalo.

Shields was carrying on his regular courses at the University and at Trinity College, was writing for the Associated Press, and, during the summers was coming into personal contact with his correspondence students by means of Institutes at various centers. During this time he wrote and published a book entitled *The Education of Our Girls* and was at work on another, *The Making and Unmaking of a Dullard,* since the subject of backward children and their treatment was one which was harassing the teaching profession. The book was built up from his own experiences as a backward child. As though all this were not enough to fill his time and energy, he and Doctor Pace were considering the necessity of a fundamental reform of the whole system used in the primary schools and the composition of textbooks based on sound scientific methods. The first volume of this series of textbooks was completed by Doctor Shields while still at Dunbarton Hall.

He used to ride to the University and back on his bicycle for the sake of exercise and economy. The distance was great and the climate debilitating. The increasing pressure of work became too great a strain even for a man who gloried in activity. He was exceeding his limit and decided he must live nearer to the University to avoid the time wasted in transit. In May, 1908, he returned to live in Brookland close to the University, where he purchased a tiny frame house at 1026 Quincy Street. This became the new home of the Press and Correspondence School as well as the home of Doctor Shields and "family" which now was increased by the presence of another niece.

Doctor Shields was facing at this time his first serious struggle with the Board of Trustees. A situation had arisen which required a solution by the Board. Bishops in various parts of the country were beginning to send young men to the University to be trained in education or *pedagogy*, as it was then called, in the expectation that such training would be provided. Yet there existed no Department of Education at the Catholic University and no provision had been made as yet for handling these subjects. Doctor Shields had met the immediate needs by a sort of camouflage. His own interest in biology and even in psychology was centering more and more on the light that these sciences could throw on educational principles. Little by little, the students who followed his courses in biology and psychology found themselves studying education. As time went on, Doctor Shields felt it irksome to continue such a fiction—was it not almost a fraud?—and his rugged integrity revolted.

He announced his intention of giving up the teaching of biology for the following year. The announcement was not well received. Pressed for his reason, Shields stated that he had given up his interest in the subject, had not kept up with the progress of the science and had devoted his best efforts to another line of work. The matter was referred to the Governing Board where it was urged that Shields had received his Doctor's degree at Johns Hopkins for biology, had been engaged to teach this subject at the Catholic University, that he must be induced to reconsider his decision. Pressure was brought to bear.

Shields was not a stubborn man but no amount of outside pressure could move him a hair's breadth once he was sure of being right. On this occasion, he wasted no words in discussion but referred the importunate pleaders to Doctor Pace, Dean of the Faculty of Philosophy to which he was attached. Pace reported back that Shields was uncompromising and that his decision was final. The Governing Board must accept his ultimatum or lose a valuable man from their teaching staff. The members of the Board, in their embarrassment, found a formula of compromise which was satisfactory to themselves. They voted to withdraw a recommendation which they had made to the Trustees previously to promote Doctor Shields to a full professorship with a raise of salary.

The man least perturbed by this tempest in a teapot was, perhaps, "the Doctor" himself. A plan had been secretly maturing in his mind: The Board of Trustees must be placed before a *fait accompli*. Courses in education had been demanded and given at the University despite the fact that no official provision had been made for such courses. The need had become acute. The camouflaged courses provided no permanent solution, though they had filled an emergency. The Rector encouraged him to go ahead feeling sure that the Trustees would act favorably at their next meeting. A Department of Education was essential and must be approved.

This was precisely what happened. The Board, placed before a *fait accompli*, approved the establishment of a Department of Education at the University, naming Doctor Shields Head or Chairman. At last he and Doctor Pace could launch a serious educational program with the full authority of the University behind them. The field had been fertilized. Now the seed could be sown.

CHAPTER THIRTEEN

SOWING THE SEED

I T was partly due to his own experience as a child, to the false educational methods of which he had been a victim, that Doctor Shields became the foremost educator of his time, a pioneer in formulating a system of Catholic education for children based upon the recognized laws of science. He was the first to vindicate those laws by showing their use in the Gospels by the Divine Teacher Himself and by the Church in her organic teachings as the mouthpiece of the Spirit of Truth. It was startling to many, to others a shock, when by tongue and pen he triumphantly proved that the universally received discoveries of modern science were discoveries only in the sense that they brought to light, in the name of biology and psychology, the pedagogical principles of Jesus as recorded in the Gospels and as applied by the Church in her liturgical and educational activities of two thousand years.

His "method" was not merely a system for a more effective and vital teaching of Religion than that in actual use. It was that and more. It was the grafting of a totally new pedagogy (based on the recent acquisitions of science) upon the stem of our ancient Catholic philosophy and dogma. It was a profound and, at the time, new approach to the art of teaching all subjects in accordance with the laws that govern the mind, laws which his own study of biology and psychology had made plain to him, and in the application of which his own genius made him a master. Religion was indeed the center of Doctor Shields' method, the principle which illumined the whole process and each individual detail of the subject matter, bringing each into its true focus in relation to the whole, both as regards this life and the life to come.

Doctor Shields' educational campaign entailed a fight on two fronts. His contemporaries among secular educators were using the new discoveries of experimental science to spread and publicize their own materialistic philosophy; men such as G. Stanley Hall and John Dewey, to mention only two, with lamentable results in the class rooms of the public schools. These false deductions and incorrect applications of science to education Doctor Shields attacked as being pernicious in their influence as well as unsound in a scientific sense.

On the other side, among his Catholic contemporaries, (teachers and a large proportion of the clergy) he faced an opposition based on mere unfamiliarity with the laws of biology and psychology, an ignorance which translated itself in suspicion of the unknown and a reluctance to accept even the most self-evident truths where they involved a change in practice, an upsetting of routine.

The struggle on these two fronts began early and ended only with the last breath of Thomas Edward Shields.

The publication of his textbooks was, once again, an interlocking activity forced upon Doctor Shields by the immediate necessities of the moment. The students of his correspondence courses complained that, however clearly they might grasp the principles of modern pedagogy, however ardently they might desire to make Religion the central theme of all education, their task in the class room was well nigh impossible since there were no textbooks in

existence based upon these principles. It was a challenge
which Doctor Shields could not resist. Theory, he knew,
was of little avail where no practical application could be
made. Textbooks must be written without delay. Who
would do this work? There was no time for hesitation. He
would write them himself with the aid of Doctor Pace if
the latter would cooperate. Pace was delighted with the
plan and lent his name as co-author, though the work was
done almost exclusively by Doctor Shields.

Religion was placed at the center of the entire system
of truths to be imparted. It was the link between all other
items of knowledge, interwoven with every concept and
activity. This idea was reinforced by the very title he gave
the series: *Religion* (First Book, Second Book, etc.) But in
spite of this title, each book contained the sum total of the
matters to be studied during the year. It was a profound
psychological approach to intellectual development in
general. More will be said about the details of the method
elsewhere. For the moment we must follow Doctor Shields
in the sowing of this new seed among Catholic educators.

As early as 1905, we find him taking a leading part in
the discussions of The Catholic Educational Association;
opening the session of the Parish School Department with
a talk on pedagogy; and before the Department of Seminaries, urging that every young priest should be made
familiar with the entire field of education in view of his
future duty of organizing his parish school. At least the
psychological and physiological aspects of the question
should be made clear to these young men in order that they
might judge competently of the value of methods. The
Seminary should not, of course, be responsible for the
formation of diocesan supervisors—The Catholic University
was the natural place for priests to receive such training—

but the strongest backing for it should come from the Seminaries themselves. Our schools were admittedly in need of better methods, of better organization, and not in secular branches only, but in moral training as well in order that strength of character be built up in the young.

At the meeting of this same Association which took place in Milwaukee in 1907, a controversy commenced which made something of a stir in Catholic educational circles and aroused a party spirit. A distinguished theologian from the Pacific coast, Father Peter Yorke, read a paper on *The Educational Value of Christian Doctrine*, pleading for a more attractive method of teaching religion to children than the dry methods in use. Both Doctors Shields and Pace endorsed the general proposition but neither of them was satisfied with the pedagogical methods advocated by the good priest and exemplified in his textbooks. An animated discussion followed. Finally, Doctor Pace remarked, in summing up the views of the various speakers, that Father Yorke had brought out the *content* of teaching; Father Finn, the importance of the teacher's personality; but, as between these two (the content and the teacher) there was a third factor, the *method* by which the teacher imparts this content of doctrine. No matter how vital the subject might be, unless that subject were handled in the right way (that is, accommodated to the growing mind of the child) the teaching would be a failure. No matter how devoted the teacher might be to his task, unless that teacher brought to his work the right sort of method, love's labor would be lost. In conclusion, he urged that this whole question of Method in the teaching of Christian Doctrine be taken up by the members of the Association and by all Catholic teachers—that they should consider not content alone (the truth to be imparted) but the method whereby that truth is to be brought within the reach of the mind of each child.

To the argument of Doctor Pace, Doctor Shields added a few words, insisting particularly on the importance of correlation, to which he was to return so insistently in later years:

> You cannot teach Christian Doctrine as a thing apart and hope to succeed in making it what it should be—the molding influence in the mind and character of the pupil.

Unfortunately, the finer points of the argument were lost upon Father Yorke, whose good intentions were beyond question but whose ignorance of biology, psychology and pedagogy was unlimited. The discussion aroused resentment and was considered a mere attack upon Father Yorke's person and publications.

The atmosphere was already strained before the meeting of the following year at Cincinnati at which Doctor Shields made the principal address on the subject: *Methods of Teaching Religion.* Copies of the proposed talk had been sent in advance to the members of the Association in order that they might be prepared to take part in a discussion of the speaker's views.

Doctor Shields had come to the meeting determined to make a frontal attack against the time-honored system of forcing children to memorize incomprehensible words and phrases under the supposition that they were thus being taught religion. The catechism with its questions and answers had, for him, none of the charm of a magical incantation. He was crippled by no superstitious belief in the power of a little paper-covered book whose success he admitted as a book of orthodox theology but whose failure he deplored as a child's textbook of religion. The theologians had planned and put together the catechism as though they meant it for a textbook of theology; thinking only of the subject matter, they forgot the child of whose mind, indeed, they had little knowledge. They were concerned only with content. Doctor Shields gave the same attention as they did to content (the dogmatic truths themselves) but he gave due attention also to the child and to the laws governing the unfolding of the child-mind. He knew that the catechism, as such, was an innovation, relatively recent in the life of the Church. It had been Luther's catechism that had led Catholic theologians to construct a catechism of Catholic belief. Catechisms, however, had always been intended for teachers, not for pupils. Thus, the catechism authorized by the Council of Trent was for the use of pastors and teachers. By what strange irony of fate had a booklet of concentrated theology been set before little children instead of the manna from heaven which was their birthright? Indeed, "all the Innocents were not slain by Herod" —as their defender loved to remark.

In making this direct attack against current methods of teaching religion, Doctor Shields realized very well that he would stir up against himself a hornet's nest. But it was high time to meet the issue squarely. That this might be a matter of personal offense to Father Yorke, probably never entered his head, nor would it have influenced his action. We quote his speech at some length because it was the first gesture in the long fight he was inaugurating and it set apart those that were with him from those that were against.

Recent developments in pedagogical science have brought to light a number of fundamental principles which the enlightened Catholic will at once recognize as the governing principles of our Lord's method of teaching. The embodiment of these same principles is the most characteristic feature in the organic life of the Church. In the teaching of Catechism, the discrepancy between these principles and the method usually employed in our schools is perhaps more striking than that in the case of any other subject. It would be difficult to find a justification for this state of affairs. There is no obvious reason why these principles should be less rigorously adhered to in the teaching of religion than in the teaching of any other subject. On the contrary, from the supreme importance which we attach to the teaching of religion in our schools, we should expect to find in the Christian Doctrine class the first fruits of every advance in the knowledge of fundamental principles.

He pointed out that this was not the case and that those who were responsible for the teaching of religion in the schools were anxiously seeking a remedy. He quoted various supervisors of schools as testifying to the fact that the mere memorizing of the catechism was not sufficient for a religious education. And he continued:

There is, in fact, a general dissatisfaction with the prevailing methods and an earnest desire to bring the teaching of religion into harmony with the accepted principles of modern pedagogy. It is believed by many that too much reliance has been placed on the mere memorizing of doctrinal formulae and too little intelligent effort expended in rendering the saving truths of religion functional in the minds and hearts of the pupils. In India and China, the cultivation of the memory is the chief object of education. In the Western world, on the contrary, mere erudition has ceased to be the goal of the teacher's endeavor. Memory is no longer valued as a permanent storehouse of forms and isolated facts.

At this point, it became evident that the opposition had heard all it needed to know: Shields was the enemy of memory! What followed was heard with inattentive ears.

With us, the function of memory tends to be restricted, more and more, to the holding of truth in consciousness while it is being assimilated by the mind. . . . The teacher is being reminded on almost every page of modern educational literature that the need and capacity of the developing mind are the only criteria of the truths to be imparted. No matter how valuable a truth may be in itself, we have come to understand that it must not be offered to a mind that is unprepared for its reception and unable to render it functional when received.

Our Savior formulated this principle on several occasions as when He said: "To you is given to know the mystery of the Kingdom of God: but to the rest in parables, that seeing they may not see, and hearing they may not understand." And again when He said: "I have many things to say to you, but you cannot bear them now." He always cast His lessons in such form that each one of those who listened to Him might receive according to the measure of his capacity. He refrained from presenting to His followers the mysteries of the Kingdom of Heaven in abstract formulations; and nowhere is it recorded that He commanded His disciples to commit to memory the exact words of any of His lessons. He established a living agency to present the saving truths of religion to each generation and to every people in forms suited to their capacity.

Shields pointed out the danger of isolating religion from life and, in the school, from the other subjects taught. He urged that it be made more attractive than any other subject,

and be so presented as to give the children a realization of the thought that God is the center of the universe and that religious truths illumine and unify all the subjects taught in the school. Religion must touch and transform the child's entire mental life: it must reach his instincts, form his habits of thinking, and guide his conduct in all the situations of life. Indeed, religious truths cannot be comprehended at all unless they are approached in the right way, and, in this right way, the Master Teacher must be our guide. In teaching the sublime truths of religion, He always appealed directly to the instincts, to the experiences, to the imagination of his disciples; and through these means, He sought to lead them into an understanding of the saving truths which He announced to them.

Moreover, Christ did not come among men to deliver to them a body of recondite truths to be carried out as a memory load by a multitude unable to grasp their significance. He proclaimed, indeed, the highest truths in both the intellectual and moral orders, but these truths were always eminently practical. They were intended to modify the conduct of all who received them. He insisted that the truths which He proclaimed could be understood only by those who reduced them to practice.

The Church had never assented to Luther's doctrine that faith without works justified, but had always insisted that the truth of which she is guardian should inspire the inward aspiration and the outward act of every member of the fold. And he continued:

The sciences which deal with the phenomena of life and mind have given us as the fundamental principles which govern the development of the human mind the foundation principles of Our Lord's method of teaching. . . . This of itself would be sufficient justification for our undertaking to outline a method of teaching Christian Doctrine in agreement with these principles but there is a still more cogent reason for this undertaking. Those who teach religion in our schools are called upon to instruct the children in the same subject matter that Christ came on earth to teach the children of men, and the principles underlying His method of accomplishing this task should be those governing the method of teaching the selfsame truths to the children of our generation.

He reminded his hearers that the purpose of teaching religion was not merely to store up information about God, but,

> Religion, to be of value, must enter into the very depths of life and affect all its ways; it must consecrate human instincts and lift them into habits that will safeguard the pathways of peace; it must shed its light on every truth that claims admittance to the mind; it must color every feeling; it must be the inmost motive of every action and the substance of every aspiration. Where religion does not mean this, it is not a blessing to the individual nor to the society in which he moves. . . . It is a stumbling block to the unwise, a cloak to the hypocrite and a thing of scorn to all honest minds.

A lively discussion followed. It appeared that while no one was fully satisfied with the existing catechism nor with present methods of teaching religion, many were convinced that a mysterious benefit could be derived by storing up in the mind matters that were not understood like a hidden treasure to be drawn upon in years of maturity. Above all, there was a general rush to the defense of "memory."

Doctor Pace remarked in his detached manner:

> Doctor Shields does not object to the cultivation of memory. What he does object to is the use of the memory in such a way as to make the mind a mere record of answers which may or may not be understood. . . . This is the essential thing in the Shields Method: we have

as our principal example the Supreme Artist and Teacher. No one could certainly have given a better example in teaching the truths of Christianity than Christ Himself. And yet how often does He cast His teaching in the form of abstract propositions? On the contrary, He continually employs the parable, the lesson from nature, the homely facts of every day life; and with these, He builds up in the minds of His hearers the great truths of the Kingdom of Heaven.

The Church follows His example in her liturgy where she appeals to the senses and reaches the intellect through symbols. What we need is to bring her methods and those of Our Lord into our own teaching of religion. And the attempt to supply this need has resulted in the preparation by Dr. Shields of manuals based on methods at once scientific and in keeping with the nature of the subject.

Manuals? That was the last straw! Father Yorke arose, slightly red in the face, attacked the speaker's principles with some warmth, and insisted that Doctor Shields' pedagogy was "nothing less than revolutionary."

Doctor Shields made no direct answer to this attack, but, with a smile, made a few closing remarks suggesting that possibly the content of his paper might not have been fully understood and that, as a natural result, his treatment of certain psychological data had been misinterpreted. Then, turning to Father Yorke, he assured him that he had not the slightest intention of deprecating the value of memory:

On the contrary, it is just because I set great store by this faculty of the soul that I am anxious to secure its proper cultivation. The issue, then, is not whether in teaching Christian Doctrine we should appeal to the child's memory, but whether memory gives the best service when it is forced to carry a burden of ideas that to the child's mind are meaningless. My contention is that our teaching should not simply provide things worth remembering, but also provide them in such a way as to help on the development of memory and at the same time bring out activity of the other faculties—understanding and feeling. He wanted, he explained, to secure a proper setting in the mind for these great truths to be remembered. However inadequately carried out, he thought that the underlying principle on which he was working was sound, namely that, "In teaching Christ's truth no less than in living His life, the Master is the best Model."

We have recorded this controversy at some length because it represented a taking of position by men in educational circles. The affair made a stir, was talked of and often misrepresented. The old fashioned members of the Association were inclined to sympathize with Father Yorke, considering Doctor Shields' theories revolutionary if not dangerous, and objecting to any radical change in practices which custom had rendered sacred in their eyes. The truths to be taught were immutable, therefore they assumed that the methods should share in that immutability. The more progressive men, especially those acquainted with modern science, were delighted at finding a leader around whom they could rally in the task of modifying educational methods which cried out for reform. From this time on, Doctor Shields became a storm center. He had a group of followers but also an organized and solid opposition.

He found this state of affairs highly stimulating. Nothing was worse than indifference. He continued to develop his points in the columns of *The Catholic University Bulletin,* filling twenty-five pages of each issue with his *Educational Notes.* The question of the proper use of the memory came up again and again in many forms. In answer to a question:

"Are not the rules and definitions which we memorized as children and which were meaningless to us then, revived at a later date, and are they not very useful to us now?" he recommended that "if the matter must be dealt with seriously" the experimental method be applied:

> Let me ask any teacher who holds this belief to set down in writing the definitions and formulae which were memorized in this way in childhood and which afterwards proved valuable. When this task is accomplished, take each of these definitions separately and estimate its value in adult life; or rather, the value that is derived from the fact of having memorized the formula in question before it was understood.

Even this would not be conclusive evidence—should the result of the investigation be positive. It would be no solution to the problem, for:

> Has the child's memory no other function than the storing of the unintelligible? If so, are we not depriving the child of the use of one of his most valuable faculties by cumbering it with a load which is of no present use to the growing mind? If it once be granted that the function of memory is to hold truths that are in process of assimilation and forms of expression that are on the way to becoming automatic, it will be evident that anything which impedes these functions is to be avoided, even if the subject matter in question would appear to have value later on. When the child's digestive system is only so far developed that he can successfully deal with nothing more complex than milk, is it wise to feed him meat which it is to be hoped he may be able to digest some years later?

Those who advocated the memorizing of the unintelligible, presumed that such a process would aid the mind to a true comprehension of the subject when the proper stage of development would have been reached. Such was not the case, in the opinion of Doctor Shields:

> The mind tends to attach *some* meaning to the memorized definition, and, not being able to grasp the real meaning, it attaches to it an erroneous concept which proves a great hindrance later on.

And he summed up his thought as follows:

> First, that it is wrong to interfere with the mental function of the child's memory by making him memorize definitions and formulae that are not understood by him; second, that such memorized definitions, instead of aiding the pupil at a later period, to understand the subject matter in question, retard such understanding and render it more difficult; third, that by clogging the intelligence with unassimilable matter, we cultivate in it a merely receptive attitude, and habits of mental parasitism which are unfavorable to initiative and self-reliance.

Perhaps had such arguments been focused merely on the teaching of secular subjects, they would have aroused less opposition. But the very idea of change in the teaching of religion, the questioning of the accepted function of memory when it concerned the memorizing of the catechism; was there not some mysterious modernism involved, something bordering on heresy? Yet Doctor Shields was not alone in attacking the problem. A contemporary, at the other end of the globe, Father Hull, S. J., wrote in *The Bombay Examiner:*

> On all grounds of psychology, economy and common sense, the formal Catechism is nothing less than a millstone tied round the necks alike of teacher and child. The formal Catechism with its official texts and technical

forms must be altogether relegated to the future and kept severely out of sight till the first essential grounding has been done. When I think of the Catechism as an organ for the first religious education of the child, I am tempted to wring my hands in despair for the radical sanity of the human race. . . . As a thing to put in the hands of an infant and make it learn the contents as the vehicle for getting religious knowledge, why nothing but the proverbial woodenness of the pedagogic mind could ever have conceived such a notion.

And a few years later, we find Archbishop Sheehan of Sydney, Australia, writing in *The Catholic Press:*

The Catechism approved for our schools, though excellent in matter and arrangement, is unsatisfactory because it is not a child's book. The chief argument of the apologists, viz., that though the child does not understand the scientific definitions, he will understand them when he grows up, contains, by implication, two false assertions, educationally unsound.

★ ❧ ★

CHAPTER FOURTEEN

MUSIC

IT was at this time that I first met Doctor Shields. He had already published two volumes of his educational textbooks and was living at 1026 Quincy Street in Brookland. It was not there but at the house of a friend in Washington that I met him.

"There are some very interesting men at the Catholic University," she told me. "You should meet, particularly, Doctor Shields who is the head of the Department of Education. He has a far-reaching plan for the revision of educational methods in the parochial schools and wants to make music an essential part of his system."

At this, I pricked up my ears. I had not been living in the United States for some years and was unfamiliar with educational developments there, but my interest in sacred music had led me to believe that the only hope of reform lay in an effective teaching of music to the children in our Catholic schools. I jumped at the opportunity of talking to a man who held such ideas and was in a position to make them triumph.

We met at lunch. Doctor Shields arrived, punctual to the minute. A square-cut figure whose clothes hung loose about him; a finely molded head with short, wild, unruly hair and a close-clipped beard of iron gray. Keen, intelligent eyes, penetrating but kind. He took little part in the general conversation during lunch. Had he not been so great a man,

I would have thought him shy. He seemed remote and pre-occupied. No doubt he was utterly exhausted, yet his personality dominated the situation even through his silence. Whenever he emerged from his apparent absentmindedness, it was fully and with such apropos that we knew he had not lost contact. His attention came and went like a firefly, sudden light alternating with drab spaces where he pulled down the blinds and shut us out. But each time the momentary flash left us with enough ideas to carry us forward into the region which he was preparing.

Finally, he began to talk. He outlined his vast plan, explaining what was lacking in current educational methods, how he proposed to reform them from the very root, and the part that music was to play in this reform. He had read an article of mine that gave him the idea that I might be able to help him in the musical part of his plan. He was convinced, he told us, that music was an essential element in any educational system worthy of the name. Teachers, and particularly Catholic teachers, must be convinced of its value in character formation. "Next to the teaching of Religion," he insisted, "the teaching of music and art constitutes the most important work in the elementary school. The real foundations of character are not to be found in the intellect but in the emotions and the will properly enlightened through the intellect. It is through music and art that the imagination and the emotions may be reached and effectively developed. Don't you agree?" he asked modestly. He outlined his plan for the training of Catholic teachers whose needs for higher education on Catholic lines had been neglected so shamefully hitherto. Suddenly, he pulled out two little volumes entitled "Religion" from a capacious pocket and pointed to the music they contained. Each section of the book, he explained, was summed up in two songs, the purpose of which was to give expression to the emotional content of the text and, through appropriate feeling, to prepare the children for what was to come.

"Look," he begged, handing me the little books. "Look at this music. I have told you its purpose. But I cannot judge whether or not it is the right kind of music. I simply don't know. I do not even know to whom to turn to get the right kind if this is wrong. Will you not give me your frank opinion?"

"Do you want me to look it over now—here?"

"If I am not imposing upon you."

I retired into a corner and examined the songs of the two books with their music. It did not take long to form a judgment. My face must have betrayed me.

"Well," he asked, "tell me—are they very bad?"

Should I tell him the horrid truth frankly, brutally? Looking into his guileless eyes, I decided that nothing else was possible.

"They are simply appalling—impossible."

"Are they as bad as that?" he asked a little sadly. "I have no doubt that you must be right, but do tell me what is wrong with them. I ask because I want to understand."

There was no vestige of offended vanity nor even of discouragement in his manner. Obviously, he was so concentrated on perfecting the work that all personal sensitiveness had disappeared. I tried to explain:

"The music is pretentious, cheap, complicated. It is much too difficult for little children to sing. It covers too wide a compass for their voices. It is poor from a musical standpoint and frivolous in atmosphere. Instead of illustrating your very beautiful text, the music brings in an element that is cheap, tawdry, almost degrading."

For a moment he looked crestfallen.

"That is about what Otten wrote about the music of my songs," he remarked, drawing out of his pocket a crumpled letter.

"Read it," he said. The letter was not complimentary.

> You ask for my judgment about the musical illustrations in Father Shields' books. I regret to have to say that they are not at all up to the required standard, with few exceptions. Taking the Reverend Doctor's standpoint that *"an idea that has been aroused by the teacher's voice, the picture and the printed word, is finally and thoroughly assimilated when it finds utterance in musical form"* to be true it must be said that, judging by the music chosen for the first volume, the *idea* has in no case been assimilated . . . the form in no sense enhances or reflects the idea, for the music (?) is positively silly and trashy to the point of irreverance. Not one number is written in accordance with the most ordinary rules of harmony.

The letter went into details. I handed it back to Doctor Shields and, though sympathizing with his disappointment, my curiosity got the better of my discretion:

"Would you mind if I asked you a question? How did you ever get hold of such music?" How could this man of superior intelligence have been so completely deceived? Why had he not exercised some prudent control of the music before printing it in his books?

He threw back his head and laughed. Is there anything more revealing than a laugh? Vanity, irony, pettiness, meanness, mere silliness can reveal themselves in a laugh though carefully concealed in ordinary intercourse. Doctor Shields' laugh was the laugh of an honest man, not of the lips, the eyes, the nervous system—the whole man laughed unreservedly. His laugh laid all his cards face upward on the table. Then he said:

"This is how it happened. My manuscript was ready for the printer, the First Book, you understand. I was in a hurry to get it out but I had no music for the songs. Eager as I was to get this book through the press and into the hands of the teachers, I think I could have compromised on most things to hurry it on, but this was a matter of principle. I could not allow a book for primary education under my signature to appear without music. That was a matter of principle," he repeated doggedly.

"So what did you do?"

"Unfortunately I did not know any musician. So what *was* I to do? Delay was impossible. I suddenly thought of an old acquaintance who occasionally strummed the piano. I went to his house. It was late in the evening. 'I want you to help me,' I said and explained to him my whole scheme. I showed him the ten songs. Everything was ready to go to press. I handed him the manuscript that he might see for himself that I was held up, now, by the mere fact that I had no music for the songs.

" 'What can I do about it?' he asked.

" 'Why you must compose the music—and while I hate to hurry you, if you *could* let me have the music by. . . .' He interrupted me with a derisive laugh.

" 'That is the funniest thing I ever heard!'

" 'Why funny?'

" 'You are illogical.'

" 'In what way?'

" 'Your book' (he had been skimming over the pages of the preface) 'your book pretends to deal in germinal form with all the basic principles of the Christian religion. You expect the music to give expression to all this. Am I right?'

" 'Certainly.'

" 'And you come to me, an agnostic, as the person best qualified in your judgment to compose music to give expression to these concepts. Are you not a bit inconsistent?'

" 'Not at all. I did not come to you with that idea in mind.' It was my friend's turn to look baffled.

" 'Did you not ask me just now to compose music for these songs?'

" 'Certainly, I did ask you, and I hope very much that you will do it for me. But I did not ask it because I believe you to be the person best qualified for the job. On the contrary, I feel convinced that you will do it so badly that all the Catholic musicians in the country will rush to my rescue before a second edition appears!' "

We all joined in his hearty laugh.

"And your friend wrote the music in spite of that?"

"As you see."

"And did the Catholic musicians of the country rush to your rescue?" A momentary shadow crossed his face.

"I got plenty of criticism like the letter you have just read, but no one offered to help me."

A lesser man would have shown disillusionment if not bitterness. Not so Doctor Shields. His face remained serene, if a little puzzled, like the face of a child. Then pulling himself together and squaring his shoulders as though preparing to carry any burden that might be in preparation, he said:

"Is it worth doing? Don't you think it is worth doing? The whole plan—is it sound and necessary? Is it not a move in the right direction? Details can always be adjusted if the principle be sound." There could be but one answer.

"Then what am I to do about this question of music? Will you help me to improve this part of the work? I can do all the rest by myself, you see, but this I cannot do."

I felt terrified because the whole plan seemed to be quixotic though tempting.

"It is a wonderful plan, indeed, but do you think, really, that it is possible for little children to sing these songs like so many little birds without ever learning the underlying principles of music? Even supposing that these songs were good from a musical standpoint, do you think the children could sing them?"

"I don't know," he replied simply. "Could they not?"

I suggested that the art of music required a preparation of voice, ear, eye and rhythmic sense; a gradual building up of taste and appreciation. Such a foundation would be required if music was ever to play the part which he expected of it in education.

"I am sure you must be right," he said, "but must there be a separate book for Music in the First Grade? I had hoped that one central book might be enough. That seemed to me essential." His mind had jumped at once to the practical consequences of my suggestion. Perhaps a teachers' book might meet the situation, I proposed, and let the children work from charts or blackboard?

"That would be better. I like the idea of plenty of blackboard work so that the matter may not become rigid." Then after a moment's silence, he turned to me suddenly:

"Will you help me with the music? Otherwise, what am I to do?" I explained that I knew nothing about teaching and that he would be seeking a broken reed to lean upon.

"No, no," he insisted, "that does not matter. I know all the pedagogy that will be required. I can carry that part of the work, if you will supply the music. Could you not at least suggest something to replace those songs, as a temporary measure, pending the working out of a fundamental scheme? Let us begin by getting rid of what is bad and substituting something better." This at least, I felt I could do and accepted gladly. For the rest, I would think over what he had said.

He looked at his watch. It was time to leave. "But we have not finished," he said to me. "Come out to see us at Brookland before you leave Washington. Come tomorrow morning at ten. I shall be there."

He had scribbled his address on a slip of paper, but the taxi driver had much trouble in finding the queer little faded cottage with covered piazzas on the corner of an unpaved street. As I dismissed the driver, I wondered how such an immense work could be lodged in this doll's house. I had hardly taken three steps inside the gate when, out of the diminutive building, Doctor Shields appeared, like a giant among Lilliputians.

"Come in, I was expecting you," he exclaimed with immense cordiality, and I followed him into a tiny room piled high with papers. The desk, the tables, the chairs, to say nothing of the floor, were completely buried. He looked about hastily for a place where one might sit down, but, finding none he started lifting great heaps of papers and carrying them out on the front porch, with stones to keep them from blowing away. But suddenly, like the chorus in an opera, a bevy of young women rushed to his rescue, making space here and there, bringing order out of chaos. "My nieces, Rose and Mary Shields," he introduced, "my secretary, Miss Askew." The chorus disappeared and we sat down. All those papers, he explained, were the multigraphed pages of the Correspondence courses, and the house was so small that every room was buried at certain critical moments in the process of uniting the pages and mailing them. Here, too, were the proof pages of *Religion— Third Book* about to issue from the press.

When we began to talk, he gave no impression of haste. He had plenty of time for the person to whom he was talking, and he went into his whole plan in more detail than the day before. He was considering the value of music, not from the point of view of an artist "as you can see for yourself," he said, but purely from the point of view of science and psychology. "After Religion, it is the most important subject in the curriculum—if we are considering the children's good," he explained rather humbly, as though fearing to shock me with such an assertion. It was the first time that I had heard a priest announce this truth. I could hardly believe my ears. We talked for an hour or more. He gave me some of his books, *The Education of Our Girls*, and *The Making and Unmaking of a Dullard*, the latter written in the midst of the confusion and crowded conditions in the cottage.

I left with the impression of a new world opening out before me. It was impossible to meet Doctor Shields, even casually, without coming under the influence of his enthusiasm, his will power and his magnetism. He made it clear that he wanted my help, not for himself, of course, but for the children in our Catholic schools and our teachers. But at no time did I feel that he was putting any pressure upon me, or seeking to influence my decision. After showing me the picture of what could and should be done for our schools, he seemed to stand aside. I only remember his asking me several times, *"Is it worth doing?"*

CHAPTER FIFTEEN

TEAM WORK

DESPITE their contrasting temperaments, Doctors Shields and Pace were united in their ideas. Doctor Pace had been largely instrumental in bringing Doctor Shields to the University, and, in the early days, they worked together as a team, consulting one another, defending one another when under attack. In their writings and lectures, the same fundamental principles prevailed, although each explained them in his own style, illumined them with his own personality. They were friends, too, in so far as two men of such different natures could be so.

Pace had been educated in German universities. He was a tall, lanky Southerner with cold, faded blue eyes that never glowed with feeling or enthusiasm, and he lacked "that little spark of love" which Lyautey considered essential to a successful leader of men. Shields, a Westerner of pioneering stock, of Celtic blood, was all temperament, fire, sympathy, enthusiasm. Pace liked to weigh, to ponder, to investigate, to turn each question inside out, forgetting that "he who considers too much will perform too little" as Schiller remarked. Prudence, from a quality, tended to become a handicap to Doctor Pace. Choice was a torture. His powers of decision were becoming atrophied. His capacity for action was paralyzed. Meanwhile Shields was developing in the opposite direction—and was moving fast. Investigation, research were necessary in his eyes but only as a basis for decision and as a guide to prompt action. Truth, once found, must be dynamic, outgiving, creative. "By their fruits ye shall know them."

Associates in a great educational work, these two men had totally different methods of teaching. The lectures of Doctor Pace were orderly, logical, comprehensive, detailed. He talked like a book. When he wrote there was a dot over every *i* and a cross over every *t*. When he lectured, no point was omitted; his students had but to listen carefully and remembered what Pace had said. He had said everything.

Doctor Shields' lectures were totally different. They sounded incoherent; ideas, questions, anecdotes, references to correlated subjects, jokes, alternated with flashes of stirring eloquence. His plan was to make the student work, to whet his curiosity without satisfying it, to arouse him to do the research work which alone would make him master of the subject. He purposely presented loose threads expecting his students to gather them up and weave them into a pattern, then present them in logical order by means of a bracket-diagram. The student must look ahead and suggest in another diagram, what, in his judgment, should be the content of the next lesson. The whole principle of Doctor Shields' teaching was to bring out the latent capacities of the pupil, to make him active, to arouse his curiosity and stimulate his interest. In a word, he was not merely teaching a subject, but teaching men and women to think.

His approach to the minds of his students may be suggested by the *Directions to Correspondents* with which he opens his correspondence course on *The Teaching of Religion*. The students had as textbooks his *Psychology of Education* and his *Teaching of Religion* to which he constantly refers. The lessons were mailed to them, one by one.

Lesson I. Forecast. Before reading this chapter, write out the topics which you think should be treated in this Course, using as few words as possible. Arrange them in their logical order and preserve them for future reference. What points do you think will be treated in the present chapter? Arrange them in the form of a diagram exhibiting their logical coordination.

Lesson II. Indexing. Read this chapter carefully and compare it with your forecast. Write a brief title to each paragraph of the chapter such as would be used in an alphabetical index of the book. Under each of these titles, write, in condensed form, any objections to the substance of the paragraph which you can think of.

Lesson III. Diagram. Make a bracket diagram of the chapter, exhibiting the unity and the logical divisions of the matter treated.

Lesson IV. Review Questions. What other subjects are taught at present by the catechetical method? What subjects were taught by this method half a century ago? Why has the catechetical method disappeared in these other subjects? What is the most striking difference between the method of teaching geography that is prevalent today and the method employed a generation ago? What do you think of the efficacy of teaching physics, chemistry or botany by the catechetical method? Would there be any real value in memorizing Boyle's Law or Kepler's Laws by pupils who understand nothing of the meaning of these laws?

Suggestions are given for collateral reading. Students are advised to devote two or three hours to discussion among themselves of such questions as: "The presence in consciousness of appropriate feeling is indispensable to mental assimilation." He asks: "What feeling should be developed in the child's consciousness to prepare him to assimilate the truths of religion?" Students are asked to send him a statement of their collateral reading and of the results of the discussion. Duplicates of the Diagrams, the Research Questions and the Formulated Questions are to be preserved by the correspondent. Such was the general plan carried out through all the Course. It assumed plenty of work for the teacher, and the student was forced to do his own thinking. Memory work would not carry him through.

We find in Lesson V—Collateral Reading—this suggestion:

> Read the Gospels and examine Our Lord's method of preparing His audience for the reception and understanding of the important truths which He came to reveal to them.

The Review Questions of Chapter VII plunge the student into the heart of *The Shields Method:*

> 1. What reasons can you assign for bringing the method of teaching religion into conformity with the current methods of teaching other subjects? 2. Was the catechetical form always used in the teaching of religion? 3. Did the catechetical form always mean the question and answer method? 4. When did the question and answer method first come into use in the teaching of religion? 5. What faculty is chiefly exercised by the question and answer method? 6. Is it more important that a child should know the letter of the law and the exact formula of the doctrine or that his conduct should be informed by the truths of religion and governed by the laws of God?

After various questions on the use of the memory in Oriental civilizations, he continues:

9. What function dominates the teaching of Our Lord?
10. What is the difference between memorizing a truth
and assimilating it? 11. What is the difference between
an assimilated truth and one that is functional in conduct? 12. What should be the chief characteristics of
the instruction given to children from six to eight years
of age? 13. How are habits related to instincts? 14. What
instincts should form the basis of Christian virtue? 15.
Where can we find Our Lord's method of teaching
exemplified? 16. In what ways does the Holy Ghost continue this divine method? 17. What use did Our Lord
make of natural phenomena in the teaching of supernatural truth? 18. What use did He make of human
emotions and passions for the same purpose? 19. What
use do you make of these same agencies in teaching the
religion of Jesus Christ to the little ones under your
care?

In the Research Questions of this same chapter, he
proposes:

1. Analyze the method employed in the parable of the
"sower went out to sow his seed" and the parable of
the Prodigal Son. (Point out the elements in the mind of
the audience to which Our Lord appealed to secure the
understanding of His lessons; the elements which He
relied upon to recall to the minds of His hearers through
the association of ideas, the truths which He taught; the
elements which He relied upon to render His teaching
operative in the conduct of His hearers.)

And again he brings his students to the consideration of
those points which are central in his doctrine, thus:

1. Man's instincts lead him to use certain objects in nature
for purposes of food, clothing, adornment, etc. What

other use does Our Lord put these things to? How are they made to nourish the mind and the soul in His method of teaching? 2. How does Our Lord use similes and metaphors and sense experiences? 3. How does Our Lord apply interest in His method of teaching? 4. What determined His choice of parables and similes? 5. Does He find it necessary to supplement His parables with exact definitions? 6. How does He prepare the minds of His hearers before presenting His supernatural doctrines? Does He give the whole doctrine at once and repeat it on subsequent occasions in the same words and with the aid of the same parables, or does He vary the words and the parables in order to bring out the meaning more fully? 7. Does this method, through the association of ideas, also tend to secure a closer relation between doctrine and practice?

In asking his correspondents to sum up the educational doctrines of the first eight chapters, he puts them face to face with the fundamental problems they will have to face in the class room:

What principles underlie Our Lord's method of teaching? What difference in mental content and environment do you find between those who listened to Our Lord's words and the children in a first-grade room in one of our schools?

What modification in method would this necessitate if we would adhere strictly to Our Lord's principles?

Compare all the catechisms within your reach with each other in the light of the educational principles developed in the preceding chapters of this work.

And finally: Compare Religion First and Second Books with the Baltimore Catechism. 2. Write out carefully all of the Baltimore Catechism which you are able to find in these two books. 3. Compare the effect on the child's

mind produced by the Christian Doctrines contained in
Religion First and Second Books and the same doctrines
as presented in the Baltimore Catechism.

We have sketched only the early chapters of his Course,
but this will suffice to give an idea of his teaching methods and also of his bold attack on the current manner of
teaching religion through memorized unintelligible formulae.

Here was a frontal attack on time-honored traditions
emanating from a professor of the Catholic University, a
Pontifical University whose Board of Trustees was drawn
from the Catholic Hierarchy. Here were new methods
reaching out through correspondence courses to a vast
number of teachers drawn from numerous religious
orders of women; reaching out to priests and educators
through the pages of the Catholic University Bulletin to
which both Pace and Shields were contributing articles
on educational psychology. The movement was spreading
and had already an enthusiastic following. What was to be
done to head it off?

A wave of opposition sprang up to the defense of
tradition. Often the opposition was based on a partial or
distorted idea of what Doctor Shields was advocating.
Despite the hearty support of many of the most distinguished
professors at the University, despite the partnership of
Doctor Pace, the whole movement became known as the
"Shields Methods." He it was who received the full impact
of the attack, and indeed his uncompromising courage was
rightly judged to be the moving force back of the movement.

How much of the original plan (the theoretical structure) was due to Doctor Pace, it would be difficult to say,
since the two men had exchanged impressions so fully, ever

since Johns Hopkins days. Pace accepted to appear as joint author of the series of primary textbooks yet, as a matter of fact, Shields alone composed these books. It was a disappointment to the latter that Doctor Pace did not give him more active help in the work but no word of criticism passed his lips, nor, indeed, lingered in his heart. The defect of Pace was procrastination. Had Shields waited for Pace, the chances are that the books would never have been published. Might they have gained in literary polish with his aid? It is questionable, and at any rate, this was an insignificant detail compared to the urgency of getting these books into the hands of the teachers. It would not do to lose the fruits of the correspondence courses. The ideas must be applied at once in the classroom by these teachers. Without a textbook, the teachers were helpless.

Thus Doctor Shields took the disappointment in his stride without fretting over the fact that he alone was carrying the work. As to Doctor Pace, it is less certain that he was entirely free from an unconscious resentment, a certain sense of humiliation at the speed with which his partner outstripped him in action. For a time, at least, the partnership held without an open break. Yet the union between the two men was cracking up imperceptibly. It was a misfortune for the cause they both had at heart.

Meanwhile, other activities were pressing, new plans maturing. The little house at the foot of Quincy Street was bursting with business which it was inadequate to contain. Something must be done.

The first books that issued from the pen of Doctor Shields bore the imprint of *The Correspondence School.* These included *The Education of Our Girls* and *Religion, Books One and Two.* His new book, published in 1909, *The Making and Unmaking of a Dullard,* bore the imprint of *The Catholic Education Press*, his own publishing house.

It had not been Doctor Shields' intention to go into the publishing business. Before bringing out any of his books, he had made the rounds of the existing publishers of text books, both Catholic and secular, with the maximum of dissatisfaction. A system based on profits, requiring large margins to cover advertising and expenses of traveling agents, none of which were necessary in his case, would have made the publication of his manuscripts far too expensive to reach the Catholic schools. In the presence of an obstacle, Doctor Shields went straight to the heart of the problem. Advertising, agents and high profits were the obstacles, not the actual cost of production. The solution was simple: profits and the rest must be eliminated. He would publish the books himself and sell them at cost to the schools. Everything must be of the best: paper, pictures, binding—nothing shoddy. There was one small difficulty, of course: he had no capital with which to launch the project. A detail like that could not stop him. He would borrow, and as fast as one volume brought in returns, he would publish the next. He set up his own publishing house, *The Catholic Education Press*.

And he financed it. Even a hard-headed banker gambled on the rugged integrity of Doctor Shields as security. Though the man of money received a warning from an official of the University that Doctor Shields was running his enterprise "on a shoe string" and that the University itself would take no responsibility for the venture, the banker found the investment a sound one. The debtor met his obligations promptly as to interest and capital.

Each new step involved another. A home for this new enterprise must be provided, as well as for the *Review* which the faculty of the Educational Department was planning. By this time, Doctor Shields knew every foot of land in the neighborhood. He had often wandered over a hilltop covered with scrub oak and brambles not far from his actual residence. The land was cheap. It commanded a fine view. He borrowed once more—and bought. Then he consulted an architect.

"Doctor Shields was my first client and my best friend," remarked, in a reminiscent mood, Doctor Frederick Murphy, now head of the Department of Architecture at the University. "His property had the appearance of a jungle the first time I saw it. But the Doctor had visualized the position of the house to be, and paced off its dimensions. He saw that house as though it already existed and he hardly noticed the brambles." This building of his new day-dream was to be a semi-monastic residence for the members of the Faculty of Education. Each man was to have his study, austere but convenient; his bedroom and bath. They would have their meals in common, but apart from that, each man would be protected in his privacy and could work undisturbed. Doctor Shields had sketched his plans: here would be the entrance, here, the stairs, here, the studies, one above the other; here, the chapels, and below, where the land dipped down, with a separate entrance of its own, the Catholic Education Press.

"The building of his home became my responsibility," writes Doctor Murphy. "He told me at once that he was sure he had not enough money to build it, but that the educational program about to be launched demanded a center where the work could be carried out." Naturally he was in a hurry. He must have plans and specifications at once. Delays provoked momentary flashes of wrath, for the Doctor had a quick temper. "He would fume for a moment, then, suddenly, he would laugh at himself and say, 'Let's go down to the Willard and have a cool drink.' " The storms blew over as quickly as they started. On the whole, however, his architect found Doctor Shields an easy client to work with since his understanding of an architect's plans and specifications was excellent, and since he attached the same value as did Doctor Murphy to landscape design as an accessory to architecture.

He delighted to keep in close contact with the progress of the work. The digging of the foundations, the gradual rise of the walls were the tonics he needed after a hard day's work. Beyond the site of his house, the Franciscan Friars had erected a huge replica of the Holy Sepulcher at Jerusalem. Pilgrims would be attracted. The neighborhood would be improved. The village would catch up with this region which was still country land. Property values would rise. Acreage could be sold and debts paid.

He consulted his architect frequently at the latter's downtown office or at the site of the new house, pressing him to hurry things on. Doctor Shields was the owner of a wheezy, broken-winded, shambling old Ford car. Worse yet, he was the driver, much to the terror of his occasional passengers. When the Doctor got absorbed in a train of thought, the steering wheel took a secondary place in his attention; the accelerator received many a kick of emphasis as the rattling old car spun around the corners on two wheels.

One day Doctor Shields was late for an appointment with his architect. Now punctuality was his hobby, for others and for himself. The members of the "family" had learned long since that it was safer to gather for meals five minutes ahead of time rather than risk provoking that look of restrained exasperation on the face of the Doctor against tardiness. Never was he late, himself, for a lecture. As the hour struck, he stepped on the platform, as exactly as a cuckoo on a clock. All the more distressing, then, was the misfortune of that day. He was late—very late. The idea of *lateness* possessed him to the exclusion of every other thought or sensation. He turned his car into the foot of unpaved Quincy Street and looking up the hill, perceived with agony the form of his friend Murphy in the distance waiting for him on the side of the road. Everything in the world vanished save that one devastating sensation of lateness and the haste he was in to retrieve his disgrace. He stamped on the accelerator, flooded the car with gas; the old frame leapt forward, emitting gasps of pain as it bounced up the hill from rut to rut. Hardly waiting to get abreast of Murphy, and with arms outstretched in a gesture of humiliation, he just jumped from the car and apologizing profusely for keeping him waiting, he forgot the machine which, well launched as it was, took the ditch in a flying leap to nose its way against the telegraph pole across the way.

"Have you been waiting long?" he gasped. Then, freed from his dominating thought, he looked behind him.

"Is that my car?" he asked. "What on earth is it doing over there?"

The teamwork between Doctor Shields and his architect grew with the years. The Doctor had much of the artist in his own temperament. He now had two arts harnessed to his chariot and teamwork to last through life and beyond the grave.

CHAPTER SIXTEEN

ACCELERATION

A LEADER who wants to make his influence effective should not be too far in advance of his time. Doctor Shields realized this danger but tried to meet it by indefatigable work in preparing the minds and souls of a vast number of students. His plans were vast. He was launched full speed. All his projects were interlocking and had to be attacked at once. He must convince the Board of Trustees of the University of the necessity of opening a Teachers College where the Catholic Sisterhoods could obtain the higher education and the degrees they required under Catholic auspices. He must get his *Educational Review* started with the prestige of the University behind it. He must organize a plan of affiliation whereby Catholic colleges and high schools could be standardized in accordance with the principles embodied in their religion. Like a race horse in a steeplechase he sprang forward, hurdling obstacles regardless of the landing spot. What could it matter whether, in the process, he might trample upon someone's flower bed?

He taught, he lectured, he wrote. In his *Educational Notes* he presented the truth from every aspect, applying his principles to specific educational problems. He analyzed the errors of the day, attacking the pseudo-scientific fads with devastating logic. He struck right and left, demolishing the stand-patters, on the one hand, and attacking, on the other, men of advanced theories whose false application of their dogmas to the educational field, he dissected with scientific precision. His operations were a veritable vivisection and, for the first time, the dogmatic pseudo-scientists were faced with an adversary to be reckoned with. The application of psychological principles, in themselves sound, to educational practices in a manner both unsound and unscientific, he exposed without mercy.

"Keep up the good work," advised a friend from the sidelines. "Your guns are big enough to reach them and you have the range." There were warnings, too. "Your notes on education have been extremely interesting. If you could blast the principles without lambasting the men and women who hold them, you would be perhaps less interesting—but safer!"

Lambast them? Why he was merely quoting. He made them expose their own ideas against a background of truth. It was his method. How could they complain? Yet they did. A friend wrote:

> The Mr. X. you slammed in the last Bulletin has a room adjoining mine. He drops in occasionally to tell me what a wonderful man he is; how deep and broad and rich and varied is his learning; what high and worthy ideals he holds. A week ago he came in to present me with a copy of his article and I, inconsiderately, told him that I had read a criticism of it. Then, of course, he had to know where, and then he must see it, and then —he didn't like it. . . . He felt he could not let such an accusation pass unnoticed. So he composed a letter with the greatest care and, I suppose sent it, though I told him you had absolutely no time for personal controversy.

Obviously, Doctor Shields was not playing for safety. He met the indignant protest with the assurance that he

knew nothing whatever about the personality of the writer
and was interested only in his ideas which he had exposed
in the author's own words and added that he was too busy
to enter into personal controversy. Yet instead of leading
to a libel suit, the affair ended peacefully with a request by
the offended gentleman for an autographed copy of *The
Dullard* of which he wrote:

> I cannot refrain from giving expression to a resent-
> ment which I felt at being dropped off at the point where
> you leave your reader. A psychologist, at any rate,
> would like to know the further progress of the hero of
> your book. It seems to me a sequel should be forth-
> coming.

Indeed few readers believed that the hero of this astonish-
ing record was anything more than an author's fanciful
personification of a theory. Yet Doctor Shields never
hesitated to admit the truth when questioned. He wrote in
answer to a question from a teacher who was dealing with
retarded children: [1]

> *The Dullard* is as faithful a record as my memory holds
> of my own development. I have not the slightest objec-
> tion to having this fact known.

As his textbooks appeared they were greeted with enthusiasm by his students. They loved the books, so did the
children, so did the parents. They were "just what little
hearts were hungering for." All the teachers agreed that
the books were bringing the children into a loving relation
to Jesus Christ.

From outside, an occasional word of intelligent appreciation reached the author.

[1] T.E.S. to Miss Regan, Nov. 19, 1910.

I have looked forward for a long time to deliverance from the bondage of the Council Catechism and, after reading your primer, feel that the promised land is in sight.[2]

It is the first intelligent effort to teach religion that I have seen from a Catholic source. Your little book marks a milestone in the right direction. As a former "wrangler" I think I can with propriety express my pleasure in seeing that the men at the ill-fated Catholic University are *doing* something besides fussing.[3]

Many correspondents touched on the fact that serious teacher training would be required before the books would give the desired results. This obvious fact was all too well known to Doctor Shields who was spending himself to bring such training to the Sisters. The books had been formally adopted in the Diocese of New Orleans but with little or no adequate preparation of the teachers. Doctor Shields dreaded diocesan adoptions precisely because of this lack of teacher training. He wanted his books to spread through the hands of the students whom he had formed though correspondence courses and summer lectures, realizing the danger of failure and reaction should the books be placed in unskilled hands. He devoted his summer vacations to lecture courses, travelling from east to west, from north to south. Rest and recreation were out of the question. What could his health matter now that the goal was in sight? In September, 1908, he wrote:

I reached home a few days ago after my summer's work on the lecture platform. I gave, in all, one hundred and forty-eight lectures and there were over two thousand Sisters each of whom listened to twenty-four lec-

[2] John M. Cooper, Dec. 17, 1908.
[3] Lucian Johnson, Nov. 24, 1908.

tures. There were a large number of new classes formed in the Psychology of Education, so that even I am beginning to be frightened at the amount of work which awaits me this year.[4]

The following year marked an increase in his schedule:

I have given two hundred and twenty-five lectures during the summer and I was so tired out at the end that I felt the absolute need of rest.[5]

I took a trip down the Great Lakes to Buffalo and thence, by way of Montreal, Lakes Champlain and George and the Hudson River to New York; and the boat, by way of Norfolk, to Washington. It was the best two weeks' rest I have ever had, and I am now facing another crowded year in good form.[6]

His friends remonstrated in vain that the sturdiest constitution could not indefinitely resist such overwork. He knew they were right in theory but it was impossible to stop or to reduce the speed precisely because he had to organize the country behind him to back the great reforms he had in mind His influence over the Religious Orders was increasing. The Superiors were beginning to seek his advice and, sometimes, to take it. They were beginning to realize the dangers incumbent in the actual situation and opening their eyes to the necessity for their subjects of an educational training in keeping with their vocation. Doctor Shields realized, for his own part, that no matter how excellent might be his system of education *per se* it would be utterly useless without teachers carefully prepared and with an adequate grasp of its

[4] T.E.S. to Sister Columbine, St. Louis, Mo., Sept. 22, 1908.
[5] T.E.S. to Rev. Thomas Devlin, Oct. 9, 1909.
[6] T.E.S. to Rev. M. Malady, Pittsburgh, Pa., Sept. 22, 1909.

principles and methods. The only logical solution, as he knew, was a National Catholic Normal College, and this was his ultimate aim. Every step that he took, meanwhile, was orientated toward the accomplishment of this purpose.

Today it seems hard to realize how Utopian such a proposal appeared at that time. The mere attempt to teach religion in a living way aroused a storm of opposition. One of the more forward looking educators of the day, the Reverend Philip McDevitt, then superintendent of the Catholic Schools in Philadelphia and later Bishop of Harrisburg, wrote, warning Doctor Shields of the type of opposition he must expect to encounter:

> I should have written long ago my word of thanks for the copy of Religion—First Book. . . . Knowing the evils which it is intended to correct and the principles on which it is based, I can but add my word of commendation to those which have come to you from so many quarters.
>
> I should, however, be very frank in stating my fear that a very general adoption of the First Book will come slowly. Actual observation of existing methods and a frequent discussion of reform in Catechetical teaching bring out strongly the widespread belief in principles directly antagonistic to those on which the First Book is constructed. . . . The proposal that an elementary book on Doctrine can have any other form than the traditional question-answer form is an absurdity in the estimation of not a few of the clergy.
>
> Another point which I cannot help stating is that the ordinary teacher needs a special training in order to use a textbook not in the form of question and answer. Hence, the First Book, in her hands, becomes simply a primer for reading. She does not see the beautiful ideas the book contains. She is unable to unfold its splendid

purpose, with the result that little tangible fruit of **her** *doctrine-teaching* is in evidence.

Often the knowledge of her class in Doctrine and her own efficiency as a teacher are estimated (by her Superior and by the Priest) from the ability of the child to repeat definitions, to answer the cut and dried questions of the Baltimore catechism.

The child, of course, is unable to formulate technical definitions unless there has been the long, exacting repetition of the words from memory. The teacher knows that a *verbal knowledge* will satisfy an examiner whose belief is that it is well for children to learn definitions, even though they may not understand what they mean. She knows, likewise, that if this faculty in repeating definitions (understood or not understood) is not seen in the children, the accusation may be made that nowadays, in the Parish schools, the teaching of the catechism is neglected.

Perhaps I am exaggerating the actual situation. I hope so. My own conviction is that a tremendous amount of preliminary work must be done before certain people realize that there is anything radically wrong with our present methods of teaching Doctrine and recognize the soundness of the principles on which the First Book is based.

There are unmistakable signs of a dissatisfaction with present methods. Your own work and that of Doctor Pace have done much to bring about the consideration of this important subject. The change for the better has begun. Your First Book will help along the good work. The difficulties, however, are many, and not the least danger is the possibility that suspicion may be excited as to the soundness of the principles of the present movement.

Now I have written of the situation as I see it. The view may not be accurate. I shall be glad to know that it is not; but such as it is, it may be of interest to you.

A mere hint from an intelligent friend. *Suspicion—soundness of principles.* It was not the first time that such a note had been sounded. Could so much originality be consistent with doctrinal orthodoxy? Could so much science be reconciled with sound Catholic faith? The whisperers asked each other where this Doctor Shields was going to wind up after starting out by "evolving Jesus Christ from a Robin." Undoubtedly there was a tinge of "modernism" in all this—hated word that could cover heresy. A natural dislike of change was exasperated by party feeling growing out of the controversy with Father Yorke of which we have spoken. One of the greatest pains to human nature, it has been said, is the pain of a new idea. Moreover, in the words of Ernest Hello, "Man is like ice toward truths and like fire toward lies." It needed some little courage, now, to come out openly in support of Doctor Shields. His ideas were not only new but they might be, conceivably, unorthodox. Was it not Shields who was undermining the teaching of religion to children, attacking the catechism, trying to make the children reason instead of learn, abolishing the use of the memory? Jokes came easily to fill up the canvas. The name of Shields became a butt for jibes. The controversy was drawn down from the realm of educators into the arena of beasts. But not for long.

How much this wounded Doctor Shields it is hard to say. He could scarcely have been totally indifferent to the casting of mud, but he never answered the criticism nor did he lose his serenity. Hours spent on replying to attack could be more usefully employed, he thought, in constructive work. As a matter of fact, the Apostolic Delegate, Monsignor Falconio had followed the movement with the most intense interest from the start and had encouraged Doctor Shields with warm sympathy. To his intimate friends, therefore, without entering into argument, he gave reassurance.

Writing to Father Boyle (later Bishop) of Pittsburgh, he says:

> The Delegate continues to be much interested in the projected Teachers Institute and in my Correspondence work, as well as my textbooks. He is very open in his declaration that this is the best work that is being done in the Catholic Church. A few days ago, I received an autographed communication from His Holiness wishing well to my "Apostolate" and imparting his blessing to me and to all who were receiving either written or oral instruction from me along pedagogical lines. So you see my orthodoxy is all right in spite of the "semi-Darwinian ecclesiasticism and the Boston mud." [7]

Father Boyle replied:

> I am glad that you are getting commendation and encouragement from the highest Church authorities; it will go far to correct misapprehension and to silence opposition.

And Father Boyle added a melancholy description of the conditions in the diocese of which he was school superintendent:

> The hopeless mess of the situation in some quarters is appalling, and the impossibility of immediate relief, maddening. It will take years and years to lift many of the schools out of their present miserable plight. Just now, one can scarcely make an impression on them. The pastors have looked upon the schools for so long a time as a portion of the parish equipment, that any concern about them on the part of the diocesan authorities is regarded as an invasion of parish rights to be resented and, if possible, prevented. Happily the attitude in its worst form

[7] T.E.S. to Father Boyle, Oct. 9, 1909.

is not common and, in some quarters, has entirely disappeared. There is a growing disposition on the part of bishops to take the schools from the control of the local pastor and to vest it in School Boards made up of priests who have a vital interest in school work.[8]

If Doctor Shields wasted no time in direct defense against criticism, he answered his detractors indirectly by reasserting his ideas with fresh energy in the pages of the *Catholic University Bulletin*. What fair-minded reader could fail to see that here was the very heart of religion, ever old and ever new, the doctrines of Christ taught by the method of the Master? One trouble may have been that those who read the Bulletin were already convinced whereas those who needed conversion never opened its pages. The new *Review* would doubtless reach a wider public. This, at least, was his enthusiastic hope. Meanwhile he kept insisting:

> No seed of divine truth will germinate or grow in human consciousness unless it finds there feeling to warm it into life. Before proceeding to plant in the child's soul the seeds of divine truth, the teacher of religion should adopt all necessary means to secure the presence of appropriate feeling and emotions in the child's consciousness.[9]
>
> That feeling plays an important role in mental development and in the building up of habits is admitted by all students of genetic psychology. But feeling has not yet won the recognition which its importance deserves from those who are occupied in the writing of textbooks and the framing of methods of elementary instruction.[10]

[8] Father Boyle to T.E.S., Oct. 29, 1909.
[9] *The Catholic University Bulletin*, Mar., 1908.
[10] *Idem*, June, 1908.

He comes back to the subject again and again, holding up the teaching of Jesus Christ as the true model:

> The first preparation which Our Lord seems to have made on every occasion was to fill the souls of His followers with feelings of love and gratitude and wonder. He turned water into wine at the marriage feast; He fed the hungry; He cured the lame, the halt and the blind; He called the dead to life and He preached the glad tidings to the poor and to the outcasts of Judea. When their minds were filled with wonder and their hearts were overflowing with gratitude, they gave glory to God because a great Prophet was raised up amongst them. With their hearts and minds thus prepared, Jesus proceeded to unfold to them the truths of the Kingdom of Heaven. And the first thing He taught them was to look upon God as a most dear Father and to serve Him in a spirit of love and loyalty. He taught them to ask of Him all they stood in need of and to offer Him the tribute of their praise. Thus you shall pray: "Our Father who art in Heaven." [11]

These, then, must be the lines on which to organize the teaching of little children. It was the principle on which his books were based. He described how Our Lord prepared His teaching by lessons from nature, and application of the homely truths that were familiar to His hearers:

> In most of Our Lord's lessons . . . there may be discerned four phases. In the first of these, Our Lord appeals to His hearers' observation of familiar phenomena in the vegetable and animal worlds. In the second phase, He appeals to human feelings and emotions, to the various circumstances of the everyday struggle for existence.

[11] *Idem,* Jan., 1909.

This phase is always present even when the first phase is omitted. In the third phase of His lessons, He leads His followers to contemplate the exalted state of the children of the Kingdom as seen in comparison with the dwellers on the lower planes of life. And, finally, He points out the obligation that rests upon the children of the Kingdom to bring their conduct into conformity with their high estate as children of God.

Step by step, Doctor Shields was following this identical plan in his own books for children, placing his feet in the footprints of the Master. His analogies were drawn from the natural phenomena that were most familiar to the children. Jesus had pointed to the birds of the air, the budding fig tree, the vine and its branches, the lilies of the field, the seed falling by the wayside. Shields chose the objects of nature that were close to the little ones, and, from the things seen and touched, through their own emotional response, raised them to an understanding of the sublime truths of the Kingdom of God.

How could he make his contemporaries understand and cease to oppose truths which were proved by the Gospels and underlined by the discoveries of modern science? How long would they continue to offer the little ones the stone of a memorized formula when the living bread alone could nourish their souls? Naturally, the doctrinal content must be preserved intact by the Church, its custodian. The only question was in what manner this doctrine was to be transmitted, what method of presentation would make it become a vital principle for right living. He wrote in the *Bulletin:*

> The deposit of Revealed Truth was carefully guarded by the early Christian teachers. Little by little the fundamental truths of Christianity emerged in clear definitions, as may be seen in the Apostles' Creed and in the

Athanasian and Nicene Creeds. The Sacred Scriptures and the commentaries of the Fathers kept the teachings of Christ in the hearts of the people. These prolific writings were, in time, summarized in convenient formularies. The catechism of the Council of Trent forms a striking example of a brief, clear resumé of the doctrines of Christianity. But all down the ages it was the Sacramental system of the Church and her Liturgy that kept the vital truths of Christianity vividly before the minds of the people and that rendered them fruitful in their lives. To the Liturgy, as a means of popular instruction, were added, in time, the resources of the fine arts. Poetry and Music lent their beauty and eloquence, while painting, sculpture and architecture joined in the building of great cathedrals which spoke eloquently to the hearts and minds of the unlettered children of the forest no less than to the cultivated mind of the philosopher and of the theologian.[12]

He quotes, as witness to this function of the Church's art, Charles Eliot Norton, the famous Dante scholar of Harvard University, in a long passage ending:

The Scriptures were displayed in imperishable painting before the eyes of those who could not read the written word. The Church became, thus, not only the sanctuary wherein to pray, to confess, to be absolved, but also a schoolhouse for the teaching of the faithful. The scheme of its pictorial decoration includes the story of the race of man, his fall and redemption; the life and passion of the Savior, and the works of His Apostles and Saints.[13]

The liturgical revival, according to Doctor Shields, must begin in the elementary school; in the hearts and minds of

[12] *Catholic University Bulletin*, 1908.
[13] *Catholic University Bulletin*, Jan. 1909, p. 75.

the baby class the seed must be planted and, from there, germinate. In this respect, as in so many others, Doctor Shields was a leader far in advance of his time.

"It is indeed a life's work," wrote the Superintendent of Catholic Schools in New Orleans, "made difficult through our lack of unity in the methods we adopt." [14]

[14] Father Kavanagh to T. E. S., 1908.

CHAPTER SEVENTEEN

THE SISTERS' CHAMPION

IN all these years the man of science, the professor of psychology and education, had not forgotten the unhappy experiences of his early years. Sympathy for the plight of the children had led him to devise a system of education which would save the little ones from the odious fate of which he had been a victim. But if sympathy for the children had been a strong motive power with Doctor Shields, a still stronger sympathy moved him to take up the cause of the teaching Sisterhoods in their embarrassing plight. Here was a veritable army of professional women who, out of love for God and the souls of little children, had made education their life vocation, who had renounced voluntarily all that the world might have to offer of ambition, of home life, of comfort, in order to devote themselves, until death, to education. Striving to become perfect in their field, what facilities were offered them under Catholic auspices? They had indeed received a normal school training in pedagogy in their own novitiates, perhaps an excellent training as far as it went. But did it go far enough? Where were these devoted teachers to obtain a higher training leading to academic degrees?

Despite the efforts of Doctor Shields and others, the Catholic University had not opened its doors to women, nor had other Catholic higher institutes of learning made provision for the needs of the teaching Sisters. Consequently the Sisters were faced with an unhappy choice, as Doctor Shields pointed out when making his appeal and pleading their cause to the University authorities. The Sisters could simply renounce all hope of the requisite training, cut themselves off from the stream of modern pedagogical science, fail to keep abreast of the times in face of strong competition from the secular schools. The Sisters who had chosen this policy were rapidly losing their pupils. On the other hand, they could decide to seek the needed instruction from secular sources. Many had made the latter decision and were taking courses in philosophy, psychology, science and history in non-Catholic institutions. The next step was inevitable: to seek and obtain academic degrees from these institutions, affiliation of their schools to non-Catholic high schools and colleges with the result that these institutions could impose their own standards upon the Catholic organizations, control the Catholic primary and secondary schools, and introduce their own textbooks quite as effectively as though the Catholic schools had belonged to the State organization.

It was a bitter choice for the Sisters. The danger was grave. The only institutions to which the Sisters could apply for the benefits of University study were indifferent, if not openly hostile to religion. Much of the science of education then offered in these institutions was unsuitable for the Sisters, not only because of its irreligious nature (the counter poison for which their own religious life conceivably might supply) but because of the inexperience of the Sister-students themselves, incapable as they then were of distinguishing between the true and the false in the doctrines fed to them. It was a danger threatening the whole spiritual structure of our educational system, and the fault was not to be laid at the door of the Sisters themselves. It haunted Doctor Shields and spurred him to the most insistent action. He knew what was needed and had expressed it clearly in a prophetic phrase in the final pages of his book, *The Education of Our Girls:*

> Here, under the shadow of the Catholic University, there will arise in a few years a Catholic Teachers College for women, to which the various teaching orders will send their most gifted members to receive the highest training that the age affords, and to carry back with them to their several communities a knowledge of the latest developments in science and of the most approved methods of teaching.

Doctor Shields' method for keeping up his own courage was to look far ahead into the future with that striking power of visualization that he had exercised in his youth. When he wrote of the Catholic Sisters College, he *saw it* with a firm inner vision; when he spoke of it—and he spoke to every one within reach—he made it so real that others saw it with his eyes. Now the groundwork had been laid. The Religious Orders were aware of the danger of their situation and were eager to follow as soon as the proper authorities gave their consent to the plan. The point now was to bring the authorities at the University to a realization of the high duty that was theirs.

Doctor Pace seconded his efforts. In a speech before the Catholic Educational Association in 1909, he brought out that:

> There are plain facts to show that our teachers, especially in the secondary schools, are eager for every possible means of improvement. But the question is: do they

find these means within the Catholic system? If they are obliged to seek aid from outside sources, then, clearly, there is a defect somewhere. A system that has not within itself adequate means of supplying its own vital elements with needed energy is a system only in name.

And at the same meeting he brought out another point no less important:

The plain man, who is little concerned about educational theories, will quickly ask why his children should get their elementary training in a Catholic school if that very school draws its strength mainly from affiliation with outside institutions.

Neither Doctor Pace nor Doctor Shields ignored the difficulties to be faced in the establishment of a central Normal College for the Sisters. The immediate but minor difficulty was financial. Such an enterprise could hardly be carried "on a shoe string" even by a financial wizard full of faith in Providence. Actually Doctor Shields was penniless. Worse, he was in debt and would remain so until his textbooks should bring in some returns or the land values rise and enable him to dispose of some building lots. The major difficulty, however, was formidable indeed. Religious Communities of women are conservative. Changes are made slowly. Innovations are looked upon as red lights of danger. The young women who give themselves to God in the religious life are said to "die to the world." To bring Sisters to Washington from all parts of the country, Sisters of many congregations with various rules and customs; to have them live together for a few years outside their convents, away from their Superiors—this indeed, would be a departure from the rigid, age-old manner of convent life and would be frowned upon by prudent and conservative

Superiors whose first care was for the spiritual welfare of their subjects.

The difficulty was one that would have paralyzed a less stout heart. Yet, in the presence of major obstacles between himself and his dream, Doctor Shields was fearless. In him was combined a high idealism inspired by Christian hope with a practical realism guided by an unbounded confidence in God.

Scholars are often dreamers and dreamer he was indeed; but to few men whose minds are occupied with academic studies is given the practical brain, the wide vision that enabled Doctor Shields to realize his dreams. The work, he knew, was for God's glory. This conviction insured his heart against discouragement. To trust in God while sparing no human effort is to demand success—and God did not fail him.

No one knew better than he the difficulties that others had encountered in the past when they tried to take Sisters from the shelter of their convents to engage them in an external work for the salvation of souls. Yet in the early Church, the religious women had not been enclosed, but had lived all their lives with their families. Only in 1298 had Boniface VIII imposed the cloister upon all communities of nuns, a regulation which was confirmed by the Council of Trent. In 1566, Pius V had decreed that no Community should exist except under solemn vows and within strict papal enclosure. Since then, it is true that a few diocesan congregations had carried their work outside of the cloister, but while tolerated, they were never approved by Rome. In their efforts to organize women to carry on the works of religion in the world, Saint Angela Mary Ward and that great doctor of the Church, Saint Francis of Sales, met with failure. It had only been during the last century that cloister bars had been removed and that Sisters had been permitted to work for God beyond the walls of their convents.

As we look back on the bold conception of Doctor Shields and his force of will in carrying it out, we are tempted to forget how great an innovation it represented in his day and how pitiless was the opposition which he had to overcome from the wise and the prudent. Diplomacy as well as force was required. He began, as we have seen, by arousing the Sisters individually to a hearty dissatisfaction with existing educational facilities, creating in their hearts a longing for something better and arousing the Superiors to a sense of the danger which their subjects faced under actual conditions.

Before the establishment of the Catholic Sisters College, there were but few colleges in the United States conducted by Sisters. When the States, one by one, began to require degrees as necessary for recognition, the problem became acute. Those Sisters who taught in colleges, academies and high schools were forced to seek these degrees in secular institutions. It was no longer a matter of choice, since the degrees were required. The attendance of the Sisters at secular universities became not only a danger to their own religious life, but a scandal to the Catholic people who were urged and even commanded to avoid sending their children to these institutions. Yet they beheld the Sisters enrolled among the students of schools from which were excluded God and His divine Son.

O felix culpa! Sometimes a few misfortunes are needed to bring about radical changes. Such misfortunes occurred, as Doctor Shields had dreaded, and they brought home to those in positions of responsibility the danger to faith and morals inherent in the actual situation. The unhappy consequences gave serious and uneasy thought to those whose tolerance had permitted the abuse. This was the sign for which Shields was waiting. "Never try to stop an abuse head-on," he used to say. "It is like trying to stop a swing just as it starts backward from its highest point. It will knock you down. But wait until it has almost reached the end of its backward radius. Then, with a mere touch, you can change its direction." It was high time to give that touch. Authorities in high places were discussing the need of change. The major obstacle was melting away. Yet so deep was still the prejudice, that only the forward-looking minds among the clergy and the Sisters were ready to accept the obvious solution. Many Bishops, many priests both secular and regular, many superiors of religious orders were openly hostile to the idea of taking Sisters out of their own houses and (what was worse) mixing up the various religious orders while they studied. So strong was the opposition, still, that when the Rector of the Catholic University went to Rome to present the plan of a Sisters College to the Pope, he was amazed to be shown letters (enough to fill a good-sized volume) from holy, conservative men and women, requesting the Vicar of Christ to withhold his approval!

The major obstacle still stood between Doctor Shields and his dream. It was his duty now to convince the Holy See that the bringing together of Sisters in a National Normal College would in no way interfere with the religious life of the individual Sister nor weaken the corporative life of the Community to which she belonged. Fortunately, Doctor Shields found his problem partially solved by an outline which had been prepared some years earlier by Bishop Spalding of Peoria who had devised a plan according to which a National Normal College for Sisters might be conducted successfully. The name of John Lancaster Spalding was one to conjure with among priests and educators who considered him something of a genius and called him "the Catholic Emerson." He had been prominently connected with the Catholic University from the first, so much so that many men spoke of him as its founder. Doctor Shields could have found no better backing for his plan, and with some modifications and elaborations, he presented this outline for the consideration and approval of the Vicar of Christ.

The project was so clear in his own mind, both spiritually and materially, that he described it to his architect and commissioned him to draw a design of the whole campus. Together they paced out the distances on the land which the Doctor had determined to purchase as the site of the Sisters College. Here on this secluded plain, he would erect the administrative and academic buildings. Around them he would arrange the sites which he would lease to the various Religious Congregations for ninety-nine years at a nominal sum that would merely suffice to take care of the grounds. On these sites each Congregation would erect its own house of study and prayer where the Sisters would live under their own Superiors and follow their rules and customs as at home. On a central knoll overlooking these halls of science and homes of prayer, he would raise a great Basilica dedicated to her who is blessed among women and whom countless nuns throughout the Christian centuries have daily invoked in the words of the litany as the *Seat of Wisdom.*

It was another and more vast daydream. No longer was he possessed by the inner vision of a material organism of wheels and levers, but he saw, already realized in all its details, a great spiritual organism directing the proper functioning of the educational forces of the Catholic

Church in America. He visualized the material center, the heart of the whole project there before him on that rolling land. He made his architect see it with his eyes and with the aid of a landscape artist they planted rows of noble shade trees on the well-graded land. Of course they must have a uniform type of architecture that all might be in harmony, and decided upon the Spanish renaissance in honor of the early missionaries. Thus the drawings were completed of the whole campus of the future Catholic Sisters College.

The saintly Pius X beheld the architect's plan of the landscaped site with its shade trees, its numerous convents, academic buildings and its stately college church. He looked upon it with astonishment, with favor, with approval, with enthusiasm and exclaimed in his admiration:

"The Sisters' City! My blessing to all who may have a share in its building!"

The battle was won. The great obstacle fell as the approval of a holy Pope placed the seal of highest authority on the Sisters' City. Voices of opposition might still whisper in corners, but no longer could they shout from housetops. Doubts would no longer disturb the consciences of those who guide the destinies of the Sisters.

To Doctor Shields, the voice of Rome was the voice of God. Peace descended into his brave soul as he realized that only the lesser difficulty lay before him now. A mere million dollars! What was that? American Catholics would soon realize the importance of the undertaking for the good of their own children, for the good of the Church—a million would be nothing compared to the treasures that would pour in. The case for the Sisters needed merely to be explained.

CHAPTER EIGHTEEN

THE HUMAN DYNAMO

IN principle the battle was won. In practice the struggle was only beginning. Open opposition had been hushed by the approval of the Pope, but the weight of inertia had yet to be overcome. The hardest years of his life lay before Doctor Shields. Nothing could quench his hope and his enthusiasm. "From long experience he had reached the conviction which abided with him always that the future of Catholic education, its worth and success, depended on the preparation of Catholic teachers. Whatever else might be done to win support for our schools, to improve their facilities, quicken the interest of parents, or increase the vocations for the religious life, the center and pivot was and must be the teacher, her training and qualifications. This conviction roused him, filled him with eagerness, stirred him to a holy impatience. It became for him a directive principle, dominating his thought and deciding the course of his action. It became, finally, the standard by which he appraised every idea, proposal and movement, whether in the field of education or in the broader field of science in which education takes root and from which it draws its vitality." [1]

In November, 1909, the Trustees of the University had

[1] Doctor Pace, *Catholic Educational Review*, Mar., 1921.

193

consented to the establishment of a Teachers Institute. They had consented in principle but great bodies move slowly. The Department of Education was directed to send out circulars to the Superiors of Religious Orders of women teachers and to the Bishops of the dioceses in which they worked, in the form of questionnaires as to the utility of such an institute and as to the conditions which they considered essential for protecting the religious life of the students. During the summer the answers came in. The majority were favorable. There existed a strong desire to see the Institute established and to obtain from the Catholic University the instruction which the Sisters were seeking reluctantly from secular sources. The plan outlined by the Department of Education met with general approval, namely, that each Community should be free to establish its own house on the campus, but that members of Communities who did not own their house should be lodged in a common home with rules acceptable to all and under the control of authorities approved by the Board of Trustees, that the academic control be vested in the University authorities, that all teaching be done by members of the University staff, that courses of instruction be provided leading to Degrees of Bachelor of Arts, Master of Arts, Doctor of Philosophy, and finally, in view of the immediate needs throughout the country and the actual requirements demanded of teachers, that professional courses in education be provided with all that was required for a teacher's certificate.

Doctor Shields was delighted with the response from the field. The goal was at last in sight. He wrote in March, 1910:

> Things are moving along here gloriously. My hopes are being more than realized in many directions. First, it seems certain now that we are to have an Institute here

for the Sisters. The matter of organization is progressing rapidly and I hope that we will be able to begin actual operations a year from next fall. It has also been settled that we are to have a summer session here for the benefit of teachers who cannot come during the year.[2]

At the next meeting of the Board of Trustees, Doctor Shields urged immediate action in view of the prospects held out to the teaching Sisters in the Circular and Questionnaire:

> I regard it as extremely important that some definite step be taken at this meeting in order to profit by the present enthusiasm of the Communities. They have been practically deterred from sending their subjects to other institutions and yet their work, in face of strong competition, must be carried on. The University is pledged to offer them, according to the terms of the proposal sent out, the facilities they require for training their teachers. Any delay at this juncture would prove detrimental to the whole work of Catholic education.

Delay! Could anything be more harrassing when the fields were ripe for the harvest? Delay, postponement, inaction— they were the enemies most to be feared. He continued:

> To give the whole matter concrete shape, I would recommend that the necessary property be secured at once and a building adapted to this purpose be erected so that, at latest, the courses be announced in the spring and opened next fall for such Communities as are willing to reside in the Community House—leaving the others free to put up separate buildings as they may see fit.

Things were not destined to move so fast. Every detail was clear in the mind of Doctor Shields, but the forces of prudence were too heavy to be moved even by a

[2] Letter to Sister Generosa.

human dynamo. Yet, through the coming years of alternate hope and fear, he let no sign of discouragement pierce through to the outer world. Doctor Turner, who had shared his friend's home for so many years and who knew him in all his moods more intimately, perhaps, than any of his other colleagues, was impressed by his steady courage:

> The difficulties which Doctor Shields encountered, especially at the beginning, the misunderstanding, the lack of sympathy which he met almost everywhere at first, brought to the knowledge of those who were close to him the splendid courage, the indefatigable zeal and the indomitable optimism which contributed so much to his final success. He simply refused to be discouraged. He so despised criticism that it seemed hardly to disturb him. He had a great idea, conceived in the spirit of unselfish devotion. To that he sacrificed literally all that he had and all that he was. He underwent actual privation at times, subordinating all personal gain and personal comfort to the cause which he had made his own.[3]

In retrospect, Doctor Pace, too, admired this steady pressure toward a goal even though, at the time, he may perhaps have thought it excessive. He wrote:

> We noted the intensity of purpose, the energy and the hopefulness which he brought to his duties and to his own generous undertakings. We saw him in the midst of difficulties, striving, persisting, forcing his way to success . . . the tireless worker, the man of initiative and courage—a singular blending of ideal aims and practical insight.[4]

The year 1911 found him carrying a heavy load of responsibilities. Fortunately he had moved into his new house on

[3] William Turner, Bishop of Buffalo in the *Catholic Educational Review*, Mar., 1921.
[4] Doctor Pace in the *Catholic Educational Review*, Mar., 1921.

the hill, in company with Doctor Turner, Doctor McCormick, and his nephew Vincent Shields, a younger son of his brother Michael Bernard. The same year that marked the approval of the Sisters College saw the founding of the *Catholic Educational Review*, publication of the textbook, *Religion—Third Book*, and the definite shaping of a plan of affiliation of high schools and colleges with the University. All these activities were closely correlated in his mind but each made inroads on his time and strength. He was like a juggler, keeping balls of many colors in constant movement. Not one could be neglected.

The new *Review* was to be the mouthpiece of the Department of Education. It was launched at this crucial time to present clearly principles of Catholic education and analyze methods in light of those principles. It was essential in fulfilling its purpose that it should have the moral backing of the University, yet this could be obtained only on condition that the *Review* should entail no financial obligation to that institution. With magnificent courage Doctors Shields and Pace took upon themselves the financial risk, wrote to the Rector, Monsignor Shahan, describing the purpose of the *Review*, requesting his approval and making the following declaration:

> We hereby express our willingness to undertake at our own risk the *Review* as above described and to provide for its publication and all expenses connected therewith out of our own personal resources. . . . According to this plan, the University will not be called upon to advance any funds for the project or to meet any financial obligations.

The letter was signed by Doctors Shields and Pace. It read like a letter from millionaires. Actually the two men were penniless. One of them was deeply in debt, for his home, for the publication of his books and for deficits incurred in financing the correspondence courses. The *Educational Review* was launched on pure hope unstained by that prudence which is cowardice in disguise. It was launched on the conviction that it was essential to the success of the whole vast plan then maturing. No part of the plan could be left weak, there must be no defective link in the chain. Naturally, the Rector accepted the proposition on the basis, as he wrote, of the offer "to undertake at your own expense the publication of a *Review* dealing with educational matters from a Catholic standpoint."

Affiliation, too, was an essential link in the chain. It was during this same year that the matter was pushed to a successful beginning. At the time of the foundation of the University, Pope Leo XIII had urged the Trustees in an Apostolic Letter to organize this matter, saying:

> We exhort you all that you take care to affiliate with your University, your Seminaries, Colleges, and other Catholic institutions . . . in such a manner as not to destroy their autonomy.

With the single exception of the affiliation of certain seminaries, nothing had been done along these lines. It needed the vision and energy of a Doctor Shields to carry through the project which he himself initiated and worked out in a manner so plastic and yet so firm that it protected the spirit and purpose of the individual organization while establishing a standard to which all could conform.

A Committee on Affiliation was named by the Board of Trustees. During the ten days that elapsed before its first meeting, Doctor Shields talked about affiliation to everyone he met, to men and women, to priests and lay people, to young and old. His whole soul burned with enthusiasm and, as he talked, his own ideas became so clear, so vivid, that he arrived at the meeting with a definite plan worked out in minute detail, which he proposed should be adopted then and there. But this was not the way of the wise and prudent. The other men were ready to consider a plan, to weigh the pros and cons, but were not prepared to act. Yet the tremendous driving power of Doctor Shields prevailed at the meeting; his plan was adopted, only to be held up for future consideration by the Rector. After due delay and when the conventionalities of prudence had been complied with, Doctor Shields' plan was finally adopted in its original form.

The first number of the new *Review* had been published in January, 1911. The Department of Education had a mouthpiece. Doctor Shields was the Editor-in-Chief. The project for a Sisters College at the University was pushed energetically. Pictures of the site and proposed buildings drew much favorable comment, particularly from architects who complimented the Dean on having made a general plan where all the units of the composition were in harmony. Meanwhile, Doctor Shields was pressing hard for a summer school to be held at the University during the summer of 1911. In this plan he had the outspoken support of the Apostolic Delegate, Monsignor Falconio, the close co-operation of the other members of the Education Department, Doctors Pace, Turner and McCormick. In May the *Review* was able to make the following announcement:

> The Trustees of the University have authorized a Normal Institute for Teaching Sisters which lay women may attend, in the immediate vicinity of the University and under its direction. The Summer School is, in reality, the first step toward the realization of this project.[5]

[5] *Catholic Educational Review*, May, 1911.

In those days the University held no summer session. Professors and students were absent. This fact made it possible for the Sister-students to use the classrooms, library and laboratories. The Sisters College itself possessed nothing in a material sense. Its beginning could be as simple as that of Christianity itself, whose first home was a borrowed cave. The point was to make a beginning, to capitalize on the permission and to function without delay.

Of course there were no residences for the Sisters. That central building was still in the realm of the imagination. The Sisters would have to depend on the generous hospitality of the nearby convents or else rent cottages in the village. It was under these conditions that the first summer school opened on July 2, 1911, and ended in a blaze of glory and general enthusiasm on August 8th. Doctor Shields might well have made his own the words of G. Stanley Hall as quoted in the *Catholic Educational Review:*

> There is always a sense in which a University does not consist of buildings, endowments or numbers of students, but in a state of mind. It is found wherever a great teacher and a few gifted pupils are gathered together.

In this case the pupils were not few. Twenty-three Religious Orders were represented among the group of 284 pioneer students. The majority came from the United States, a minority from Canada and even from England. The Superiors who visited the Summer School were satisfied that the religious life of their subjects, far from being endangered, was reinforced and enriched by their studies. The students were touching in their gratitude. "How good it was to feel that we no longer stood alone and unchampioned," wrote one. "Years of waiting added zest to enjoyment," wrote another. And a third, "To me and to many others the Summer School has been more than a Retreat, for practical religion was blended with all that we heard and saw." Of the Dean himself, a student wrote: "His endurance like his patience and his erudition was inexhaustible. Never shall we forget the hours we spent thrilled through and through by the rare qualities of his eloquence and the delightful charm of his conversation."

Doctor Shields and his collaborators had triumphed in this first experiment. The stages of preparation had not been in vain. As they sat, in the evenings, on the porch of their new home, the men of the Education Department could look back at an honest continuity of effort: in 1904 the formation of Diocesan supervisors undertaken almost in spite of itself by the University; in 1905 the launching of articles on educational topics by the Catholic Associated Press, followed that same year by the Correspondence Courses; in 1907 the opening campaign in the Catholic University Bulletin under the title *Notes on Education*; in 1909 the formal establishment of the Department of Education at the University, and now, at last, the approval by the Board of Trustees of the establishment of a College where the Sisters could receive the needed instruction from the same faculty that taught at the University.

But a summer institute is not a College. The six weeks had but whetted the intellectual appetite of the students. Must they wait a whole year for another brief summer session to continue their studies? The Superiors of several Communities appealed to the Rector to allow their Sisters to continue their studies during the academic year. They won the Rector's consent. Suddenly the Sisters College had become another *fait accompli*. It was there to stay.

It was a strange beginning. Of material resources Doctor Shields had not even a promise. Classrooms, library, laboratory, chapel, housing facilities, all were lacking. Co-education being forbidden at the University, the Sisters must look elsewhere for borrowed necessities. But Doctor Shields had no intention of letting the thin edge of the wedge, once in hand, slip out of his grasp. No matter under what conditions, the Sisters must remain. They must be taught and they must be lodged.

In this crisis, the Benedictine Sisters of Brookland came to his rescue. The Convent took in as many Sisters as possible; the others rented cottages in the vicinity. The Benedictines shared their chapel with all the Sisters. The classrooms, occupied during school hours by the children, were turned over to the Sisters College early in the morning, late in the afternoon and in the evening. There was hardly time to ventilate the rooms between the changes of occupants. The professors generously added these hours of teaching to their already heavy schedule. Doctor Shields was filled with enthusiasm. The Sisters College had an official standing. The University was committed. There could be henceforth no drawing back. The inconveniences could not dampen his ardor nor that of the students. For the Sisters College had had its formal opening on the third of October, 1911, and on the seventh, the Apostolic Delegate had celebrated a solemn Mass to the Holy Ghost with Doctors Shields and Turner as Deacons. The Rector of the University had preached the sermon. It was the formal inauguration of a great movement in the Church, a humble beginning in absolute poverty but with riches incalculable of faith and hope. Here was the first tender shoot springing from the seed planted and tended through the years with foresight and intelligence by Doctor Shields.

CHAPTER NINETEEN

IMPEDIMENTS

DOCTOR SHIELDS sat at his desk in the new house. His apartment consisted of a bedroom no larger than a monastic cell, a tiny bathroom and a large, airy study. The floor was bare. The walls were lined with books. A few stiff chairs, an ample desk, a typewriter and a dictionary on a revolving stand made up the sum total of what, in his eyes, constituted luxury. Space, light, air, working materials under his hand—a dream of many years realized. His study opened on a large, covered porch from which, to the east, he could see the Franciscan monastery, to the south Quincy Street, still unpaved, and to the northwest, across rolling country, the coveted land on which the future Sisters City was to stand. A hemlock hedge made a dark line of privacy around the Quincy Street property; a magnolia, planted by his hand, was ready to burst into bloom; a purple wistaria to shade the southerly porch was rising rapidly as befitted a Shields project. All this was responding to the master's hand. Yet Doctor Shields was worried. The man of hope was frustrated. He was facing a job for which he felt totally incompetent. With success all but won, his optimism for the first time in his life was deserting him.

Yet, in December, 1911, he had prevailed upon the University authorities to purchase the coveted land, those forty-seven acres adjoining the University grounds that had been pictured in the plan sent to Rome. He had, of course, promised to find the funds to pay the interest on the loan and, finally, to pay for the land itself, as well as for the necessary academic buildings. There would be no difficulty in securing funds for so noble a purpose.

Already the Sisters were clamoring for permission to build their convent residences on the campus—and there was no campus. They could not be permitted to build until the land was graded, roads designed, a central heating, lighting and plumbing system installed. All this required funds, and there were no funds. The Sisters City could not be financed on a shoestring. Delay was impossible. Under pressure from all sides, Doctor Shields sat at his desk facing the distasteful task of begging for money. A financial campaign—a veritable nightmare to him—imposed itself inexorably.

He had always financed his other enterprises on a strictly business basis. He borrowed and he repaid. Such operations left his self-respect and his independence intact. This new role of beggar did not suit him. He was unhappy and felt that he did not know the rules of the game. His attitude toward money was that of a master to a slave. He spoke of money in a tone of lofty and rather offhand contempt. Yet he was a good man of business, liked clean-cut contracts and sound methods. And now, suddenly it had dawned upon him that, with success within easy reach, he was going to be thwarted by this unreal element, money! His friends, like himself, were intellectuals and, like himself, poor. They could neither help nor advise him in this crisis. He must grope. And while groping, he must spend his time, so limited and so precious for teaching and writing, in persuading reluctant givers to open their hearts and their purses. The idea made him shudder and hesitate.

Yet this hollow unreality was setting itself between him and the realization of his dream. He had not the vaguest idea how to begin a financial campaign.

A few months earlier, he had launched successfully the new *Catholic Educational Review* on borrowed funds and his credit was strained to the breaking point. Yet his self-respect was intact and his enthusiasm knew no bounds. He wrote:

> I am simply overwhelmed with work, but I want to tell you about the *Review*. It is going to be a glorious success. We are determined to make the magazine a great bulwark against the enemies of religion. We must create a public opinion in favor of our schools and colleges or we will soon find ourselves in a position similar to that of our friends in France, Spain, Portugal and other European countries. Dr. Pace and I have been able to borrow a few thousand dollars to get the enterprise started and we do not expect to be able to pay this back for many years.

And in another letter he explained:

> We are building an encyclopedia of Catholic education literature. There is practically no other literature on the subject available. . . . The financial burden of the magazine will be very heavy for some years; D. Pace and I will have to bear it alone.[1]

Yet he asked no aid, save that his friends in the various religious orders should advertise their colleges and schools in the pages of the *Review*. When offered direct help of a financial nature, his reaction was characteristic:

> If we cannot make the *Review* self-respecting and self-supporting after a fair trial, the sooner it dies the better.

[1] The letters quoted in this chapter are written to Sisters of teaching communities and to J. B. Ward.

I believe, however, that it is going to have a vigorous life and accomplish great things for Catholic education.

This was the man doomed to become a beggar! For the Sisters College, he was willing to face even this. The very success of the infant college multiplied responsibilities. The applicants, each year, were increasing in number. By the summer of 1912, students had registered from twenty states and represented fifty communities. The University facilities would take care of the summer session, but what was to be done for the winter? The Brookland convent had already become totally inadequate to accommodate the classes, to say nothing of suitable residences.

On the advice of Cardinal Gibbons, Doctor Shields had written to various wealthy Catholics outlining the whole plan in detail. A millionaire sent him a check for a hundred dollars which disheartened him more than a blunt refusal. He began to lose hope of the millions that were to flow in from a grateful public. As a matter of fact, he was not an able beggar. His very tact made it all too easy to refuse what he asked. "I know you will gladly help me if you can find the means" was a formula that brought many disappointing answers. There was another difficulty. The whole project was so vast and so complex, it required so much familiarity with the educational situation in the country, as to make the appeal almost unintelligible to the small group of wealthy Catholics who could have financed his plan had they been willing to do so, but whose sympathies were more readily aroused by the needs of the body than by those of the mind. Finally, the poor Doctor, himself, who was so eloquent before his students, became tongue-tied when forcing himself to beg. The whole project was so close to him—as close as the beating of his own heart or as the circulation of his own blood—that he felt humiliated in speaking as though he were asking something for himself. He, who was accustomed to see eyes light up with enthusiasm when he spoke, must stiffen himself to speak to an audience in full resistance, drawing down the shutters of the mind to protect the purse. It was a new experience. Finally, he had no time, literally none, in which to make these appeals. He was teaching winter and summer every day except Sunday. He was editing a *Review*, composing textbooks and carrying on his duties as Dean of the College. Those few weeks of interval between the summer and winter sessions, the few days after Christmas and those before Easter were his only free moments.

In those few days when he should have rested, he travelled and appealed for funds. His first experiment was absurd and completely ineffective. He displayed stereopticon slides of the University and proposed Sisters College, talking of the project and its needs as he commented on the pictures. Beforehand he wrote in 1912:

> I never talked at a picture show in my life and I am also entirely green in the matter of collecting money so the present undertaking seems to me an ordeal greater than you can possibly understand. However, I will go through with it as best I can. The cause itself should be sufficient to supply the place of eloquence. I cannot believe that the American people will hesitate to supply the necessary funds once they understand the nature of the undertaking.

Of his project, he wrote at this same time:

> I hope to raise a million dollars that will enable me to present the grounds rent-free to the various Communities, prepare the grounds, heating plant, put up public buildings and to offer free tuition. Whatever may be the difficulties, some way will be found to remove them.

But in February of that same year, a note of dismay sounds in his correspondence. He had traveled, written, lectured, shown the lantern slides, and the million dollars were still as far out of reach as the gold at the end of the rainbow.

> I returned from the West a week ago, worn out and with a severe cold. I am just beginning to get back into some sort of working condition, but am almost discouraged at the amount of work ahead. I got practically no immediate returns from my Western trip. I wish I could get $25,000 or $30,000 pledged before the Board of Trustees meet in April for in that event, I feel sure they would permit us to proceed at once with the erection of the first academic building. Our present cramped quarters would be wholly impossible next year. . . . I must get some rest before I can think clearly on any line.

Many more years were to pass, years of hope constantly deferred. The Board of Trustees met and decided to "make a careful study of the various problems involved and to report with recommendations to the Board at their next meeting in November." There was to be no hasty action. Prudence in the garb of delay was holding its own. Unfortunately Doctor Shields had not captured the funds that might have broken down the objections. The decision hit him hard but no word of complaint passed his lips. He even tried to justify the decision. He wrote:

> This was at first a great disappointment to me but, on thinking the matter over, I believe the action was both wise and fortunate for us. It will enable us to get the grounds ready and to attend to the problems of drainage. It will enable the Sisters who wish to build to consider their plans in somewhat more leisurely fashion. . . .

Of course it will make the work of the Sisters College
next year a difficult problem to deal with, but we shall
do the best we can and I hope that by the first of
November, we may have sufficient means to proceed at
once with our building projects and have things in readi-
ness for the summer school July, 1913.

From year to year, his hope was deferred. In 1914, he
wrote in the *Catholic Educational Review:*

> The Sisters College is still in its infancy. It is almost
> entirely without funds. The ground on which the build-
> ings are to be erected is still to be paid for. The Com-
> munities, out of their very slender incomes, are eager
> and willing to build residences at the Sisters College, but
> laboratories, libraries, lecture halls and chapel must be
> provided. . . . The benefits of the Sisters College of the
> Catholic University will be felt in every parish school
> and in every Catholic home throughout the country in
> the immediate future. . . . The Sisters give their lives
> unsparingly for the children of the Church and of the
> Nation. They should not appeal in vain for the necessary
> equipment for the worthy discharge of their sacred
> duties.

But year after year, Doctor Shields appealed in vain.
His face bore the mark of strain, though he would not
admit failure. He traveled, lectured and collected a few
thousand dollars with the maximum effort for the most
mediocre result. He managed to pay the interest on the loan
and devised a temporary solution to the classroom problem.
He purchased a large portable building that served for
many years as chapel and classroom. It could accommodate
several hundred students and was set up, first, on the
grounds of the Benedictine Convent and, later, was moved
to the site of the Sisters College. Bearing the dignified name

210   THE EDUCATOR

of *Sedes Sapientiae*, the Seat of Wisdom served its purpose during the rest of Doctor Shields' life.

A wooden, portable structure, however useful, was not of a nature to overcome the objections of the University authorities. The Board of Trustees remained adamant. Meanwhile, all prejudice had died out among the religious orders. Religious Superiors who visited the School were deeply impressed by what they heard and saw. The student-Sisters formed a family of which Doctor Shields was the head. They appealed to the Dean for everything they needed, materially, intellectually and spiritually. He found lodgings for them at suitable prices, sorted out those who wished to share a common home, became liaison officer between the Superiors and the architect, examined specifications, criticized contracts, took up their cause with the contractor. The Sisters, like himself, were pioneers. They deserved all the help he could give them. The sleeping porches were to be enlarged a few feet, a laundry was to be added in the basement; it was to the Dean that such appeals came in. To each he replied with courtesy and good humor, with the attention to detail of a man who had no other occupation in life than to attend to their individual problems. There was nothing too large, nothing too small to bring to his attention. One thing alone terrified him, that painful duty of collecting money. Again he set out for the West and wrote, as though trying to hammer the point into his own head:

> My main object is the getting of money. It is a new experience for me and one that I dread more than I can tell you, but the splendid promise of the Sisters College can only be realized on condition that the University pays for the grounds and erects the academic buildings. I can find no one else willing to take up the matter and

so I must do it myself. . . . Of course I hope for some success but I must confess to a very cowardly feeling. I find myself calling upon all my reserve strength to keep me from running away from the task. I believe if there were not so much at stake, I would readily find excuses for remaining at home.

Returning, baffled and exhausted, from one of these trips, he remarked that he would like to get out and work to earn the money required; he was sure he could earn it by honest work in less time and with far less expenditure of energy than he was using up in these travels and appeals to unwilling givers. Then, he pointed to his Roman collar with a smile and a shrug, and the moment of weakness passed.

There was but little change in the situation until the year 1914 when two events took place which affected the financial campaign, the one beneficially, the other, catastrophically. Through the efforts of Cardinal Gibbons, Chancellor of the University, a priest was secured to assist Doctor Shields in the task of raising funds. The Reverend James M. Hayes of Dallas, Texas,[2] undertook this work energetically, visiting various cities to explain the work of the College and its needs, organizing a Sisters College League, founding and editing the *Sisters College Messenger* which explained in simple language the aims of the work and reported its progress. He appealed particularly to the Catholic women of the country, the poor as well as the rich, since it was to their interest that the Catholic schools should be raised to the highest possible level by providing the educators of their children with proper facilities for higher studies. Thus

[2] Father Hayes had been pastor of the Cathedral parish and had financed and built a splendid Cathedral for the diocese. He continued to work for the Sisters College for ten years, three of them subsequent to the death of Doctor Shields until a severe illness forced him to relinquish the task.

Father Hayes lifted a painful burden from the shoulders of Doctor Shields and provided the College with a steady if modest income.

The plan had barely begun to function when the Rector of the University returned from Rome and announced that he planned to erect a great basilica on the grounds of the University. He brought with him the Pope's approval for the project. In November, the Rector was made a Bishop. Immediately, he organized a national collection of funds for his project. The women of the country were urged to make the erection of this basilica their dearest preoccupation. Committees were organized in every city and even in small towns. The basilica was to be the gift of all American Catholic women.

The noble plan was a death blow to the financing of the Sisters College. Here were two appeals to the women of the whole nation both emanating from the Catholic University at Washington. What was wanted: a College for Sisters? a church for the University? As happens when there are confusion and cross currents, both projects suffered. The organized channels, doubly appealed to, resisted, and even individuals drew back. Friends became discouraged. The ground had been cut away from under the Sisters College at the precise moment when the work was becoming known, when interest had been aroused. There was no longer any hope for a successful general appeal. The only chance that remained, and it was a slim one, was to find a generous person who would provide the College with at least one central building which would move the Trustees to final action.

It was with a heavy heart and with hardly a spark of his old optimism that Doctor Shields kept an appointment made for him in New York on the afternoon of Good

Friday, 1915. He knew that the appointment had been granted reluctantly. He knew what that meant—a courteous refusal. He faced another fiasco, of that he was certain. The day was sombre and his spirit low. But he was at the end of his tether. He gritted his teeth and went.

When he returned two hours later Good Friday had blossomed into Easter without waiting for the Liturgy. He was pale and could hardly speak. A Catholic woman had understood his great plan. She had opened her heart to generosity under the fire of his faith, his sincerity, his personality. The long battle was won. He would have the central portion of the new building at once, the wings, perhaps, later. But that was enough. The Normal College for Sisters was a reality at last. All his optimism came flooding back to his heart, spreading joy around him. From the mountaintop of vision he saw his college as a permanent source of light and strength to all the teaching Sisters of the nation. He saw its graduates in all the schools of the country raising the standard of education, lifting their scholars to a love of mental culture, preparing them to take their place in the world as champions of those truths and those laws which are God's revelation to man, the source of human happiness and the welfare of society. Could it be that with this little word "yes" a woman had made this possible?

On May 5, 1916, the central building of the Sisters College was solemnly dedicated by Cardinal Gibbons. Already the Board of Trustees had consented to the formal establishment of the Sisters College as an affiliated College of the Catholic University, with its own Board of Trustees of nine members chosen from the Board of Trustees of the University. A ninety-nine-year lease of the necessary ground was granted to each teaching community wishing to erect a convent home, twenty-five communities having already selected their sites on the campus.

Immediately following the incorporation of the College, work was begun on the land: the grading, the cutting of roads, the bringing in of water, electric light and sewers. *Sedes Sapientiae* was solemnly transferred and placed on the basement of one of the future wings of the central building. The building itself provided the Sisters with a library, two classrooms, a chapel, a dining room, a kitchen in the basement and living quarters upstairs. These quarters were for the lucky ones. There were still some hardships to be faced by those who lived far away, but what Sisters would not face them cheerfully when this splendid prospect was, at last, unfolding before their eyes? All might have echoed the thought of Doctor Pace a few years later as he laid a wreath of words upon the bier of the worker who had given his life for a great cause:

> In every diocese and parish, in every religious novitiate and scholastic council, academy and elementary school, there are debtors to Doctor Shields,—teachers who owe him the best that is in them, men and women who are living by his direction, children unnumbered who are growing to knowledge and virtue on the fruit of his thought and endeavor.

PART FOUR

CHRISTIAN EDUCATION

Learning is immanent activity.—
St. Thomas Aquinas

What art can be compared to that of guiding and forming the mind and character of the young? He who has the ability to do this ought to use greater care than any painter or sculptor.

—*St. John Chrysostom*

CHAPTER TWENTY

ORIGINALITY

THROUGHOUT the years that Doctor Shields struggled to establish a permanent center for teacher training, his creative work continued uninterrupted. Books and articles flowed from his pen. From a *Philosophy of Education* to textbooks for the primary grades his thought reached out to meet the needs of all classes, of all degrees of intellectual development.

The question presents itself, perhaps, to the reader: to what extent was Doctor Shields a discoverer, an innovator? How much was he carried by the current of the forward movement which influenced all the educational thought of his day?

Undoubtedly he had precursors as well as imitators. Many basic principles of the *Shields Methods* were common property. In this country, William James had already stressed the importance of activity, the educational value of the motor element, the vital connection between impression and expression, refusing to separate the activities of the pupil's body from the development of his mental processes. James had urged the need of spontaneous interest for obtaining the attention required for assimilation; he had insisted that the positive and constructive should replace the inhibitory and the negative; he had explained the need of association in ideas. All these things which were fundamental elements in the Shields Methods were not original discoveries for there were many other men working along these lines of thought.

John Dewey had written before Doctor Shields of the need for a center of correlation to link together the various subjects presented to the pupil. Correlation became, to Doctor Shields, one of the principal leit-motifs of all his teaching. It was essential to assimilation and to a balanced development. With most of his contemporaries, Doctor Shields held that the child, his needs and his capacities should be the center of observation in contrast to mere attention to a formal curriculum, and with them, he believed that only by the child's own activity could the truths presented to his mind be assimilated. The child and his needs, his stage of development, the adaptability of a truth to the mind of a child, this was the test of when and how to present it. As he put it: "The temple of life and mind can be built by none other than by the inward dweller." In all these fundamental points of view, Doctor Shields was a man of his time.

Moreover, all these American educators, whether they agreed or differed in detail, were rooted in the soil fertilized by the German psychologist and educator, Herbart,[1] and were influences by the experimental methods of another German, Doctor Wundt.[2] They all felt the need of a concrete approach to ideas, they all stressed the importance of developing the child's powers of observation and reasoning, and all of them applied the principles of experimental psychology to education.

To this extent, Doctor Shields belonged to the general educational movement of his time. He differed radically from his predecessors and contemporaries in his philosophy, in his concept of the nature of man, which profoundly

[1] 1776–1841.
[2] 1832–1920.

affected the ultimate end of education, and he stood out from among them all by the originality and power of his application of theory to concrete practice.

Not every man of genius is a discoverer of new facts or principles. The great Bach, for example, made no musical discovery. He used the material that was familiar to all his contemporaries but used it in a manner that had never been equalled and that, conceivably, will never be surpassed. He took what everybody could handle, the musical conventions of his day, and transformed them by his genius. In the same way, Doctor Shields worked in the educational field with common material which he transformed into an imperishable work of art. "Psychology is a science and teaching is an art," wrote William James, "and sciences never generate arts directly out of themselves. An intermediary inventive mind must make the application by using its originality." [3]

Doctor Shields possessed the needed science. He also possessed an original and inventive mind. He towered above his contemporaries in the field of education principally by his original application of principles which they held in common. Where he differed radically from the men of his time was on questions of philosophy, on the type of human being to be brought out through educational means rather than on those educational means themselves, on his concept of the nature of man and his eternal destiny.

From a superficial standpoint, therefore, the educational technique of Doctor Shields might appear to have much in common with that of John Dewey and the other men of his time. All these educators worked to supplant the passivity of the old school system by activities within the normal experiences of the child. All agreed that, for a truth to become vital, it must be presented in a form adapted to the

[3] *Talks to Teachers on Psychology,* 1899.

child's actual stage of development. Abstract formulae were rejected for this reason. Perception, imagination, memory, judgment and reasoning were stimulated. All held that education was a life to be led and not a mere preparation for life. All trained for adjustment to a changing environment, but Shields, in contrast to the others, held that certain fundamental values remained unchanged, among these the ultimate reality of a personal God ruling all creatures and directing them to their final end. Dewey believed neither in God nor in religion of any sort and considered that moral teaching had no place in the classroom. "Apart from participation in social life, the school has no moral end nor aim," he wrote.[4] To Shields, an education which ignored God and His moral laws was an incomplete affair, an organism lacking a directive principle.

Again, Dewey and his contemporaries made much of socialization. So did Shields, but the latter placed greater emphasis on idealization as the motive power. Both men believed in developing the child according to the laws of his nature, but Shields objected to letting nature, unguided and unrestrained, dominate the child's activity. Though the child entered the world with a definite body of instinctive tendencies he held that not all of these tendencies should be encouraged to develop along native lines. The object of education, as Shields saw it, was precisely to transform some of these tendencies into their opposites. The child must learn to give instead of grabbing, to love instead of selfishly demanding, lest these instincts, untransformed, should make of the child an undesirable member of society.

Dewey's philosophy and that of the other men of his time aimed at a man-centered society; that of Shields was focussed on a God-centered world. Dewey's class room was

---

[4] *Moral Principles in Education*, p. 11.

child-centered; that of Shields, Christ-centered. The various subjects to be taught were, to Shields, like scattered bits of stone destined for a mosaic, meaningless until gathered into a pattern by Religion. *Science* could teach the child his relation to his physical environment; *Letters* could bring him knowledge of the experience of the race; *Institutions*, such as home, school, church, state, could acquaint him with their capacity to realize the higher aims of life and instill a respect for legitimate authority; *Aesthetics* could open to him beauty in all its forms, but these units of knowledge remained incomplete and inorganic until *Religion* placed them in their true perspective and developed the child's full capacities as a social and ethical being. Religion, to Shields, was the core of all knowledge. Other subjects must radiate from that central point. Thus, the function of religion in the classroom was not merely to convey information about God but to consecrate human life. Religious truth must unify and illumine all the subject matter and transform the mental life of each child, guiding his actions in all possible situations that might occur. Thus, while Dewey and his contemporaries held many technical practices in common with Shields, their educational aims were poles apart. No one was more keenly alive, indeed, than Doctor Shields to the dangers inherent in the use of educational skills and techniques of a high order in the service of materialistic doctrines. In a sense, the better the technique, the greater the danger to the child when that technique was not directed to a high aim.

Another point of difference between Shields and his contemporaries lay in this fact: many of the principles which other men of learning had grasped in the laboratory or from books, seated comfortably in an armchair or at a desk, had been burned into the brain of Doctor Shields by the tragic experience of his childhood. A secret emotional memory backed up his scientific convictions. He held "the point of view of the frog"—to use his own words. Other educators looked down from the height of their superiority upon the submerged mass of the ignorant and incapable. Doctor Shields, too, looked down from a height, but in the submerged mass he found himself, smarting under errors of psychology and under mistaken teaching methods. He had no need of experiment or research to discover the importance of sensory and motor reactions in the development of mental faculties. Every nerve in his body, every faculty of his soul bore the imprint of those truths. All he needed to find out was the how and the why of these things, in order to help others. Thus he approached each one of the principles underlying the new methods with a two-fold grasp of their importance: an intellectual conviction and a personal experience. Of course, he neither expected nor desired that every child should be subjected to the conditions or should face the experiences of his own childhood. His had been an extreme case. But it was his confirmed opinion based upon statistics that dullards were being ground out in increasing numbers in the schools of the country by unsound psychology and mistaken methods. Normal children were being transformed into dullards, and this was true in public and parochial schools alike. The conviction lent wings to his words and power to his actions.

In another respect, Shields stood out from among his contemporaries. Leaders of thought on educational lines theorized, formed their students and guided them in a general way. Doctor Shields did this and more. He took upon himself the arduous task of making a practical application of his theories. He composed a series of textbooks for little children which illustrated all the principles that he had been advocating in his lectures. It was not a vague ideal that he set before his students but a realization. Here was a concrete example of how to create spontaneous interest, how to use the emotions of the child to reinforce impressions, to make truths easy to assimilate, to aid the memory. In a word, he gave his students both principles and application. He did it with the reasoning powers of a scientist and the simplicity and subtlety of an artist. He spoke to little children in accents of profound beauty. Those little books called *Religion*—though they included all the subject matter which the pupils were to study during their first and second years at school—are literary masterpieces for children. They are simple yet profound, true to the science of earth yet glowing with the overtones of heaven. No wonder that a great foreign artist described them as "the most beautiful things since the Fioretti of Saint Francis." To Doctor Shields, beauty was a byproduct. He had sought truth.

Yet the most original feature of Doctor Shields' contribution to modern education was neither its theory nor its application. It was in his philosophy that he broke away radically from his contemporaries. The other forward-looking men in the educational field were either definitely atheists or vague idealists of a pragmatic cast of mind. Not one of them thought of religion as basic. They were occupied with the physical and the material. At best they aimed at training for good citizenship. Doctor Shields did this and more. He knew that man was composed not only of a body but also of a soul and that the two elements, body and soul, made up a complete person. To treat the child as a higher animal with no eternal vocation was to rob him of his spiritual inheritance. Doctor Shields wished every child to be prepared not only for good citizenship in this world but prepared to be a worthy citizen of the world to come. It was to Doctor Shields that belonged the honor of placing God Himself as the center of correlation. To John Dewey, the correlative center was geography. "The unity of all the sciences," wrote Dewey, "is found in geography. The significance of geography is that it presents the earth as the enduring home of the occupations of man. . . . The earth is the final source of all man's food." [5] To Doctor Shields, on the contrary, the earth was but a temporary home; the final source of all man's blessings—including his food—was the divine Master and Creator. The human home was but a symbol of the eternal home; the human father, but a symbol of the Father in heaven; the arts of man, but a borrowed ray of beauty from the treasure house of the eternal Master-Artist. Consequently, for the earth and its geography, as correlative center, Doctor Shields substituted the Kingdom of Heaven and its laws; for the earth as final source of our food, he substituted God, the giver of all human sustenance, and he taught the children to say: "Our Father who art in heaven . . . give us this day our daily bread."

Moreover, Doctor Shields was the first among modern educators to point out that all the psychological principles that are being brought to light in our time and applied to education had already found their highest efficiency and most typical functioning in the teaching of Jesus Christ Himself. These same principles, he pointed out, were the basis in the whole teaching practice of the Church from earliest days. We must quote him directly to show how he concentrates in a few paragraphs an epitome of a vast body of psychological data, conveying in a vivid and vital setting those principles of psychology that have been advo-

[5] *School and Society*, p. 16.

cated from the days of Pestalozzi to our own and showing
how the organic teaching of the Church makes application
of these principles. If it took a Herbart to formulate clearly
the principles which made the teaching of Pestalozzi a
psychological success, it needed a Shields, perhaps, to make
us conscious of these same psychological principles in their
application by the Church down the ages. It is a theme that
runs like a leit-motif through the teachings of Doctor
Shields, reiterated with force and conviction. He writes:

> The Church in her teaching, reaches the whole man,
> his intellect, his will, his emotions, his senses, his imagina-
> tion, his aesthetic sensibilities, his memory, his muscles
> and his powers of expression. She neglects nothing in
> him; she lifts up his whole being and strengthens and
> cultivates all his faculties in their interdependence.

He describes the process in detail; how the Church does not
limit her teaching to the spoken or written word but teaches
through the liturgical functions, carrying the mind back to
the ages when faith flowered in the mediaeval cathedrals,
when faith was witnessed by saints whose pictures and
statues adorn her temples, while the stations of the Cross
recall to the ignorant as to the sage the great tragedy of
Calvary with its story of love and self-immolation. The
cloud of incense carries the mind back to the smoke of sacrifices of ancient days, and of the long history of Messianic
longing leading to the great sacrifice of redemption. Music
stirs the feeling and emotions of the worshipper, directing
them heavenward in harmony with the uplift that is being
experienced by all man's conscious life. Nor is the worshipper permitted to be a silent witness of this drama; he
constitutes a living part of it by his song and his prayer; by
his posture, he enters into the liturgical action. After describ-

ing these and other methods used by the Church to influence the lives of her children in a manner in keeping with the laws of life, Doctor Shields continues:

In this manner of teaching there may be plainly traced many of the recognized fundamental principles of education. We find here embodied sensory-motor training, the simultaneous appeal to the emotions and to the intellect, the appeal to the memory of the individual and of the race, the authority of the teacher and the faith of the hearer, and the principles of cooperation and of imitation.

That the educators of today have lost their understanding of this great educative function is due in large measure to the revolt of the sixteenth century. In order to escape from the influence and control of the Church, the reformers set to work to frighten the people away from the fascination of her teaching and of her worship and, in doing so, they went counter to the great fundamental principles of education through the exercise of which the Church had succeeded—and has succeeded even to the present hour—in preserving in the lives of her children the great doctrines of revealed truth, not merely as apprehended by the intellect or stored in the memory, but as living, active forces in their lives.

Psychology is revealing to the educators of today the fact that a conscious content strictly confined to the intellect lacks vitality and power of achievement. Every impression tends by its very nature to flow out in expression, and the intellectual content that is isolated from effective consciousness will be found lacking in dynamo-genetic content because it has failed to become structural in the mind and remains external thereto. From the evidence in this field, we may safely formulate as a fundamental educative principle: *the presence in consciousness of appropriate feeling is indispensable to mental assimilation.*

He remarks on the general recognition of this truth but the difficulty experienced in the embodiment of the principle in working methods in the schools and continues:

> He who would see its perfect embodiment must turn to the organic teaching of the Catholic Church.

He analyzes the Sacramental system providing each crucial moment in life with the proper elements of mental and emotional food; the models for her children's imitative faculties offered by the Church in the lives of her Saints, the guidance of intellect and emotions at each great stage of development.

> The Church, through all the forms of her organic teaching aims at cultivating feeling, but she does not allow her teaching activity to culminate in feeling, which she values chiefly as a means to an end; she employs it to move to action and to form character, and she never leaves it without the stamp and guidance of the intellect. As the feelings glow to incandescence, she imparts to them definite direction and animates them with a purpose which, after the emotions and feelings subside, remains as a guiding principle of conduct.

Again, he describes the Church's use of the child's imitative faculties:

> As light is lit from light, so virtue springs from virtue, and through imitation noble deeds multiply themselves in the lives of others. But, unfortunately, imitation is not limited to the propagation of virtue; it is equally potent in transmitting vice and multiplying evil deeds; hence the necessity of controlling the imitative instinct in the light of larger experience and a higher wisdom than that possessed by the individual. In this respect the Church brings to her task the long experience of the ages and

the wisdom of supernatural guidance. The conformity of her methods to the nature of the imitative phenomena is becoming increasingly clear in the light of our growing knowledge of psychology.

He describes in detail the Church's use of imitation, her obedience to the laws of unity and continuity, her preservation of symmetry in development, her cultivation of the aesthetic faculties, her use of instincts and reflexes as the bases of habits with many other educative practices which occupy the thought of modern men of science and continues:

> The embodiment of these principles in Christ's method of teaching is obvious. He constantly appealed to the emotions and instincts, to the love of parents for offspring, to physical appetites, to human ambitions, to the desire for wealth and power, and He made these purely human tendencies lift the soul into an understanding of the higher truths of revelation. He appealed to the whole man and developed every faculty by which the soul is endowed. He did not let the minds of His followers rest in dry formulae or in the things of sense which He constantly used to lift up the mind to a view of immaterial truths. He always adjusted Himself to the attitude of His followers and answered the questions that formed themselves in their minds.
>
> These and similar educational principles have (without having been understood by her children) always animated the organic teaching of the Church. They were all clearly embodied in her ritual and in her life during the darkest hours of the ninth century, as they were during the brilliant centuries that were adorned by the Fathers and by the Schoolmen.
>
> Those who left the fold of Christ during the sixteenth century carried with them as much of human science as

was possessed by those who remained in the bosom of the Church. No longer guided by the spirit of the Church, the reformers abandoned those principles: they suppressed feeling as an unworthy accompaniment of revealed truth; accusing the Church of idolatry, they extinguished the lights on her altars and banished the incense from her sanctuaries; they broke the stained glass of her windows and the images of her saints; they suppressed her sacraments and her ritual; ignorant of the laws of imitation, they would have neither guardian angels nor patron saints; not knowing the vital necessity of expression, they taught that faith without works was sufficient for salvation; with the warning of the Apostle ringing in their ears, "the letter killeth, it is the spirit which quickeneth"—they accepted the rigid standard of the written word in lieu of the living voice of the Church.

As a consequence of their failure to embody these educative principles in their teachings, revealed truths were extinguished, one by one, in their midst, thus leaving the descendants of confessors and martyrs wandering in exterior darkness where, like the Children of Israel, they were compelled to make bricks without straw. But the day of salvation is at hand. Delving in the natural sciences, the children of this generation are gaining a clearer realization of some of the laws that underlie the life and growth of the mind, and, lifting up their eyes, they find these laws embodied perfectly in the organic teaching of the Catholic Church which, like a cloud by day and a pillar of fire by night, will lead them back into the Kingdom.[6]

These quotations give but an imperfect and inadequate summary of the important study made by Doctor

---

[6] The quotations are from *A Philosophy of Education*, Chapter XVIII.

Shields in his *Philosophy of Education* regarding the Church and her application of what we are pleased to call modern psychology. The chapter should be read in full to be appreciated at its true value.

Certainly Doctor Shields has made us conscious in a new and vital way of those psychological principles which the Church has used through the ages. He was the first to point out that the advances in psychology and the discoveries in education which modern educators were using in his day were but bringing to light the principles that were basic in the educational methods of Christ and of his Church. He was the first among modern educators to make a twofold test of each psychological discovery: the test of science and the test of revelation. He was the first to place before Catholic teachers the methods of Christ as the supreme model for their imitation, not merely as a stepping stone to eternal life, but as their daily pattern in the classroom. He was the first to place God as the center of correlation for all educational thought and activity. In this consists his most important contribution to modern Christian education. Here lies his true originality and genius.

CHAPTER TWENTY-ONE

THE WRITER

DOCTOR Shields was a prolific writer. Among his better-known works are *The Making and Unmaking of a Dullard*, *The Education of Our Girls*, *Primary Methods*, *A Philosophy of Education* and, last but not least, his *Catholic Educational Series of Textbooks for the Schools.*[1] In addition to these books, he wrote for the *Catholic University Bulletin* and *The Catholic Educational Review*. Some of the best things from his pen are hidden away in these pages.

We do not find in Doctor Shields, the writer, those clear, well-rounded phrases that constitute the charm of William James. Shields had no time to polish a phrase. His thought rushed out pell-mell like a torrent uncontrolled. He dictated to a typewriter, his impatient thought outstripping the slow pace of the keys as he walked up and down his study with energetic stride. His terminology was too technical, at times, for the general reader, but his striking, homely illustrations hammered home his points. When a phrase of pure eloquence appears, it is the emotional content of the subject matter which carries him away, a golden shower of truth shining through his words, free from any forethought as to literary style. Indeed, he was so pressed for time that he hardly stopped to read over what he had dictated. Whether it was because the typewriter moved so slowly, or

---

[1] All published by The Catholic Education Press, Washington, D. C.

because of the more formal attitude of mind engendered by the thought of cold print rather than the immediate contact with living souls, it is certain that Doctor Shields was more eloquent and brilliant when talking than when writing. His lectures were more vivid than his books. Other minds stimulated him. His brief articles, such as book reviews, contained gems more engaging than the formal statements of principle in his books.

The impression left by Doctor Shields' writings is cumulative. He was a master of thought if not a master of style. A reader risks disappointment at a first contact, but he will be rewarded if he perseveres. The work of Doctor Shields is like a theme with variations. Fundamental principles are presented in constantly varying perspective. They are examined from this angle and that; here a bird's-eye view from a mountaintop, there a summit seen from a valley. It was the Shields system for avoiding monotony and dry repetition. The richness of his presentation, the original illustrations that fasten themselves to the memory, the correlation of all things human and divine in the service of truth, as though each sound produced an infinity of overtones unfamiliar to the casual ear—these are the characteristics of Doctor Shields as a writer rather than any literary perfection. His were rough and ready sentences but not rough and ready thoughts. He might have written with more finish had he had more time, but he would not have written differently as regards content. As it is, the reader cannot miss his meaning. His writing is logical, clear, persuasive, convincing. If it is not literature it is life. Each phrase, unpolished, in the rough, sets the reader thinking, and that was the purpose of the man who wrote—rapidly, in haste, for the time was short and art too long for the measured years that lay ahead.

"Perhaps the easiest task the savant is called upon to perform is to write a technical treatise embodying the work of his researches," wrote Doctor Shields in one of his book reviews. "It is much more difficult to present this same matter freed of technical terms so that it may reach the intelligence of educated adults who have not mastered the technicalities of the particular field in question. It requires a high order of genius to present the same matter so that it may be understood by a popular audience of uneducated or semi-educated people. But the supreme test of genius is to be found in presenting great fundamental truths or discoveries to a little child in such a manner that he may comprehend and utilize them in the growing structures of his mind and in the development of his character."

Doctor Shields was not referring to his own work evidently. But he could not have given a more exact description of what he himself accomplished in his books for little children. They are masterpieces of principles, of methods and of style. They succeed in bringing the highest truths of philosophy and theology to the child in such a way as to make these principles an active force in his life. We are far, here, from the dry formulations of the catechism. These books represent what Doctor Pace has called the contrast between "the method that seeks only to deposit an idea in the mind and the method that aims at setting the idea to work." One of the laws that Doctor Shields sought to illustrate in practice is thus expressed: "The human mind grows in knowledge under the law of development wherein it is written that each subsequent phase shall be attained through the reconstruction of the previous phase. In the human mind you cannot build with naked truth, the mind cannot look upon it and live." Then followed the homely illustration with which he always drove home his points: "The crayfish can grow only by casting off its shell from time to time, but if in your mistaken zeal to help it in its growth, you proceed to tear off its shell, you will kill it instead of helping it."

His schoolbooks apply this principle of reconstruction. A truth experienced in one context is translated to a higher application. A bit of scientific knowledge is applied in the home life of the children and is finally raised to all its eternal implications in the realm of the spirit. It is the principle of the parable.

We find, too, the principle of correlation applied with skill. A single book contains all the subject matter that is to be presented to the children during their first (and even their second) year at school. The Books are entitled *Religion—First Year—Second Year*, etc. In each book the central, correlating element is God. Yet the books contain "germinal concepts" of all that is to be taught later in the secondary schools and even in the universities, during the years that the human crayfish casts off one shell after another. In Doctor Shields' own words in his directions to teachers:

> First Book is designed to serve as the child's first reader, but it has a far more important function than this to perform. It is, in fact, the child's first book along all the lines of his development. It is a reader, a nature study book, a book of instruction on home life, an elementary textbook of religion, an art book dealing with the three-fold root of the aesthetic faculty, viz., form, color, and rhythm. These five lines are not dealt with separately, but are woven into organic unity.

The instincts of the child are the starting point, but these are gradually transformed and guided in the task of equipping him for adjustment to a changing environment. Though Doctor Shields believed in the necessity of conquering environment, he emphasized that "it is a much greater privilege to be able to conquer oneself."

The growth of intelligence, the strength of muscle and the persistence of will power required to conquer environment have a value in themselves which is much higher than the value which they possess as a means of modifying the outer world. Nor does education concern itself alone with the development of these powers. It must aim at bringing about a multitude of subtle internal changes in feeling and emotion, in volition and insight, which are not immediately related to the outer world. . . . It has a still higher mission to transform the inner man and bring him into conformity with the ideal of perfect manhood revealed to us by Jesus Christ. Christian education should be conscious of its redeeming mission. It must never forget that its chief business is to transform a child of flesh into a child of God.

In his schoolbooks Doctor Shields applies these principles in detail. In his suggestions to teachers he writes:

The First Book is divided into five sections each one of which has for its aim the transformation of one of the instincts which helps to determine the child's dependence on its parents. The thought material in each of these parts is developed in a manner resembling a Gospel parable. The work begins with a nature story in which an attempt is made to lead the child into an understanding of some vital phenomenon, and thus lay the foundation of his future scientific development. In accordance with this aim, great care has been exercised in the selection of themes and in their mode of presentation as well as in accuracy of statement. These nature stories are intended to be dramatized. By this means the children are freed from detail and put into possession of a generalized truth which they may be led to apply elsewhere. The nature story is . . . developed as the basis of a parable which discloses its inner meaning in the lessons immediately following. . . . What he learns in the study of nature must find immediate and practical illustration in his home life. That which he dramatizes in his nature study he must put into actual living in his home.

The truth embodied in the nature story and in the home scene which follows it, is developed in the third part of each section in a religious instruction which in every case revolves around the person of Our Lord. These three parts of each section parallel the three elements usually found in Our Lord's parables.

"*Behold the lilies of the field*" is the analogue of the nature story; "*and which of you—if your son should ask for bread—would you reach him a stone*" is analogous to the domestic story in which parental love is the central theme; finally, "*How much more your Heavenly Father knows how to give good things to those who love Him*" is the analogue of the religious theme.

In all Our Lord's parables, as in the several sections of the first and second books, there is a progressive development of a central thought from a concrete setting to its abstract formulation, e.g., "*Seek ye first the kingdom of God and His justice and all these things will be added unto you.*"

This was the process by which a child of flesh was to be transformed into a child of God by a path as ingenious as it was direct.

The fundamental ideas of method involved are: to suit the form and substance of teaching to the needs of the child mind; to correlate religious truth with mental content and experience; to promote growth and assimilation according to the laws of natural development.

Coming down to specific detail, he writes:

> At the age of six the normal child is unable to deal with the abstract or with the complex but this does not justify the conclusion . . . that the child mind calls for the trivial and for the fragmentary. . . . Nothing is too big for the child mind if it is put in simple lines and it is only the big that interests him permanently. The thoughts that are presented to him in his first book should be the germs from which the whole of his conscious life will unfold as naturally as the plant unfolds from the seed.

And again:

> Everyone with the slightest experience knows that the child of six is unable to comprehend anything that is presented to him in abstract terms. That God is a Spirit that cannot be seen with bodily eyes; that He has one nature and three Divine Persons; that He created Heaven and earth and all things out of nothing—are statements quite beyond the child's grasp. He can reach a knowledge of God only through a knowledge of Jesus Christ. . . .
>
> In Religion First Book, the nature study and home scene . . . are so constructed as to prepare the child's mind directly and immediately for a knowledge of our Lord. . . . He must be presented to them in His humanity in order that their imaginations may lay hold of Him and their hearts may warm with love towards Him. But it is not less important that He be presented to them as He is, that is as God the Son, the Second Person of the Blessed Trinity through whom they are to gain a knowledge of God the Father, Creator of Heaven and earth.

Thus the home idea is utilized to bridge over the chasm between the human and the divine.

This was Our Lord's method who taught us to say "Our Father who art in Heaven." He taught us to ask of our Heavenly Father just those things, on a higher plane, that children are accustomed to ask of their earthly fathers, and He taught us to yield to our Heavenly Father that love and obedience which natural law exacts of every child towards his father.

The way in which the home idea is made to accomplish this end in Religion First Book, may be seen by examination of the lesson entitled "The Home of Jesus": "The birds have a pretty home in the trees. They are happy and sing sweet songs. We have a happy home with father and mother. We love it better than the robins love their nest. But the home of Jesus is more beautiful than our home. It is Heaven. Jesus came from Heaven where His Father lives. He came to show us the way there. When Jesus was on earth He lived in Nazareth."

Then immediately follows the response, the active side of this knowledge of Jesus:

A Welcome to Jesus

The birds welcome Jesus because His Father gives them their sweet songs.

His Father teaches them how to fly and how to build their nests.

He fills the hearts of the birds with love.

The trees wave a welcome to Jesus because His Father makes them big and strong.

The roses and lilies open their hearts to Him.

They fill the air with sweet smells because His Father sends them the sunshine and the rain.

Jesus loves the sunbeams and the breezes.
He loves the sky and the stars.
He loves the birds and the flowers.
He loves the sheep and their shepherd.
He loves all who work for others.
No one is so kind and gentle as Jesus.

A Secret

Wherever Jesus goes the people follow Him.
They are made glad whenever they hear His voice or
    look into His face.
He gives the secret which He brought from Heaven to
    every one who loves Him.
When we learn this secret we love one another.
Then joy grows in our hearts like a beautiful flower.
It fills our lives with sweetness.

Dramatizing the relation of the children to Jesus, they learn from his lips many of the truths (the "secrets") which will make of them good citizens of this world and prepare them for the world to come.

By the same developmental procedure, the food motive is carried through; from the robins feeding their little ones, to the family scene at the breakfast table and, finally, to the miraculous multiplication of the loaves and fishes by Jesus to feed the hungry crowds.

The rescue from danger motive moves from the robin saving her babies from the cat to the human mother saving her child from an excited gander and finally to Jesus saving Peter from the waves, and rescuing the apostles by commanding the storm to cease. The healing of the sick follows the same lines of development, and, finally, the original theme is sounded once more in a new tonality:

Jesus does not want us to live on earth always. He says
to us, My little children, love one another as I have loved

you. He says, be ye perfect as your Heavenly Father is perfect.

Our Heavenly Father loves us so that He wants us to be ready to live with Him. He knows that we cannot be happy in Heaven until we have learned how to live there.

He sent His only Son to be our model. Jesus became a little babe and grew into a man to show us how to live. If we try to be like Him we shall learn how to live in Heaven.

The Christmas scene is then introduced and the children begin to follow Jesus from his coming as a baby through various scenes of His life to be developed in future volumes. Each book is an organism—the ideas are connected psychologically and enriched by practical suggestions. The great fundamental notions are dramatized; they enter into the thought and activity of the children in their first school year. To give an adequate idea of the continuity and ingenuity of these ideas as embodied in the Shields Readers, we should carry these brief descriptions through the whole series, for there is not a thought to be found which has not been planted in the form of a seed in the first book. As with the crayfish, the shell has been cast off again and again, as each idea reappears in more developed form. In another chapter, we shall give some account of the effectiveness of these books when tested in the classroom. For the moment, we must say a word about Doctor Shields and his book reviews.

When a book was important, when it represented a trend that was likely to influence educational theory or practice in this country, Doctor Shields reviewed it at great length, quoting the author generously, then using the occasion to set forth sound doctrine as against the background of the false. An example was his total demolishment of the so-called

"Culture Epoch Theory" for the propagation of which, in our country, Doctor Stanley Hall and John Dewey were responsible, though it was their students who translated these doctrines into textbook form. The theory, today, is totally discredited and precisely on the scientific grounds upon which Doctor Shields attacked it. According to Hall, "The child learns and becomes adapted to practical life by passing through all stages through which the practical activities of the race have passed." These activities were "the highest type of culture which he can absorb." A series of textbooks appeared in Chicago, wherein the children were encouraged to practice and relive the primitive savagery of their presumed ancestors. To Doctor Shields this was "an error in transfer of thought and theory from biology to education" with pernicious effects. It was a confusion between matters of structure and of function. "Not one of the repeated or recapitulated structures which occur in embryonic life are destined to function. It is necessary to emphasize this truth that we may understand how wholly unwarranted is the application of this doctrine which is put forth in the Culture Epoch Theory." Whether the recapitulation theory is true or false as accepted in current biology, it lent no support to the application of the doctrine in education. The movement was already becoming discredited among those educators who had an adequate scientific training but, according to Doctor Shields, its ravages were felt by thousands of innocent children in the public schools of the United States.

"Those who have undertaken to carry this theory to its logical conclusion," wrote Doctor Shields, "are demanding that we set aside the child's social inheritance and frankly accept his physical inheritance as the guide to the development of his mental and moral life."

If Doctor Shields was severe in unmasking the dangerous

tendencies in pseudo-scientific textbooks, he was no less severe in dealing with the so-called Catholic textbooks which defied all pedagogical laws. His pen could raise a blister at every stroke.

With less important books, he flicked them away as one would chase an importunate fly from one's hand. Thus:

"The date of this textbook is 1920 and not 1820," was his caustic remark, and, after a summing up of the contents, he added: "The ordinary reader will hardly be impressed with a textbook whose chief recommendation seems to be the egotism and self-satisfaction of the author."

Books with scientific pretensions drew sparks from his pen:

> This is the usual clap-trap, betraying a complete igno-
> rance of physiology on the part of the authors and dis-
> torting the truth in the interests of what they conceive
> to be correct policy. Half-truths are worse than whole
> lies and these chapters are filled with half-truths.

Reviewing a book which accused the sciences of the day of materialism and of sapping the foundations of religious belief, he remarks:

> That there is all too much truth in this paragraph we
> may readily concede without committing ourselves to the
> view that the remedy is to be found in invective and
> abuse. Those who have in their custody the higher truths
> of salvation should be the leaders among those who have
> no other guidance than the uncertain light of human
> reason. If they have abandoned their posts, they cannot
> escape a share of the blame for the undesirable conse-
> quences. . . . There is a large body of men and women,
> both in the Church and outside its fold, who willingly
> and eagerly turn to those who have any truth to offer or

any light to shed upon the great problems of life here and hereafter. There is no disposition on their part to sneer at truths that they would listen to reverently if reverently and seriously advanced. And as for the others, the shallow, scoffing kind, who mistake sarcasm and ridicule for arguments,—who would waste a single brain cell on them, whether they call themselves Catholics, Protestants or infidels?

An "edifying" novel is dismissed with this flip:

> The incidents related constitute a bit of extravaganza and the love thread which runs through it is more wholesome than artistic.

A book on art draws forth these comments:

> He [the author] has cultivated the art of suggesting a train of thought and the restraint that prevents him from interfering with its natural course. The book has a message for those who have eyes to see and ears to hear, but its message must remain inaccessible to the untrained mind, to the thoughtless and to those who deal only with the obvious.

This caustic and, at times, ironic touch that appears in his book reviews and which, not inconceivably, gave offense, was wholly absent in his conversation. His humor was quick and subtle but he avoided wounding others, humiliating them or provoking a sense of inferiority. He had, on the contrary, that rare quality of making each person that came in contact with him feel himself more competent in leaving his presence than he had felt before coming. He stimulated his intelligence and brought out his best qualities. He had an immense tolerance for the opinions and even the failings of others. This appears in another book review from his pen:

Well meaning people who are over rigorous or who, instead of being animated by the broad tolerance of the Catholic Church, are controlled by the narrow bitterness of the Scribe and the Pharisee, or of the Jansenist, have always waged relentless war upon those of their fellow religionists who look upon human nature and its ways with kindlier eyes. . . . Nor need anyone be surprised to find that the abuse and recrimination was to be found on the side of the rigorists; the real Catholic is usually denounced and seldom does he denounce in return. It will be a consolation to many to realize that what they may have suffered in this respect has been the common experience of the great body of Catholics at all times and in all stations of life.

With this last phrase, which may contain a note of introspection, we close this chapter on the writings of Doctor Shields, which, to be appreciated, should be read in their continuity, for this author is not one from whom to quote, as are poets and litterateurs, nor a man whose phrases can be enjoyed fully out of their context, but a profound thinker who requires a reader's whole attention, ready to follow him in the fullness of his doctrine. Otherwise his message "must remain inaccessible to the thoughtless and to those who deal only with the obvious."

* ❧ *

CHAPTER TWENTY-TWO

VOICES OF CHILDREN

"EDUCATION is not a mere knowing or remembering; it is preeminently a matter of *doing*," wrote Doctor Shields. The classroom of his dream was not a prison where little children sat immobilized before desks "like so many little tombstones," but a scene of joyous activity. "The primary room," he wrote, "instead of being a quiet, sad place where little children fear to move lest they should disturb a nervous teacher or break in upon the profound train of thought whereby their young companions are learning to master the A.B.C.'s, presents a joyous, active scene." [1] Each child delighted in carrying out tasks that were exactly suited to his individual capacity. Some sat at low tables absorbed in modeling clay, drawing in colors or matching designs with little sticks as a basis for mathematics. Others worked at the board, writing action words or melodic themes. Music and rhythm animated the scene. Stories were dramatized and the children moved about the room freely, each child delighted with his or her assignment. The Teacher passed among them with motherly interest, encouraging, suggesting, criticizing, but keeping outside the domain of the "inner worker." It was a different picture, indeed, from that melancholy schoolroom of Shields' own childhood which had all but wrecked his life.

A new note had been sounded in Catholic education. God

[1] *Primary Methods*, p. 35.

245

had been "restored to His place in the textbook"; He was there, the center of all thought, all feeling, all activity; a glance at the new books made that clear. But something else had changed too. "The teacher is, of course, the most important factor in any schoolroom; if she is a failure, the rest matters little." [2] These teachers had been trained by Doctor Shields in his own Sisters College, for which he had worked so long and which was now a reality. They had gone out into the field as pioneers, enthusiastic for the work ahead.

The educational standards of the day in Catholic schools were based exclusively on content and, at best, on a logical plan of presentation. To Doctor Shields, content was as important and as carefully chosen, but his order of presentation was psychological. Moreover, the selection of material and the time of presentation was based upon the content of the child's mind, the child's interests and his capacity for understanding and applying. Thus, Doctor Shields fecundated the dry bones of knowledge, aiming, not at mere accumulation of known facts, not at mere information, but at the formation of mind and character.

In the State schools, modern principles of education had been tried with considerable success, but the children profited by the modern methods only to be led into a contempt for religion. The Catholic school authorities, horrified by the abuse of applied science in the public schools, reacted by clutching tightly to the dry letter of the law, to the memorized formula, to the unassimilated memory load, which developed neither the intelligence nor the will of the pupil.

In both camps the experiment of Doctor Shields was looked upon with curiosity but little sympathy. It was still in the realm of theory. Would it work? Doctor Shields was

[2] *Ibid.*, p. 76.

applying many of the same principles that were used in the public schools but his application was different. To him, all knowledge, whatever might be the specialized branch, was centered in God. All knowledge must be correlated. No isolated truth could function in a vital way, not even religion. Specialization had no place in the primary school; this was reserved for a later stage of education. In the primary school, all items of knowledge must be woven together like threads in a tapestry, the design of which would appear later. Due proportion must be maintained between the various subjects taught, that a proper balance in development be maintained. The task of the teacher was not to impose knowledge from without but to provide the proper material, to stimulate, guide, encourage the child's own efforts. Obviously such teaching required pedagogical skill of a high order. Nothing was to be taught that would not be put to immediate use by the child in his actual stage of development. The assimilation of a few great truths and the setting of these truths to work, was more important than a dead knowledge of many facts. Knowledge that set the will in motion, that gave it power and energy, was the aim of Doctor Shields. The capacity to read, to write, to spell, to count, were useful accessories of life but they were not life itself and should not be considered fundamentals in the educational process. Character—that was fundamental. Character depended on the power of the will guided by the intellect. The will itself had its motive power in the emotions. Hence the importance given by Doctor Shields to music and the other arts in the primary classroom.

"What progress did you make in music?" he asked some Sisters. They replied that there had been much illness in the schools that winter, and having fallen behind in the general subjects, there had been no time left for them to teach music.

And Doctor Shields' comment in telling the story startled his listeners: "Had they had the real interests of the children at heart, they would have dropped everything else, if necessary, but taught the music."

Since those early days when I first met Doctor Shields, a music course had been prepared which followed as closely as possible the pedagogical principles embodied in his other books. I had felt incompetent to undertake the work and we tried several more experienced authors, only to meet with the comment from Doctor Shields: "It is the same old rigid stuff!"—and the stuff was discarded as useless. Finally, in desperation, I offered to try to carry out his ideas and apply them myself to the field of music. "That is what I wanted from the start," he remarked. We worked in partnership as regarded the pedagogy, and I obtained precious collaboration from a Jesuit priest, Father J. B. Young, for the formation of the child voice and many problems of sight reading. Father Young was enthusiastic about the whole proposition. "You cannot refuse this task," he urged. "Think what this will mean for liturgical music with the prestige of the Catholic University behind this work for music in the schools." As the books appeared, and were tried in the schools, the results were satisfactory. Doctor Shields and I visited many of these schools together to check on the development of the work.

I shall never forget the first time I sat in a classroom with Doctor Shields while the children of the first grade dramatized his "Welcome to Jesus." There were tears in his eyes as he watched the babies playing around the statue of Our Lord. Here were the birds with their sweet songs, flying with rhythmic gestures; here were the trees waving a welcome to Jesus and the roses and lilies opening their hearts to Him; here were the sheep and the shepherd—and one little

boy had insisted upon being the shepherd's dog! The drama-
tization was so spontaneous and naive that the children
revealed the contents of their innocent hearts in every loving
gesture and in the song "A Welcome to Jesus" which
sprang from baby lips. Doctor Shields could not speak
when it was over; he was too deeply moved. He had written
—yes but here was the realization:

> The first task of education is to bring the emotional
> life of the child . . . into subjection to law and under
> the control of the intelligence. Reading, writing and
> arithmetic are only tools, the skilled use of which will be
> helpful throughout life, but it is utterly absurd to think
> of them as fundamental. It is music and art which consti-
> tute the enduring foundations of education, and not the
> three R's. When this truth is forgotten it is not surpris-
> ing that the effects of education are seen to be superficial
> and unsatisfactory.

And again he wrote:

> Next to the teaching of religion, the teaching of music
> and art constitutes the most important work in the
> elementary school. . . . The real foundations of character
> are not to be found in the intellect but in the emotions
> and the will properly enlightened through the intellect,
> and it is through music and art that the imagination and
> the emotions may be reached and effectively developed.

His theories had fallen on dull ears in a decade when
music was supposed to be a fad or an accomplishment for
the privileged few. He had written and he had talked, and
here, at last, was the realization of his dream. As we moved
from room to room, he saw happy, interested children,
active, responsive, working out their own problems, concentrated, enthusiastic. His whole being responded to the

sight and he was speechless as on the day when the grubbing machine had succeeded. But this dream had been long in coming true.

The diocese of Cleveland had been among the first to adopt the Shields Methods. The superintendent of education, Doctor Kane, had been formed for his task at the Catholic University and had, in turn, formed the local teachers. The new books were introduced into the first grade of each school, no changes being made in the other classes in order that results might be compared. Doctor Shields waited eagerly for the report of the first year's work. "The method surpassed our fondest expectations," wrote Doctor Kane. "The children of the First Grade are thinkers." They knew more about their religion than the pupils of the fourth and fifth grades who had been taught by the rigid question-answer system. The things of God had been made beautiful, joyful, in a form that they could understand. These results had been obtained with a technique that was new to all the teachers. Yet, though in the beginning the cry of "new-fangled ideas" and doubts as to success were heard, the work had been a pleasure to teachers and pupils. Regarding the music, Doctor Kane wrote.

> What these children have accomplished in the reading of notes astonished the audience (composed of all the diocesan teachers). Their accuracy in writing on the board melodies which were dictated by their teacher was something many an adult might have emulated.

During the first few months, parents wondered what the children were doing. There were no books in sight. Were they merely playing? They were learning to use their minds and the next months showed the results of that slow preparation. By the end of the year, the first-grade children were the attraction of every school.

The second year was even more convincing as Doctor Kane's letters revealed:

> Astonishing results were obtained in sense training, dramatization and singing. A test in reading was given to some children in the second grade. . . . Two were given Third Readers, books they had never seen, and were asked to prepare a lesson. Three minutes were allowed for this preparation. Then each child in turn stood before the 650 teachers and read the lesson with an understanding that could not be denied. . . . The last child told a long story after preparation lasting five minutes. Not a detail was omitted.
>
> These children had not been drilled in this, nor did they know they would be called upon for such a test. I dared to make the test because I felt certain that our method of teaching reading compels the child to see in words only symbols expressing thought, and that when the thought is suitable for his years, he will have very little difficulty with words at the end of the second grade.

Each year, the reports from Cleveland grew more enthusiastic. The teachers were entirely won over to the new educational process. As for the children: "The children of the primary grades are thinkers and they can talk," wrote the superintendent. "In regard to Religion the children are familiar with a great part of the Old and New Testaments and can answer readily, not in the language of dry formulae, but in their own words, questions of Christian doctrine that come under the assignment. They have a better understanding of the matter than those children who have only studied the catechism."

> In music, I have found that the children of the third grade master in ten minutes exercises for which those of the eighth grade require an hour.

2

The teachers are delighted with the Series. In the beginning they were doubtful. The books seemed very difficult and the method was strange. Now the teachers confess that the results are far superior to anything of the past.

And he concluded:

I am convinced that nothing in the educational field will contribute more to the honor and glory of God and the salvation of souls than the Catholic Education Series properly handled in our schools.

We have quoted the news from Cleveland at some length because it was the first diocese to organize the work on a vast scale and to send in detailed reports of progress to the author of the books. But the isolated schools sent in their comments from all parts of the country. From Texas, a Sister wrote:

We find our second grade pupils better readers—better students in every way—than the present fourth grade pupils.

and the principal of a school in Michigan wrote:

It would do your heart and soul good to see the wonders that are being achieved by your readers and Sisters' teaching. . . . The children in the second, third and fourth grades surpass in their reading and in their powers of expression and interpretation, the children of the sixth grade who have not had the benefit of your method. Many of the second grade children read fluently from any ordinary story book or even from the fourth Reader.

Success is contagious. Attention was attracted all over the continent. Pittsburgh, one of the largest dioceses in the

United States, adopted the books, and the history of the
Shields Method in Pittsburgh was a replica of its success in
Cleveland. The superintendent of education at that time
was Doctor Ralph M. Hayes.[3] During the third year that
the books were in use, he wrote in answer to an inquiry:

> When the Readers are taught according to the
> Method, they have given the greatest satisfaction. Where
> the teachers did not prepare seriously for the work or
> attempted to teach by a conflicting method, they did not
> meet with the results expected.

This remark is one that hit the crux of the matter. Teacher
training had to precede the use of the system and Doctor
Shields, himself, feared diocesan adoptions of his books lest
the essential training be lacking. Doctor Hayes, after citing
instances of the amazing results obtained where the system
was properly taught, continued:

> Community supervisors write to me in this strain:
> "The majority of our first grade teachers are more than
> satisfied, they are enthusiastic. The subject matter . . .
> could not be improved. The method, its arrangement
> and presentation, all appeal to the children. . . . They
> are encouraged to think and to express their thoughts by
> word and action and song and art work. They are al-
> ways ready to respond, so ready, indeed, that at times it
> is difficult to curb their enthusiasm . . . !" You know
> that the Second Book is not an easy one, yet I have seen
> Polish and Slavic children who came to school almost
> entirely ignorant of the English language, after one year's
> training in the Method, handle that Second Reader with
> ease and even with an understanding that no one can
> doubt. . . . The Religious studies have been equally

[3] Later, Bishop of Helena, Montana, then Rector of the North America
College in Rome and now Bishop of Davenport, Iowa.

successful. While there is no cut-and-dried question-answer teaching, the children acquire a wonderfully exact knowledge of their faith and a remarkably extensive grasp of Bible history. Religion is made a live thing to the children.

Many letters that reached Doctor Shields, during those years, commented on the development of the children's imagination and powers of expression as well as the ethical applications which the children themselves drew from the material presented in the books. Doctor Shields never wished the moral of a story to be pointed out; it must be so embodied in the story that the children would discover it like a hidden treasure. Among the examples, we quote the following:

The second grade children were deeply impressed by Father Tabb's little poem:

"Thou hast fallen," said the Dewdrop
   To a sister drop of rain,
"But wilt thou, wedded to the dust,
   In banishment remain?"
"Nay, Dewdrop, but anon with thee,
   The lowlier born I,
Uplifted, shall I seek again
   My native home, the sky."

After they had finished reading the poem, a little girl looked up into Sister's face and said: "I was the little rain drop when I missed Mass last Sunday." It is a constant source of wonder to me to see how deeply impressed these babies are with the stories. Their dramatizations are wonderful and their compositions are unlike anything we have ever had before. . . . Sister had a hard time in convincing me that these stories were all written without any help from her.

We have heard from the superintendents and teachers. Let us listen, now, to the voices of the children. The first to speak is a little girl who was seven and a half years old at the time. She draws from the pen of Doctor Shields this comment:

> The little girl in question exhibits just such a knowledge of religion as we hoped would be imparted by the use of our method. By the time this little girl shall have passed through the work of the fourth grade, she will find no difficulty in gaining a clear understanding of the formulations of the catechism.

The incident, which is vouched for by Doctor Kane, was recorded by the child's teacher:

> Last Thursday during the noon recreation, I noticed a number of high school girls grouped around a little child from the third grade. She was amusing the girls by telling them the story of Zan and Bobo.[4] Finally, coming to that part of the story where Zan's pride leads her to wish to be like God, the little girl told this part of the story with a great deal of indignation, shaking her head over the dreadfulness of Zan's pride. The girls were much amused by the child's earnestness and thought it a good chance to draw her out.
>
> "Well, Marie, why was that so bad in Zan? If she were good, couldn't she be like God?"
>
> "Of course not," promptly answered Marie. "She couldn't possibly be good enough to be God."
>
> "But Sister over there—she's good. Couldn't she be God?"
>
> "No, she couldn't. Even the Pope couldn't be good enough. Besides, there can be only one God and He is so good that nobody could ever be nearly that good."

[4] A story from Shields' *Third Reader*.

At this point, the Sister joined the group and she said:

"Tell me, Marie, who is next to God?" When asking the question, she had in mind the Blessed Virgin, but the child's answer took her breath away:

"Why the Son of God as man."

"Where does the Son of God live?"

"He lives in Heaven and in the little tabernacle in the Church."

"But the tabernacle is such a little house."

"Yes, I know," she hastened to assure us, "but He doesn't mind that because He takes the form of a tiny white Host. It isn't a Host, though (and she kept shaking her head to emphasize the fact) but it looks like one. It is really Our Lord."

"Why did Jesus take that form?"

"Because He loved us and wanted to be with us."

"Marie, perhaps you can tell these girls how much Jesus loves little children?"

She then told the story of Christ blessing the little children and she dwelt with such fondness on the description of the little girl on His lap [5] that I thought it a good chance to test her further.

"That is a beautiful story, Marie. Wouldn't you love to have been that little girl on the knee of Jesus?"

"Yes indeed," she answered, and then, after a moment's thought, "But you know, Sister, we can get much closer than that little girl."

"How, Marie?"

"Why, in Holy Communion. He comes right into our hearts, and that's closer than being on His knee."

With that, Marie ran off to join her playmates. The older girls, impressed when the teacher told them that any child in the class could have answered as well as Marie, asked:

[5] A picture illustrating the story in *Religion First Book.*

"What catechism do they study, Sister?"

"They have not had any catechism; religion comes into all their work."

Another child, this time in Pittsburgh, speaks next. The story was recorded by a parish priest.

I was examining the children in one of my primary rooms to determine which of them might be allowed to make their First Communion. There was present a little girl younger and smaller than her classmates. I decided that she was too young to go to Communion with the others and told her that she would have to wait till the next time. Leaving the school, I met this little girl in the corridor, crying bitterly. I picked her up, set her on the radiator and inquired solicitously concerning the cause of her tears. Through her sobs, I learned that her grief was caused by my postponement of her first Holy Communion . . . I said:

"My child, you do not know what Holy Communion is."

"Yes I do, Father! In Holy Communion, Jesus comes to live in our hearts."

"What would you do if I gave you Holy Communion?"

She replied instantly: "I would love Him! I would love Him!"—and she illustrated with her little arms how fondly she would embrace the welcome Guest.

Signs and symbols seemed to vanish in a faith so vivid that the child contemplated Jesus Himself (not "it" but "Him") as she spoke of the Blessed Sacrament, and lifted her heart to Our Saviour in all the majesty and sweetness of His personality.

Similar instances of the love of little children for Our Lord fostered by the use of his books reached Doctor

Shields from every side. Week by week the evidence came
in. "All that we had dared to hope for and more," wrote
Doctor Shields, "has been achieved."

It was not only in the field of religion that Doctor
Shields' methods were triumphing. They were giving
amazing results in general education. A specimen of the
work of a child in the fourth grade of a school in Cleveland
is given in the Appendix [6] which illustrated concretely the
results of true education as Doctor Shields conceived it. The
mind, the heart, the soul, the emotions were all active and
all united. History, geography, ethics, religion were all correlated. As these reports came in, Doctor Shields tasted at
last that peculiar joy that comes to the dreamer when his
dream takes life. He had met that supreme test of genius:
he had presented great fundamental truths to little children
in such a manner that those truths had been understood,
assimilated and utilized in the growing structures of their
minds and in the development of their characters. The
voices of children were bringing to their unknown champion the assurance that his heart craved.

His work had been conceived in faith. He might take to
himself in a special sense the words of St. Augustine: "Credo
ut intelligam," words that were "true in the natural order
and in the supernatural," as he had remarked himself.
"Always faith ceases in vision and man attains to no vision
which has not unfolded from a germ of faith."

[6] Appendix III, p. 294.

* ✿ *

CHAPTER TWENTY-THREE

ON THE HOME
STRETCH

A T that time, there were more than six thousand
Catholic schools in the United States, educating a
million and a half children. The number was constantly increasing but the schools lacked system, the thirty
thousand teachers lacked adequate training. Teacher training had been, from the beginning and remained until the end
the leit-motif of the Teachers' Champion. When the first
group of Sister-students graduated with honors in 1912, his
optimism knew no bounds. He wrote:

> I feel that the long fight has been won. The record of
> the eighteen Sisters who took their degrees on the 5th
> inst. has gone out to the whole United States and has
> made a tremendous impression. This is the sort of thing
> that will give confidence to our people and make them
> realize the qualifications of our religious teachers.

It was only a beginning, but the Sisters College was to
solve the problem by training leaders for the whole country.

In the spring of 1913, the Catholic University conferred
the degree of Bachelor of Arts on twenty-three Sisters and
the degree of Master of Arts on twenty-four. The required
credits had been obtained in part by correspondence work,
in part during summer sessions and, finally, during a year of
residence in Washington. These Sisters were the pioneers in

a long line of Catholic teachers who peopled the daydream of Doctor Shields and for whom he had won the privilege of obtaining higher education without the sacrifice of their religious principles. Each summer session surpassed the previous ones in the number of those who attended and in the extent of the work accomplished. The University professors generously made the sacrifice of their time, doubling their teaching hours in order to help the Sisters.

The students, in 1913, came from forty-eight dioceses, from twenty-nine States and from the Dominion of Canada. Doctor Shields kept in constant correspondence both with the Superiors of the religious orders and with the individual students. His advice was always on the side of action. To a Sister who sent him eight pages of hesitations and worries, he answered: "I would advise you to quit fretting and come down here and get to work." Difficulties never bothered him. There was always a solution.

During the summer of 1913, he gave his usual lectures, attended to his duties as Dean, and gave his personal attention to the most minute details of physical and spiritual comfort of the students. He was a man who found it difficult to turn over to others, who would willingly have helped him, the routine details of the days. The result was to be foreseen. By the end of the summer session, August 6th, his health was visibly breaking. For the first and only time in his life, Doctor Shields allowed himself a real vacation. It was none too soon. He took a slow steamer, the *Prince Adelbert*, and with a few colleagues from the University, he sailed for Europe. From the boat, he wrote to his mother, then in her 98th year, under date of August 19th:

Dear Mother,
    We are passing through the English Channel today. We expect to sight the Isle of Wight in a few minutes.

We have had a beautiful trip thus far. No one was sick and the weather was delightful.

We left Philadelphia at eleven o'clock Thursday morning, August 7th, and expect to reach Hamburg Thursday morning, August 21. Every minute of our time has been restful. . . . We purpose to leave Hamburg in a few hours to go to Cologne, thence up the Rhine to Bonn, Mainz, to Basle in Switzerland. We will travel about the Swiss lakes for a few days and then go over the mountains to Northern Italy where we will visit Milan, Verona, Venice, Bologna, Florence, Pisa, Genoa, thence along the Riviera to Marseilles where we must be on September 13, our day of sailing. I will send you cards along the way.

I hope you are quite recovered by this time. I am looking forward anxiously to seeing you which I hope will be some time in October. May God bless you and make you well and happy.

Your loving son,
Tom

The schedule could hardly be considered restful unless on the theory that a change of activity is the only form of rest possible to a busy man. The party survived the rest and reached the United States late in September completely out of funds. The Customs had gathered in their last dollars for duty on a picture that had captured the heart of Doctor Shields, who wanted it for the children's books. Doctor Murphy found the party engaged in animated discussion as to how to spend their last pennies—whether on lunch or fare to Washington. His presence made a more comfortable solution possible.

Late in July Doctor Shields had received my manuscript for the first volume of our music series for the elementary schools. He turned the manuscript over to the printer hoping to find the proof ready on his return from Europe. He found the whole thing in a mess. The pages containing staff exercises had been cut up that these might be set up by a music printer and no record had been kept of the place where these examples belonged. Humiliated at this mistake, and not wanting me to be worried by it, Doctor Shields set to work himself to decide from the context where each example belonged. What followed was characteristic. He had not told me at the time, but admitted later, that he had never liked the idea of the number notation to represent tones. He saw in this system merely a duplication and he felt that the children should not be taught two symbols for the same sound, the number and the note on the staff. Due to the printer's error and his self-assigned task of fitting the staff exercises in their proper place, Doctor Shields realized that the numerals were not a duplication but the key to the whole art of staff reading. He became an enthusiast of the number notation and explained his conversion with a hearty laugh at himself. Incidentally, when the proof came through to me, every staff exercise was in its proper place.

Doctor Shields did not consider himself a musician. He could play no instrument nor could he sing a tune. I found him, however, a most intelligent critic, and no one wrote more profoundly of the influence of music in education than he. As an example of his penetrating criticism: I remember his telling me that the rigid gesture by which we used to beat time in the old days distressed him. Children should develop a rhythmic sense by large, free gestures of the arms, preferably by movements of the whole body. The small, restricted movements should come later. It was not until many years later that I discovered the wonderful system of chironomy invented by Dom Mocquereau of Solesmes for the direction of Gregorian Chant, and found that this plas-

tic system of curves could be applied to the rhythmic training of little children, giving them their first impressions of
rhythm through just the means that Doctor Shields had
desired—large, free movements from the shoulder, rising
and falling of the whole body. He had been right both
pedagogically and musically.

Long before the liturgical revival of our day, Doctor
Shields had been a pioneer in this direction. Before undertaking the music work, I had asked him whether it was part
of his plan to bring the school children into the liturgical
singing. Of course, he had answered, that was the ultimate
aim. His fourth book centered around the Mass. Could I
bring the children to the Gregorian Chant by that time? I
found by experience that we could do so even earlier.
In 1920 Doctor Shields had the long-awaited joy of
hearing ten thousand little children succeeding each other
for three days, filling the huge Cathedral of St. Patrick in
New York with their young voices. It was on the occasion
of the International Congress of Gregorian Chant at which
Dom Mocquereau himself was present. Here were the first
fruits of our music series.

With what kindness, patience and humor he had watched
over the education of his collaborator! A vivid memory
comes to mind. I was worried because Doctor Shields expected this series to be taught by grade teachers and not
by music teachers. These Sisters, presumably with no training in music, how could they teach music to children? The
subject came up again when courses in music were to be
given the Sisters. It was difficult to teach those who knew
nothing of music. His face lighted up with amusement:

"Are you sure they know nothing of music?" he asked.

"Oh yes, quite sure. They know absolutely nothing!"

"Then you can teach them nothing."

By that time I knew him well enough to expect an explanation, and it came. He had been drawing me out in view of making me understand that nothing could be taught to anyone except by connecting it with something already in the mind. The first task of the teacher was to find out what was there to build on. In the case of music, was it possible that these teachers could not hear the difference between a very loud sound and a very soft one? Between a sound that was very long and one that was very short? Between the timbre of a stringed instrument and that of a trumpet or drum? All these crude notions were there and the art of the teacher was to engraft upon them more delicate distinctions in regard to pitch, timbre, duration, rhythm. When Doctor Shields gave a lesson it was not easily forgotten. I give this one as an example among many of the way in which he formed, little by little, the one whom he had honored by selecting her as partner in the work.

There was no detail too troublesome to merit Doctor Shields' personal attention. When the Sisters began to clamor for charts embodying the singing exercises which they had no time to transfer to the blackboard, Doctor Shields came on to New York himself and measured out each line, making diagrams for the printer that the music might successfully be transferred from books to charts. For three days he worked over this affair as though he had no other responsibility in life. When I protested, he answered: "This is a real vacation for me!"

The books were well received by critics with one notable exception. A Bishop who had given his endorsement to a public-school music method on condition that the firm should add a Gregorian Chant supplement, wrote to Doctor Shields in no uncertain terms of his indignation at the appearance of a music course as part of the Catholic Education series. The Bishop was a member of the Board of Trustees of the University. He was difficult to soothe. Indeed he was never soothed at all. When the Bishop of Cleveland retired in 1920, this very bishop succeeded him. He remembered his grievance. An ultimatum was sent to Doctor Shields to the effect that the Ward music must be dropped in the diocese if the Shields Methods were to be retained. The Bishop's favorite music course must be substituted. Had Doctor Shields been willing to compromise on this point, his books would have remained in use in the diocese. But he felt that the music was an intrinsic part of the success of the whole method and refused to bend to the Bishop's ultimatum. The Shields Methods were thrown out of the diocese over night. Doctor Kane, superintendent of education, was sent to a country parish, and relieved of his educational work. In all this tragedy, this clash of human passions higher up, who thought of the thousands of innocent children in the classrooms of Cleveland, doomed to be cut off like spring buds about to blossom? Who thought of these children robbed of food for the imagination, from whom had been snatched away that beauty which their aesthetic faculties craved? Who cared when the little ones were imprisoned, once more, in the land of mechanized tombstones? No one, perhaps, but the little ones themselves, the teachers and the man who had rescued them once but was now compelled to keep silence in his grief. He had seen his work succeed, had witnessed the breaking down of prejudice, the triumph of the truth in the minds of teachers, pastors and children. With one stroke of the pen the work had been slain for a whole diocese.

From the year 1914, Doctor Shields' health had been visibly breaking. Mentally, he was at the peak of his power, but physically, he could but recognize that he was paying the debt of long years of excessive work and worry. On the surface, he seemed to hold out for a few years more while the pressure increased on every side. Success was his; he had the confidence of the heads of the religious orders and could, as he put it, "do more good in five minutes than formerly in a six weeks' course." Indeed, many of the present Superiors were his own students. Unfortunately, however, the world was not made up of his former students. There were opponents as well as collaborators around him. Evidently, a man of Doctor Shields' energy and driving force is not a comfortable man to have at your elbow if you are not in a hurry.

In every forward step he had taken, Doctor Shields had felt himself pushed by necessity. Each need had been so obvious that he was forced to act. Others, indeed, admitted the necessity, but quite a long time after it had been pointed out by him. The strain for Doctor Shields was represented by that interval—by those weeks, months or years—that elapsed between the date when he felt forced to act and the date when that action was approved by higher authority. He was self-possessed and calm externally at a great cost to himself, for he was far from being insensitive. When, occasionally, his hot Irish temper burst out in a flash, it left devastation behind it as the colder temperaments of his associates froze into a state of permanent resentment. Yet he was forced to move forward. He knew that his days were numbered and he took action without counting the cost to himself. While others weighed, analyzed, dissected, his quick synthetic mind had translated thought into decision and decision into action. It was this characteristic, combined with an exceptionally clear vision, that explains his whole career and his impact on other minds. Some admired this leader of thought, this innovator, this dynamo. Others found it uncomfortable to live in his immediate radius. His ceaseless activity was a silent reproach to their own inertia. His arguments were unanswerable but his energy was intolerable.

St. Augustine and St. Jerome had their moments of friction. In more modern times, Cardinals Newman and Manning were in open opposition. Ideas had something to do with these differences but temperament was, perhaps, a fundamental element. In the case of Doctor Shields, ideas were not the principal cause of his troubles. One of his chief enemies, in later years, was a man who shared his ideals and ideas more closely than any man living. What separated the two men was a matter of temperament. Differences of speed were but part of the friction. There was this and more. "Saul slew his thousands and David his ten thousands" had been the song of those imprudent girls when the head of Goliath fell, and, from that very hour, David's life was in danger. Silence would have served him better. The very distinction of a man's services can play him strange tricks. Success is a treasure to hide as long as possible. When it bursts forth it may play the part of a bomb.

Each year new volumes from the pen of Doctor Shields stretched out along the bookshelves of the University. Yet minds more brilliant in academic estimation were producing little or nothing. Shields was employing architects, landscape gardeners; buildings were rising on the right hand and on the left. Shields was known through his lectures and books in every corner of the vast continent, students were flocking to his courses, his name was on many lips, he was praised and admired. Rome had singled him out for approval; the Holy Father Pius X had sent a personal gift of money for his Sisters College. The Apostolic Delegate was telling all who cared to listen that Shields was doing the most important work of the century for the Church. Why Shields? Were there no other prophets in Israel?

And such books—hastily written, dictated to a type-writer, lacking polish and literary style! Others polished and re-polished their phrases and when their works were published, if published they were, they received little attention from the public at large. How mediocre was the space occupied by these works on the library shelves compared to the endless output from the pen of the prolific Shields! His books succeeded each other with exasperating frequency. The last was a Philosophy of Education, the first book in English to treat this subject from the Catholic standpoint. Once more, why Shields? Were there no other men at the University who could have treated such a subject with more competency? And the *Educational Review*, and the publishing house—where would all this activity end? Was the man a millionaire to launch all these projects and carry them through without involving the University in debt? Where, in short, did the money come from?

Why should Doctor Shields live in a spacious house of his own surrounded by shrubs and vines and flowers? Why on the Sisters College campus should convents spring up like mushrooms? Had he been wrong to push through these projects? Were the ideas unsound? No. Doubtless he had been right, but what was the hurry? Why look so far ahead? The Church was working for eternity. Why persistently think of tomorrow when one could more comfortably think of yesterday, or, if need be, of today? Men can accept a *fait accompli* if they must, and resent it. Who likes to have his hand forced?

Crops of red tape abound in big institutions. What is easier than to fetter a disturber of the peace with mazes of red tape? Let him cut his way out if he can. Some shreds will stick and hamper his forward movement. Energy will be consumed. Time will be gained and the slower-moving minds will set the pace.

Suddenly, this man of dynamite requires more land. His keen eye has discovered a farm in the immediate vicinity of the College which must be purchased to protect the Sisters City from the ravages of real estate operators, to save it from undesirable neighbors. The farm, he insists, could be made to pay for itself in crops and food for the students. The land was about to slip into the hands of agents. The utmost haste was demanded. Again Doctor Shields took matters into his own hands, mortgaged his home and the good will of his publishing house, in order to borrow the purchase price. He used the name of a third party to conceal the identity of the real purchaser. To one of the most prominent bankers in Washington he announced: "I must have this loan today." Impossible; such a sum could not be loaned without an action of the board of directors. When would they meet? Next week. No, that would be too late. The transaction must be concluded at once, that very hour. And it was. When all the documents had been signed and the money was in hand, Doctor Shields drew from his pocket a map which showed the piece of land he was purchasing. The banker put on his glasses, looked, and drew back in amazement and disgust:

"Why that is the very piece of land that I have been trying to purchase myself. Do you mean to tell me that I have loaned you the money to buy that farm?" The affair ended in a hearty laugh, for the banker was a good fellow and could appreciate a joke, even at his own expense.

The Board of Trustees of the University, for its part, was not going to be pushed into any hasty decision. They resisted on principle. The Rector would have none of this land. A painful interval followed, one of those which contributed to the breaking down of the health of Doctor

Shields. He was deeply hurt, this time, and embarrassed financially. How could he carry the interest on the debt? These were bitter days. He said little, but his vitality was put to a heavy strain. Ultimately, the Trustees reversed themselves and the land was turned over to the College.

Inertia can turn, by imperceptible stages, into resentment. No one thought of throwing a spear to pin this modern David against the wall. Yet what was dearer to him than his life was endangered. The slower partner was winning the race. One can be slow yet subtle. One can be frank and guileless even though rapid. Accumulated resentments can pile up unnoticed. There had always been a group of men at the University who were unfavorably disposed toward the movement initiated by Doctor Shields. He and Doctor Pace had won their battle while their forces were united. And now, with a sudden shock, Doctor Shields realized that the Board of Trustees had become antagonistic to his plans, perhaps to his person. When he sought approval for some matter of detail, of mere routine, he was met at worst with a refusal, at best with delay. It reached a point, as he told me in a rare moment of expansion, that when he needed an action by the Board, he had to argue from the opposite point of view. Then, thinking to oppose him, these men granted what he needed.

From 1916, until his death, Doctor Shields was seriously ill with valvular heart trouble. When we made our last trip together for a Teachers Institute in Pittsburgh, he had to rest flat on his back before and after each lecture. The doctor had warned him about the gravity of his condition, insisting that he should cut down his work. He, himself, had no illusions about his condition but to cut down his work was impossible. The only thing he could give up was the Ford car. He had suffered many a heart attack cranking that old machine by hand. Yes, he would give up the Ford and buy an electric car that needed no cranking. The new machine gave him no physical strain as it went dashing around corners as gallantly as its predecessor. Meanwhile, he grew thin and gray. The heart attacks came more frequently. He knew that his years were counted, perhaps they were numbered by months rather than years. The nervous tension of the Washington situation undoubtedly shortened his life. But the necessary things must be carried through to completion no matter what might be the cost. It pained him to seek by devious paths the approvals which were his due. It pained him more deeply still to realize that the source of the opposition was a man who had been his close friend and collaborator, a man for whom he had a profound admiration and for whom he never lost his deep affection, one whose ideas ran parallel to his own. Why this opposition, why this studied antagonism? With all his psychology, Doctor Shields never suspected the reason. It is perhaps true that hatred and love are close of kin. On the part of Doctor Shields, his love for his slower partner never wavered. Even when he realized at last how matters stood—and he was slow to believe it—he avoided all criticism and, as much as possible, all mention of the friend of earlier days. For the loss of his friend was more painful by far than any complications caused by the organized opposition. Doctor Shields kept this sorrow to himself. It was the greatest trial of his last years, the most profound sorrow, perhaps, of his whole life, touching as it did, his work and wounding his generous heart.

On his death bed, Doctor Shields was to receive a visit from his old friend. At so solemn a time, mediocrity disappears. Assuredly, the two men parted friends.

★ ❀ ★

CHAPTER TWENTY-FOUR

ECCE QUOMODO MORITUR JUSTUS

"SOME men die of their own death, others of their entire life." [1] Doctor Shields was one of these last. He had never spared himself in the pursuit of truth nor in its generous communication to others. He did not spare himself after the mortal malady which he carried in his breast was known to him and was gaining ground each month, each week. There were still many things to be accomplished. What could it matter whether they were done quickly in a short life or more slowly in a life that petered out? He was too deeply involved as leader in the rush of events he had himself set in motion to draw back now or even to reduce the speed. With a word, today, he could guide where before he had had to persuade. It was the time of golden harvest.

In the electric car that needed no cranking he drove with the dash and distraction of old; up through the country lanes, muddy and bumpy, that led to the Sisters College, he bounced and skidded with never an instant to waste. When the Summer School, the last one for him, had ended he was in a condition where only a hospital would have been adequate. But he had promised to visit me in the Adirondacks for three weeks of complete rest. He took the train.

For some days, I had been expecting a letter or a telegram.

[1] Charles Péguy.

His little house was ready close to the lake and shaded by giant trees. But the message never came. Instead, one morning, before sunrise, I heard the sound of oars in the distance, looked out, and saw a guide boat approaching with Doctor Shields sitting in the stern. He had traveled all night with a mind so intent on arriving, on getting the rest he so sorely needed, that he had totally forgotten to notify me of the day and hour of his coming.

That he was very ill was all too evident. His heart attacks were frequent and terrifying. He paid little attention to them himself and tried to hide them from me. When he managed to get his breath, he was the same delightful companion as ever. He was as full of projects as though he were just beginning his life instead of facing death. As we sat looking across the lake to the distant hills, he described in detail the eight books that were composed in his mind and were simply waiting there to be dictated to a typewriter— if only he could find the time to dictate them and someone to take his dictation. His old secretary had broken under the years of strain and had become a nervous wreck. Could no one else replace her? Materially, yes, but it would be too painful a humiliation for the old woman to be set aside, she who had come to his rescue in the early days when no one else believed in him. To pension her or retire her would be cruel, for she felt herself a part of the work, had spent herself for its sake. Now that she had become a liability, in a sense a menace to his own work and health, nothing would persuade him to set her aside as a war casualty. It would be unjust. Finally a bit of diplomatic charity was the cause of my being present with Doctor Shields during the last months of his life and at his death. He begged me to take the top floor of his house in Washington, bring my secretary and lend her to him for the dictation of those eight books.

This could be done, he thought, without putting aside his old assistant.

The eight books were to contain the development into specialized lines of activity of those germinal concepts contained in his elementary books. They would represent those enlarged circles of ideas restated for minds in more advanced stages of development. The core of his method existed, and was working wonders. Yet, it was only the seed, at best, the central trunk of the great tree the branches of which must appear in due time. Who would complete his work if he died now? Doctor McCormick had been close to him for many years but was too busy. There was one man of whom he spoke often, Doctor George Johnson, one of his most promising students. Doctor Shields was watching him with keen interest and hope. He was working over problems of modern education, was young, energetic and sympathetic to the Shields movement. Perhaps he could carry on the work and complete the needed books. But in reality, Doctor Shields still thought he would have time to finish them himself.

The weeks at camp slipped by. The work at Washington began. Of course the eight books were never dictated. The struggle was appalling to get through the essential duties of each day. First there was Holy Mass at six-thirty. That, he never missed until he went to bed never to rise. After Mass, he rested flat on his back before starting off to give his eight o'clock lecture at the Sisters College, fasting still, lest nourishment should bring on a heart attack. When he appeared on the lecture platform of *Sedes Sapientiae*, the portable hall, no one could have guessed that he was a dying man. He was full of life, energy, wit and enthusiasm. Returning from his lecture, gasping for breath, he rested for another hour before taking a light breakfast. He never missed his lectures at the University nor his weekly seminars with his students though each of these activities had to be prepared and followed by a rest flat on his back. How painfully he came up the long flight of steps that led from the street to his house and then climbed those to the second floor where he lived. Resting after each step, gasping for breath, he was a painful sight for those who watched the final months of a heroic life.

There was the new farm, too. It must be made a success. Here the one-time farmer was in his element. He kept in close touch, metaphorically and literally, for, ill as he was, he had to have his hands in the mixture for the silo, he had to determine which soil would adapt itself to which crop. The Italian farmer stood open-mouthed in amazement as the dignified Dean of the Sisters College stooped down, picked up a handful of soil, felt it and said: "Here, Louis, we shall plant potatoes," then gathering another handful of dirt in a far corner of the field, "Here is the place for the corn." By what magic, Louis wondered, did the crops always succeed just as the Doctor had prophesied? The Doctor was always right, at least as regarded the crops.

But there was a tug of war between the two men. It was about a tree. In a corner of one of the richest fields of farming land there stood a great elm, a giant of noble proportions. Shields, the farmer, knew as well as Louis that the tree interfered with the ploughing. Shields, the inventor of the grubbing machine, knew exactly what ought to be done about it. Shields, the artist, knew that its beauty made it safe. "We will plough all around that tree," he said to the reluctant Louis, who knew that the Doctor was always right except as regarded that accursed tree.

During those few months of 1920–21, I was able to be present at all Doctor Shields' lectures at the Sisters College.

They were a feast for the intellect and for the soul. He was eloquent in a way peculiarly his own which was so simple and direct that the word *eloquence* seems too grandiloquent to describe it. His words were like a search-light illuminating our hearts and consciences. He was irresistible because there was no barrier between his mind and ours. He felt our pulse and knew by intuition, perhaps by a long experience of souls, just where a resistance was likely to occur, and met the difficulty in advance. Often his questions did the trick. We convicted ourselves of ignorance and error, yet the experience was full of delight and not of humiliation. Fresh insight made us forget our inadequacy, even despise it, in the joy of dancing in the light of new perceptions of truth. We knew that we were sitting under a great teacher—more than that, under a great witness.

He was disappointed that so many religious orders sent him the older members of the community instead of the younger Sisters who would be more plastic and less the slaves of custom. Yet these elderly women must be won. They sat before him with what he described as "that keep-off-the-grass expression" and he aimed all his remarks, his choicest jokes, in particular, at the most severe among them. When he succeeded in provoking a smile from his chosen victim, better yet, a hearty laugh, he felt that he had won his audience. From then on, they were his to form and to mold.

He disliked constraint, artificial efforts at attention. Effort must be free and joyful. In this connection, I remember a remark he made to the astonished Sisters: "I don't like to see wrinkles on the faces of Sisters. Smooth faces are a sign that you are fully in your vocation."

Our meals were sandwiched in between rests for Doctor Shields. He could eat very little because of the added strain on his heart caused by digestion. Outside of the members of his immediate household, no one realized how rapidly he was sinking, for when he appeared in public he carried himself gallantly as of old and his mind was keener than ever. Fatigue took the form of absent-mindedness. Once at Mass, he omitted one of the prayers. Someone spoke of it. He was much pained: "Are you sure?" "Yes, Doctor." "Then why did you not stop me and tell me?" On Sundays when all the members of the household gathered before his little chapel for Mass, he used to preach us a ten-minute sermon. The custom had been introduced in Dunbarton Hall and had never been broken. I am sure that he prepared those sermons as carefully as though he had been going to preach to a large congregation. His subject, usually, was some phase of the Gospel story of the day. His talks were full of wit, deep wisdom and a strong, communicative faith.

I think he realized better than we did how close he was to the end. Though he rarely spoke of this, he discussed with me quite often the dispositions he was planning to make, that his work would continue after his death. The Catholic Education Press was safely taken care of by a corporation whose board of directors was of his own selection. The stock, however, and the Quincy Street house were his personal property. How could he be sure that all this would be used for the advancement of the work to which he had consecrated his life? To leave it to an individual would be dangerous—the person might die and find no successor. An organization was best. Then he thought of his own Sisters College which would surely carry on his traditions. He made his will leaving all his personal property, save a few legacies, to the Catholic Sisters College.

The end came rapidly. One afternoon, he returned from

a meeting and saw that his ankles were swollen. He looked up quickly to see whether I had noticed it. I had. Nothing was said but we both understood. He continued his lectures at the Sisters College for a few days more. His last words in that strangely informal *Sedes Sapientiae* were more solemn than those he usually uttered. It was on February 2, 1921. He ended his lecture thus:

> God works with noiseless majesty—in the return of the seasons, the fall of the snow, in the song of the bird, the ripple of the stream, in the surge of the ocean, the strength of the wind, and above all in the mysterious silence of the stars.

Then just before his usual rapid movement to begin the prayer, he added:

> God looked upon His work and saw that it was good.[2]

It was that same evening that he had a sudden chill. With great difficulty we persuaded him to go to bed—from which he never rose. For ten days the doctors and nurses did what was possible to save him, but it was too late to do anything effective. He sent for his confessor and received extreme unction on the 13th. On the night of the 14th, he sank rapidly. His sister had come from St. Paul, and his nephew, Vincent Shields, was living in the house. They were by his bedside. It was nearly midnight when the last moments approached. At the foot of the bed in that tiny cell stood two priests, Doctor McCormick, the friend of long date, and Father McVay. They were reciting the prayers for the dying.

They feared that the struggle would be long and painful. A man with the sturdy physique and the strength of will

[2] Quoted in *The Sisters College Messenger*, Apr., 1921.

of Doctor Shields would leave this world only after an agonizing battle. This was their thought as they read the psalms and as they called on the saints of heaven to come out and meet their departing friend.

"Mayest thou see thy Redeemer face to face and, standing always in His presence, behold with happy eyes the most clear truth!"

Did the man lying immobile on the bed hear these words —or was he already too far away? That truth had been his object all his life; he had sought it with unremitting zeal, had spread it far and wide, and it would be no strange sight to those eyes which were losing contact with material surroundings. For Doctor Shields was not resisting death. Until now, while life had been the goal, his mighty will had focussed all its concentrated power on living—living with every ounce of energy he could command; but tonight his job was to die, and all his will power was focussed on dying —rapidly, as was his way. We all saw him, apparently calm and probably conscious, sigh deeply. That was all. The nurse leaned over and closed his eyes. "Is it all over?" asked his sister, incredulous of the rapid passage. Yes, it was the end. The two priests looked at their watches to determine whether it was before or after midnight. They decided that it was the 15th of February, 1921.

Doctor Shields had always been a man of prompt action. Death was no exception. Without a struggle, without resistance, with a face of utter serenity and a deep sigh of contentment, he had left us. The heart of a great servant of God had ceased to beat. We thought that his emaciated face, drawn by suffering but almost without a single hated wrinkle, resembled that of the dead Christ.

Vested in a white alb and purple chasuble, Doctor Shields lay for three days in a coffin set in the middle of the little parlor of his home on Quincy Street. His sister was there and his three nephews, the only living members of his immediate family. But his vast spiritual family kept watch by day and by night around his bier. Sisters from the College and other religious institutes, children from the schools, succeeded each other, spending the days in prayer. Priests and Seminarians divided among themselves the night watches. Tears were mingled with the prayers. These were no mere formal expressions of grief. The children did not know what they had lost but the Sisters knew, all too well, that they were mourning their fearless champion. They were orphans weeping for a father. Others, like Doctor Pace, saw "with sudden realization" the largeness of the place which he had left vacant, the distinction of his services to the Church and to the Nation. And the prayers they offered may well have been mingled with regret of a nature which we may not analyze.

Expressions of sympathy poured in by telegram and letter from all sides: from the Apostolic Delegate, bishops, archbishops, superiors of religious orders, from simple parish priests and humble teaching sisters. "In every diocese and parish, in religious novitiate and scholastic council, in college, academy and elementary school, there are debtors to Doctor Shields, teachers who owe him the best that is in them, men and women who are living by his direction, children unnumbered who are growing to knowledge and virtue on the fruit of his thought and endeavor." These were the words which Doctor Pace was to pronounce a few days later. Now, the body of Doctor Shields lay still in our sight. But where was the communicative fire of his word? The energy of his movement? Was this really the human dynamo, our friend? We had never before seen him in repose.

Three days later, on the 18th of February, 1921, the funeral took place. He was carried to the University gymnasium, not an inappropriate place for the final appearance of the athlete of Christ. It was the only hall large enough to hold the crowds that came to mourn him. There, a pontifical Mass of Requiem was celebrated by the Rector of the University, Bishop Shahan, assisted by the Vice-Rector with Doctor McCormick as Deacon and Father McVay, sub-Deacon. Bishop Turner of Buffalo gave the absolution and Doctor Pace pronounced the funeral oration. Friend and foe had awakened to "sudden realization" of that irreparable loss which had come too soon, far too soon.

"The final tribute remains to be paid," said Doctor Pace to the weeping multitude, "not by one but by all, not in words but in deeds. The work which he began must be continued. The noble aims which he pursued must be completely fulfilled. . . . Thus shall we build the only monument that is worthy of him. None other would he have desired."

Then the body of Thomas Edward Shields, dullard, scientist and sage, martyr to his zeal for the truth, now silently awaiting the day of the general judgment like the humblest of his mourners, was buried in the cemetery of Mt. Olivet in the northeasterly section of Washington. A few years later, permission was obtained to transfer his body to the grounds of the Sisters College. He was interred at the precise spot over which the high altar was to be erected in the collegiate church planned by him and incorporated in those drawings sent to Rome which had so delighted the Pope. A temporary monument marks the spot until such time as the church shall rise according to his plan. Meanwhile he rests close to the Sisters College which he loved and on that land which he purchased at a great price. The final tribute remains to be paid. The spiritual monument, the completion of his work, when will it spring forth in all its perfection?

During the transfer of the body of Doctor Shields and after the solemn ceremonies had ended, after his own eloquent eulogy of his master, Doctor George Johnson, then a member of the Department of Education of the University, remarked to a friend:

"He was a hundred years ahead of his time. That is why we are having so much trouble in keeping up with him."

EPILOGUE

A QUARTER of a century has passed since the death of Thomas Edward Shields. His full dream remains to be realized. The only monument worthy of him awaits erection.

He planned a system of education based solidly on religion and science, an education which was to begin in early childhood and be carried through to its culmination in the university; which was to develop organically from a seed into a mighty tree; an education wherein religion, music, art, liturgy, letters, history, geography, mathematics, science, social inheritances and patriotism were all correlated and centered in God, in whom they found their source of unity, of authority and of order. He lived long enough to prove that his ideas were sound and easy to realize in practice. He died too soon to see them triumph fully.

Since his death, others have groped along the paths so brilliantly blazed by Doctor Shields, the pioneer. But, as Monsignor McCormick points out,[1] "None of those who came after him has aimed as high or built his method on as firm a scientific or psychological foundation." A renaissance seems close at hand. If the seed sown by Doctor Shields was, in reality, the word of God, then the last phrases have not yet been pronounced.

A prophet of old looked out over a field of dry bones. The voice of God asked him, "Son of man, dost thou think

[1] Introduction, p. xiv.

these bones shall live?" The prophet answered, "Lord, Thou knowest." Then, listening, he heard these words: "Come, Spirit of the four winds, and blow upon these slain and let them live again."

APPENDIX

APPENDIX I

"A distinct motive which we keep always before us and for which we are always striving our best is what gives power and vitality to our actions and insures the success of whatever we have in hand."

"There is a greater and higher pleasure in conferring benefits than in receiving them. In conferring good we resemble the Creator; in receiving it we resemble the creature. A good conferred will receive an hundredfold reward. A good received can merit none."

"Reputation is good only in so far as it may enable us to serve our neighbor and is dangerous in so far as it exposes us to pride. Scarcely anything can render us more unhappy than over-solicitude for our good name, especially when the solicitude springs from pride and self-love."

"We should try to be what we wish to be thought, but never try to be thought what we are not. What we believe and feel it is cowardly to wish to conceal, and it is waste of time to try to cover up what we are ashamed of. The time would be well spent in removing the cause of concealment."

"Every additional talent accompanied by due humility is an additional power in attracting and subduing our fellow-men. But the greater the talent and the less the humility, the more repulsive to them we become and the less they are

287

THOMAS EDWARD SHIELDS

influenced by us. Abstain from all injudicious display of talent. An unnecessary display is always injudicious."

"Common sense is the highest spirituality. Go quietly about your own business and leave others to God and their own consciences. When it becomes your duty to interfere, do so, for then it *is* your business. This course of action will preserve your own peace of mind and add materially to the peace of the community in which you live."

"By putting the most favorable interpretation possible on our neighbor's words and actions we will do ourselves no harm, do him good, avoid rash judgments, slander and calumny, and practice charity."

"He who tells us the evil spoken of us is our worst enemy. Kindness and good offices are the best means of vanquishing an opponent. It will invariably win the crowd to our side and shame our opponent into being a faithful friend. This is much easier done when we know not the evil done us, for, in the contrary case, we are only too apt to be vanquished by losing temper."

"What must be borne should be borne manfully. It may sometimes be well to refuse submission to unjust demands, but it is unworthy of a man to submit to them with a bad grace. Grumbling is self-destruction and never tolerable in a rational being."

"To be a successful teacher a man must be learned. His knowledge must have become a part of himself and then his instructions receive a vitality from him that rivets attention and develops the powers of the pupil. Mere erudition is dead and has no more power of instruction than the book itself, and, often, not as much. Force of character is also a very powerful means in the hands of a teacher."

"Men who would be teachers should first solve each problem that presents itself and then carefully study out the way they reached the solution. The results of our mental labor may be sufficient to such of us as will lead the lives of the solitary. But those of us who would lead others to the same results must know every step in the process by which our mind arrived at the solution."

"If we would win others to think with us, we must first place ourselves with them and show them that we understand their position and hold all the truth there is in it. Then we will be able to show them the way to our position. If we commence by thinking with them they will end by thinking with us, whenever the truth is on our side."

"It is the resisting atmosphere which impedes the bird in flying that speeds her on her flight. It is her weight which ties her down to earth that mounts her up on high. It is the trials and temptations which impede our progress home that speed us on our way. It is our lowliness and meekness which tie us down to earth that lift us up to heaven."

APPENDIX II

SERMON PREACHED BY THOMAS EDWARD SHIELDS ON
EASTER SUNDAY, 1891, AT ST. MARK'S CHURCH,
ST. PAUL, MINN.

Today, my brethren, Christ celebrates His victory over death and over the world. It is the great day of His triumph over sin and over the powers of darkness. Today He fulfills the promise He so often made His friends, the challenge He so repeatedly flung out to His adversaries that they would destroy the temple of His body and on the third day He would build it up again.

In His resurrection He gives the world proof of His divinity. He submits to human reason the credentials of His divine mission with the seal of His Father upon them, credentials in which 19 centuries of keenest criticism have failed to find a flaw. You are familiar with the proofs, the attacks of adversaries have but served to bring their truth out into clearer light.

But there is another phase of the resurrection which interests us no less deeply. Christ's resurrection is the type and pledge of our own resurrection into life everlasting. Jesus extends to us all this morning a glorious participation in His own resurrection. He gives us a resurrection from the wilderness of doubt and skepticism to the light and certainty of divine truth. A resurrection from the death of sin and selfishness to the life of grace and love.

Have you and I risen with Christ this morning? Can we with a good heart say with St. Paul: "Christ is risen; He now dies no more"? Look well into your hearts and see. If the voice of the risen Christ speaks to you today, harden not your hearts against Him. This is the day of His victory and triumph; do not refuse to join Him. Let the full tide of His grace flow in upon your souls, the full tide of the life Christ earned for you on Calvary and that He brings to you today in His resurrection. Let it be the tide of life that shall ever surge in your veins, impelling your every act. Then indeed you shall be risen with Christ to die no more.

But what is this life of grace into which we have risen this morning? It is life and love flowing into our souls from the throne of God's mercy, illumining our intellects to see the truth and warming our hearts to love the good and the beautiful; it is the God of majesty and glory stooping down to our poor, weak nature and lifting it up to a level with His own, so that we may see as He sees and love as He loves and, in the light of His own knowledge, that we may partake of His own life, His own infinite, entrancing happiness. This is the life of grace.

But what is grace to us? See how the sun is warming into life the vegetation around you. See how it lifts up the juices through their stems and converts them into living matter in their leaves. See how the sun's activity converts cold, dead earth into the spotless purity of the lily and into the blushing rose; see how it loads your vines with purple grapes and crowns your orchards with rich and mellow fruit. Such is grace to us. It is a force entering our souls from without and changing all that is there from death to life. It is not of our nature or from our will and yet without our will it cannot act. Without our cooperation grace would be as powerless to produce the flowers and fruits of eternal life as the sun without seed is powerless to evoke living fruit from earth.

Have you ever observed a polished hollow hemisphere with its open side toward the sun? It is filled with an intense light and heat, which are not from its own nature but from without, and yet a light and heat which by appropriation and correspondence, it has made its own. Turn its open face away from the sun: all within is cold and dark. The sun still sends out his light and heat, but our hemisphere had turned its back upon it and fails to take up and correspond with its movement. So it is, my friends, with the grace of Christ. It is a participation of God's own nature and life, just as the sun's light and heat are a participation of the sun's nature and life. It was earned for us on Calvary; it comes to us from without and gratuitously. If we let it flow into our souls and correspond with its movement, it will convert all within us into the glorious and joyous life of the risen Christ. All within our souls will be beauty, activity, life, light, love and happiness.

Christ has risen; He now dies no more. He has risen in the body that was broken for us on Calvary. That body is now glorified, impassable, incapable of suffering or death. It is seated at the right hand of the Father. We shall not see it again until we see it coming in the clouds of heaven, clothed in the power and majesty of God, to judge the world.

Christ has risen in His Church. He now dies no more. All the power and majesty of pagan Rome sought in vain to falsify this statement. With her immense armies under whose tread the world trembled, with her boundless wealth, with her ingenuity of torture, with her power of organization and her inexhaustible resources, she bent herself with all her might and with her characteristic perseverance, to destroy Christ risen in His Church, but the waves of her attack were flung back upon her bosom; as the ocean's waves from a rocky beach they beat against Christ who is risen and who now dies no more!

For eighteen hundred years, all the powers of darkness have leagued against Him; heresy, schism, scandal, the indifference and treachery of His children, every form of attack, every instrument conceivable by malice have been hurled with all the power of demons and of men against Christ risen in His Church, but they only beat against immortality. Christ has risen in His Church; he now dies no more. He has placed it beyond the power of creatures to reverse this sentence in His glorified humanity or in His Church.

But Christ has a third resurrection this morning, in which He still leaves Himself subject to the mercy of His creatures.

Christ has, we hope, risen in your soul and in mine this morning, crowned with all the glory of His resurrection, breathing peace and mercy and love, filling our lives with the gladness and the sunshine and the glory of His grace; planting in our hearts the fountains of living waters that shall spring up into life everlasting. And yet Christ risen in our souls in all His power and glory stands a petitioner on our goodness, pleading with us for life, pleading with us to make it true of Him in this resurrection also *"Christ is risen; He now dies no more."*

What shall be our sentence? Shall we join with the per-

fidious Jews in crying out: "Crucify Him, crucify Him"?
Or shall we exhibit ourselves in the role of the weak and
cowardly Pilate and yield to the tumult of our passions, to a
passing whim or to the jibes and scoffing of the rabble?

Oh! my friends, let Him not plead with us in vain! How
can we contemplate Christ and sin—and choose the latter?
We blame the blind mob for preferring Barabbas to Christ,
but Barabbas was a king compared to the monster we prefer
to Christ. How can we turn our backs on goodness, mild-
ness, charity, peace and happiness itself and choose the
monster, sin? What could be more unreasonable, more
against our own nature and happiness than this perfidious
choice of a base satisfaction rather than the glory of Christ's
resurrection?

Have you risen with Christ? then you will love the things
that are of Christ. You will sorrow over your past sins that
you may sin no more. You will seek to know Christ
and His teachings. You will follow Him over the plains
of Judea and see Him diffusing gladness and sunshine into
all hearts. You will see Him healing the sick, blessing the
children, comforting the sorrowing, consoling the widow
and orphan, bringing the soft, sweet tears of repentance and
love to the eyes of hardened sinners. You will see Him
everywhere loving God and loving and assisting fellow
man. Look well upon this picture and happy for you should
you recognize in it your own features; it is the picture of
one who has risen with Christ, of one who has passed from
the death of ignorance into the risen life of Christ in grace
and truth. Imitate His example, love all creatures, for they
are all His. Take upon yourselves the yoke of Christ for it
is sweet and His burden, light. His only aim, His wish is to
promote your happiness.

How can we refuse to obey the teaching of One who
comes to us as Christ does this morning, clothed in all the
glory and majesty of God, Who lived among us and for
us, Who came down from the bosom of His Father to be

our way and our life, to teach us how to find heaven, happiness, His own infinite, eternal bliss, One who gives us every proof within the broad range of infinite possibility, of His surpassing, enduring love for us, One who loves you so much and who knows so well what is for your happiness? What foolishness, what consummate folly to hesitate in obeying Him! Truly, those whom the powers of evil wish to destroy they first make blind.

My friends, open your eyes to the light of Easter morning and your hearts to its love, and let this light and love of the risen Christ ever abide with you and be your guide. Then, indeed, you shall have risen into the joys and glory of Christ's resurrection.

APPENDIX III

TEST IN HISTORY AT CLEVELAND, JANUARY, 1919

Together with a Statement of the Superintendent of Catholic Schools, Doctor Kane, regarding the conditions under which the test was made.

"I am enclosing a report of a talk given by a pupil of the fourth grade to the girls of the high school. I can vouch for the following.

1. It is a stenographic report and, in the transcribing, no corrections in language have been made.

2. No special preparation had been made for the talk. The girl had not given the talk before and did not know she was to give it till that day.

3. The talk concerned facts that she had not studied since September.

4. It was not a memorized talk, as is evident from the fact that the girl has given it three times since then in language and construction quite different from the first speech."

The Sister Introduced the Child

"Girls, this is little Alma Donnellon of the fourth grade. She is going to tell us about Attila invading Rome."

"Sister, Attila didn't invade Rome. He only came to the gates of Rome and then went away without entering the city."

"Oh, I beg your pardon, Alma. Then tell us please, what happened before and after he came to the gates of Rome."

Alma's Story

"Attila was king of the Huns. He was said to be a mower of men. He was born in the western part of Asia near the forest of Tartary in the fifth century. He was short, broad-shouldered and had a huge head. He had a thin black beard. He received his company seated on a wooden stool and ate from wooden dishes, but his men ate from golden dishes.

"After some time Attila came down from Asia and pitched his tents on the banks of the Danube River. He had an army of five hundred thousand men. He was warlike by nature and he thought that he would like to go into France and pillage and burn all the cities of that country.

"With his men, he crossed the Rhine River into France and burned and destroyed as he went along. The people had no time to offer any resistance. When he came to the city of Metz the people of this city held out a little longer than the others.

"From Metz he went to Troyes. The Bishop of Troyes was a very holy man. He promised his people that he would save the city for them. He went to meet Attila dressed in pontifical attire. Attila was so astonished at the bravery of this holy man that he left the city unharmed and went back to his tents. Then he moved towards Paris. The people of Paris were dismayed. They prayed to St. Genevieve, the patron saint of their city, and she told the people to be comforted, that Attila would not destroy their city. This came true, for Attila for some reason turned in a different direction and left Paris unharmed. He then turned toward Orleans. Orleans was noted for miracles. The people in Orleans were frightened, for they thought that in a few days Attila would come into their city and pillage and burn it. The Bishop of Orleans asked a Roman general if he would send his men to fight for Orleans. Just at the critical moment when the people of Orleans were going to throw open their gates to Attila, the Roman general came and they had a battle and Attila was defeated.

"After his defeat at Orleans, Attila crossed the Alps into Italy. Soon he was at the gates of Rome. The people of Rome were terrified. They walked up and down the streets talking in low, anxious voices. As the soldiers passed along the people watched them, for they felt that the future of their city depended on the soldiers. Valentinian and Theodosius, the two Roman Emperors, went out to Attila to ask him to be a general in the Roman army. But he sneered at them, saying that his servants were generals and the Roman generals were servants. He boasted that he was 'the scourge of God' and that 'grass never grew where his horse had trod.' Valentinian and Theodosius went back to their palaces and Attila sent them this insolent message: 'Prepare a palace for me this day.' This meant an invasion. Valentinian, who was a coward, sent the message to the senate as though he did not know what to do.

"The Roman senators selected Celestus, one of their number, to go to Valentinian and make a last attempt to induce him to defend the city. Just as Celestus was coming down the steps of the Roman Forum, he met Justus, a tribune. Justus asked Celestus if there was any news that he might carry to the people, who were very anxious. But Celestus had no good news and said that he feared that the barbarian Huns would come in and pillage and burn their city. While they were talking, the people gathered around to hear. Celestus asked Justus if he had seen Attila and if he knew how terrible a man Attila was. Justus said that he had not seen him. Then Celestus said that he would tell Justus about him so that he might give the description to the people.

"Celestus told Justus how he had gone out to Attila's camp the day before to see if he could make a truce with him. Attila came out of his tent and his soldiers and the women and children gathered around him. They were all very ugly and were very much afraid of Attila, who was very fierce and wicked-looking. Celestus said that Attila made fun of the Romans and boasted that he had burned every town and field of grain between the Alps and Rome.

"Then Celestus told how he had left the camp of Attila feeling sick at heart and that, as he came back into the city, he thought of the Holy Father and of how he loved the people. This strengthened him and he went to see Pope St. Leo. The Holy Father promised to help him if Valentinian still refused and said that he would meet him at three o'clock the next day. Valentinian refused to leave his palace and so Celestus arranged to meet the Pope. He invited Justus to go with him. At first Justus said it was too great an honor for him, but after awhile he agreed to go.

"The Pope did not want any soldiers to accompany him and said that only Celestus and Justus should go with him. Celestus and four African slaves carried the chair of the Pope. As they approached the tent of Attila they could hear the singing of rude songs and rough merry-making. When Attila's people saw them they shouted that they were lords of the world and the Romans were coming to bow before them. Then St. Leo turned to Celestus and Justus and said that Attila was justly called the Scourge of God; for God uses strange means with which to punish people for their sins. He sometimes lets them be punished by other men and sends them war, famine and sickness. Then they see that they need God and they turn to Him and the world becomes better.

"Attila came out of his tent and rode toward St. Leo. He was mounted on a shaggy pony. When Attila came near, he began to sneer at St. Leo and his companions and to call them slaves. But St. Leo just looked right through Attila and did not speak a word. Attila tried to look back at St. Leo but the Pope's eyes were so full of holiness that he had to drop his for shame. Then St. Leo began to speak to Attila and to ask him why he had come to Rome to injure their city and to pillage and rob when they had never injured nor stolen from him. Attila could not answer. St. Leo then told him of the power of God and how it could conquer all men, and as he talked, his eyes glowed like fire. Attila began to feel afraid and to tremble and moved toward Thuros, one of his generals, who had accompanied him. He whispered to Thuros that he was afraid and asked him to hurry with him back to camp. Then he sent Thuros back with a message to St. Leo, saying that he would go away to the east and leave the city unharmed. Celestus was not satisfied with the promise of Attila and wanted St. Leo to demand his written word. But the Pope said that there is no faith in the word of a barbarian, but there is faith in the word of God and God had told him to be consoled.

"Then St. Leo and his two companions turned back towards the city, and St. Leo, as he rode along, bowed his head in a prayer of thanksgiving that God had spared their city."

Questions

Q. "What river did he cross in going into France?"

A. "He crossed the Rhine River."

Q. "When he left France and started towards Rome, what mountains did he cross?"

A. "He crossed the Alps."

Q. "When he left Rome and went back to his own country, in what direction did he go?"

A. "He went east."

Q. "Alma, why was Attila called a mower of men?"

A. "Because he went through the cities and killed and cut down men as if he were mowing."

Q. "What do you think about Valentinian?"

A. "I think he was a coward and mean to his people."

Q. "Alma, you said that Attila sent an insolent message to Valentinian. What do you mean by an insolent message?"

A. "He sent a rude, bold message. He wasn't particular about how he worded it."

Q. "Why were Attila's people afraid of him?"

A. "Because he was cruel to them."

Q. "Why couldn't Attila look the Pope in the eye?"

A. "Because Attila was wicked and the Pope was holy; and a wicked person can never look a good person in the eye."

Q. "Is there anyone of whom you have heard that resembles Attila?"

A. "Yes, the Kaiser."

Q. "Why?"

A. "Because he, too, went through cities killing people that had not harmed him."

Q. "Did the Kaiser go into the same part of the world as Attila?"

A. "Yes, the Kaiser pillaged and burned Belgium and about three-fourths of France. He tried to get into Paris, but the Allies wouldn't let him."

Q. "Is there any difference between Attila and the Kaiser?"

A. "Yes, Attila went at the head of his army, but the Kaiser stayed home in his nice palace and sent out his men to fight and pillage and burn the cities of other people."

Q. "Well, then, do you think that the Kaiser was worse than Attila?"

A. "Well, neither one of them was any good."

Alma Donnellon was just beginning her work in the fourth grade, and was, presumably, in her tenth year. The basis of her talk was the opening lesson of Doctor Shields' *Fourth Reader*, yet if anyone should compare Alma's talk with that lesson, he would realize that the child did not memorize the lesson but used freely the materials contained in it. This was Doctor Shields' aim, to let the child break up and reconstruct material in new forms. Alma simplified the facts but all those facts were organized and vitalized so that her hearers were made to see with her Attila, his generals, the rabble, the invasion of France; to feel with her the awe of Attila at the courage of the Bishop of Troyes, his mysterious turning aside from Paris and his defeat at Orleans. When her interest shifts to Rome, her audience accompanies her; it feels the cowardice of the Roman emperor, the terror in the hearts of the populace and its pitiful dependence on the soldiers. It approaches the Pope with reverence and listens to his preaching of sublime truths, sharing in his gratitude.

The child showed no apparent effort of memory although three or four months had elapsed since the facts narrated had been studied in school. The fact that the child used different language and construction in subsequent talks proved that her work was vital and not mere memory load. She had never been taught formal grammar, yet her grammar was faultless. Thus when the proper time should come for that study she would need only to analyze the forms of speech to which she had been accustomed. In history, in language, in religion, all depended upon the preparation. No child could have gained this vital mastery of thought and expression through the old procedure of passing from form to content, nor attain that fecund knowledge under the guidance of a teacher who deliberately aimed at building up mental structures in the mind of the child according to his own prearranged plan. The child showed the effect of true education as Doctor Shields conceived it.

INDEX

Abstract proposition: avoided in Christ's teaching, 144; cannot be dealt with by children, 237; vs. concrete reality, 37; vs. germinal truths, 144, 236, 237

Achievement and its subjective value, 63

Aesthetic development in education, 150–1, 157

Affiliation of high schools and colleges with Catholic University, 133, 170, 197–9

Apostolic Delegate (See Falconio)

Art: as used by the Church, 182; in education, 249

Assimilation, 160; and attention, 217; and feeling, 160, 223, 226, 247; and interest, 217; of religious truths, 161; through activity, 217–8; vs. memorizing, 161

Association of ideas, 162, 217

Astor, John Jacob, 5

Attila: history told by child, 294–9

Authority and infallibility, 114

Bach, Johann Sebastian, vii, 219

Baltimore, Md., 56, 108

Benedictine Convent and Sisters College, 202, 206, 209

Binet, Alfred, 112

Biological studies and experiments by Shields, 109–10, 111–3; transfer of biological thought to teaching, 109, 127–8

Biology and education, 109–10, 111–3; danger of misapplication, 111–3; example of misapplication, 241; ignorance of, 113; taught by Shields at St. Paul's Seminary, 116–7; and at Catholic University,

121, 127, 132; then abandoned, 132

Board of Trustees, Catholic University, 131, 133, 170, 193–4, 195, 198, 201, 208, 210, 213, 269, 270.

Bombay Examiner (Fr. Hull, S. J.) 147

Boniface VIII, Pope, 188

Boyle, Most Rev. Hugh C., 178–9

Brookland, D. C., 127, 131, 156

Catechetical Methods, 138–40, 159–60, 161, 163, 175–6, 177–8; discarded in all subjects save religion, 159

Catechism, summary of orthodox theology, not children's book, 138, 147; comprehensible after training in religion, 255; Baltimore Catechism compared with Shields Books I & II, 163–4

Catechisms, 138, 143, 147, 163, 175, 181; intended for teachers, not pupils, 138

Catholic Associated Press, 124, 128, 129, 201

Catholic Education Press, 124, 166, 277

Catholic Education Series (Shields Textbooks), 124, 231, 233–4, 252–8, 264–5; results in Cleveland, 250–2; in Pittsburgh, 253; and elsewhere, 252–3, 254–5

Catholic Educational Association, 136, 137, 186

Catholic Educational Review, xiv, 125, 170, 197–8, 199, 200, 205, 209, 231

Catholic Free Press, Sydney, Australia, 148

Effect of Odours and Irritant Vapours and Mental Work Upon the Blood Flow, The (Shields), 112

Emotions and assimilation, 160, 179–80, 222–3, 226, 247, 249; and memory, 10–2, 223; as motive power, 76, 247; reinforced impressions, 223; under control of intellect, 249

Emotions and permanency of mental record, 11, 62

Failure, effect of, 53–4, 62; memory of, 21

Falconio, Most Rev., Diomede, 177, 199, 202, 267

Farming, 17, 19–20, 20–9, 25–34, 269, 275; and machinery, 39–40, 42–4, 48–52, 55–77

Feeling: and mental assimilation, 160–1, 179, 222–3, 226–7, 247–8; and mental development, 179–82, 226–7, 249; and memory, 144–5; as used by Christ, 179; by Church, 227; by Shields, 180–1; neglected in preparation of textbooks, 179; to prepare truths of religion, 160–1, 179

Fight on two fronts, 135

Financial operations, 149, 166–7, 187–8, 197, 203–8, 210–1, 212, 214, 268–70

Financing a parish, 119–20

Fort Snelling, 5, 6, 47

Franciscan friars, 168

Galtier, Rev. Lucien, 100

Germinal concepts and truths: as developed in Shields' books, 240, 274; vs. abstract principles, 39, 40; in geometry, 25–33; in mechanics, 22–3, 25–6, 32–3, 39, 40, 42; in Religion, 129

Gibbons, Most Rev. James Cardinal, 206, 211, 213

God, center of all knowledge, 247;

center of correlation, 141, 224, 247; restored to His place in textbooks, 246

Gregorian Chant, 90, 262, 263, 264

Grindstone, experiment with, 42–4

Grubbing machine, invention of, 54–60, 66–73; effect of, 61, 62–3, 66–73, 76

Habits, as related to instincts, 162; as related to feeling, 179

Haggerty, Michael Gamble, 78–84, 97–8, 101

Hall, G. Stanley, 109, 135, 200, 241

Hayes, Rev. James M., 211–2

Hayes, Rt. Rev. Ralph M., 253–4

Herbart, Dr. Johann Friedrich, 218, 225

Hill, James J., 88

Hopkins (see Johns Hopkins University)

Ideas, concrete approach to, 218

Illusions and their value, 64–5

Imitation, as used in Church, 227–8

Impression and expression, 84, 217, 218

Index Omnium (Shields) 94–6

Inheritance of child, physical, 241; social, 249; spiritual, 223

Instincts, consecration of, 143; five fundamental, 235–6; related to habits, 162; must be reached by religion, 141–2; are starting points, 234; form basis of Christian virtue, 162

Intellect and sense training (see Sense training and sensory-motor reaction)

Interest vs. drill, 217, 223

Ireland, Most Rev. John, 87–8; 90, 93, 101, 108, 111, 121

Irish scholarship, 80–1

James, William, 217–8, 219

Jesus' method of teaching (see Christ's methods)